Literature in the Digital Age
An Introduction

Literature in the Digital Age: An Introduction guides readers through the most salient theoretical, interpretive, and creative possibilities opened up by the shift to digital literary forms such as e-books, digital archives, electronic literature, and videogames. While Digital Humanities (DH) has been hailed as the "next big thing" in literary studies, many students and scholars remain perplexed as to what a DH approach to literature entails, and skeptical observers continue to see literature and the digital world as fundamentally incompatible. In its argument that digital and traditional scholarship should be placed in dialogue with each other, this book contextualizes the advent of the digital in literary theory, explores the new questions readers can ask of texts when they become digitized, and investigates the challenges that fresh forms of born-digital fiction pose to existing models of literary analysis.

Adam Hammond is Assistant Professor in the Department of English and Comparative Literature at San Diego State University. He is coauthor of *Modernism: Keywords,* and his articles have appeared in such journals and newspapers as *Digital Scholarship in the Humanities, The Globe and Mail, The Walrus,* and the *Literary Review of Canada.*

Literature in the Digital Age
An Introduction

ADAM HAMMOND

San Diego State University

CAMBRIDGE
UNIVERSITY PRESS

CAMBRIDGE
UNIVERSITY PRESS

University Printing House, Cambridge CB2 8BS, United Kingdom

One Liberty Plaza, 20th Floor, New York, NY 10006, USA

477 Williamstown Road, Port Melbourne, VIC 3207, Australia

4843/24, 2nd Floor, Ansari Road, Daryaganj, Delhi - 110002, India

79 Anson Road, #06-04/06, Singapore 079906

Cambridge University Press is part of the University of Cambridge.

It furthers the University's mission by disseminating knowledge in the pursuit of education, learning and research at the highest international levels of excellence.

www.cambridge.org
Information on this title: www.cambridge.org/9781107615076

First published 2016

A catalogue record for this publication is available from the British Library

Library of Congress Cataloging in Publication data
Hammond, Adam, 1981–
Literature in the digital age : an introduction / Adam Hammond.
   pages cm.
Includes bibliographical references and index.
ISBN 978-1-107-04190-5 (hardback) – ISBN 978-1-107-61507-6 (pbk.)
1. Literature – 21st century – History and criticism – Theory, etc.   2. Information theory in literature.   3. Literature and the Internet.   4. Online authorship.
5. Computer literacy.   6. Hypertext literature – History and criticism.   I. Title.
PN98.I54H36   2016
801–dc23   2015026052

ISBN 978-1-107-04190-5 Hardback
ISBN 978-1-107-61507-6 Paperback

To Marta

Contents

List of Tables and Figures

Tables

Figures

Preface: The Excess of Seeing

In August 2013, I traveled to Brighton for the annual gathering of the Modernist Studies Association (MSA), the biggest academic conference in my field. I had been to the MSA conference many times before, but this time there was a twist: I was going to participate in the conference's first-ever "poster session." Humanities conferences normally consist of oral presentations and seminars, and the MSA's decision to include a poster session – a common model in the sciences – was meant to recognize the growing prominence of Digital Humanities (DH), the area of humanities research concerned with and conducted with the aid of digital technology.[1] Much of my work in the preceding years had focused on developing computational methods of tracking multi-voicedness in modernist writers such as T. S. Eliot and Virginia Woolf, and I was glad for an opportunity to present this digital work to my fellow modernists. After a long intercontinental flight with an unwieldy poster tube and several computers in tow, I arrived brimming with enthusiasm.

However well intentioned, the poster session was a disaster. In an effort to attract maximum traffic, the conference organizers had set us up in the refreshments area. My booth – I sat behind a table with a large poster to my left and a laptop in front of me to "demo" my work – was directly across from the coffee station. On the first day of the conference, I was asked many questions ("Where is the toilet?"; "Which way to room 312?"; "What time is the plenary?"), but none pertaining to my research. In the visual vocabulary of the humanities conference, a person seated behind a desk, in the vicinity of a laptop, was staff – not someone with something to say about literature. On the second day of the conference, in a novel if somewhat desperate effort to attract attention to our work, the conference organizers suggested we set up during the wine and cheese reception, always a popular event. It was indeed packed – though no one, it seemed, was in the mood to discuss natural-language processing. One conference goer, gesticulating wildly in the course of a lively conversation with a colleague, knocked my poster off the wall. My booth was quickly identified as a convenient place to discard empty wine glasses and dirty napkins. The final straw came when one scholar, needing both hands free to illustrate the point he was making, carelessly deposited a half-eaten piece of cheese on the keyboard of my MacBook. I packed up my things in a rage and spent the rest of the conference attending panels and plenaries, leaving my booth unmanned.

I present this story as a parable of the place of Digital Humanities in literary studies today. On the one hand, there is enormous excitement about digital approaches. Ever since William Pannapacker declared it the humanities' "next big thing" in a much-discussed blog post written from the 2009 Modern Language Association conference,[2] DH has served as a beacon of hope in a field perpetually beset by existential angst. At a time when jobs, funding, and public attention are in short supply in literature departments, DH promises all three. Yet for all its attractiveness and its practical and material advantages, literature departments have had a hard time embracing DH. This reluctance has been partly a question of ideology: many scholars, having imbibed the Romantic opposition of art to technology, remain deeply suspicious of the application of quantitative scientific methodologies to something as uncertain, elusive, and, well, as *human* as literature. It has also been simply a question of time. Although scholars have been using computers to conduct humanities research for more than a half-century, the term "Digital Humanities" is barely a decade old, and its methods and assumptions are still slowly trickling into the consciousness of most scholars.[3] Laudable as it is for a conference organizer to include a poster session in a major humanities conference, it is unreasonable to expect all the attendees to know what a poster session is. Depositing a half-eaten piece of cheese on a laptop remains, sadly, a more natural reaction for many established humanities scholars than, say, grabbing the mouse, exploring the digital exhibit, and asking a series of probing questions about machine-learning models and *p*-values.[4]

In *How We Think* (2012), N. Katherine Hayles explores the rift between digital and so-called traditional humanists. Surveying a number of DH centers in the United States and the United Kingdom, she describes two prevailing models for digital scholarship in the humanities: an "assimilation" model, in which digital resources are deployed primarily to assist established researchers in traditional text-based interpretation, and a "distinction" model, in which digital scholars increasingly work outside of literature departments, focusing their attention on digital theory, digital culture, and born-digital forms such as videogames, whose relationship to "literature" is uncertain and problematic. Hayles warns against both these polarized models, calling instead for balanced "approaches that can locate digital work within print traditions, and print traditions within digital media, without obscuring or failing to account for the differences between them."[5] Hayles's call for hybrid approaches is important, in part, because literature and literary research are themselves quickly hybridizing. For all the rivalry between digital humanists and print-focused traditional humanists, it is increasingly difficult today to locate pure specimens of either digital or analog scholarship. Even if you reject algorithmic analysis of Shakespeare (see Chapter 5) or stop short of teaching the Flash poetry of Young-Hae Chang Heavy Industries (see Chapter 8), you would be hard pressed to avoid writing up your research on a word processor, communicating with colleagues via e-mail or social media, or disseminating your research in digitized periodicals. Likewise, it is difficult to discuss Flash poetry without discussing the traditions of oral and printed verse – and even more difficult to discuss an algorithmic analysis of Shakespeare without discussing Shakespeare. This is why Matthew Kirschenbaum and Sarah Werner reject the notion of a "transcendental 'digital' that somehow stands outside the historical and material legacies of other artifacts and phenomena." The field of the digital is rather, for them, "a frankly messy complex of extensions and extrusions of prior media and technologies."[6] To understand this "messy complex," we must become, in Maryanne Wolf's memorable coinage, "bitextual":[7] conversant both in print and digital literary conventions and aware of the complex ways they intersect and overlap.

Given my training in literary modernism, Maryanne Wolf's call for bitextuality immediately calls to mind Virginia Woolf's description of androgyny in *A Room of One's Own* (1929), where she argues that the creative mind becomes "fully fertilised" only when its male and female halves are able to exist "in harmony together, spiritually co-operating."[8] Hayles's appeal for mixed scholarship that acknowledges the differences between digital and print-based approaches, yet strives for fruitful combinations of the two, in turn reminds me of Mikhail Bakhtin's concept of the "excess of seeing." In his early ethical philosophy, Bakhtin notes the way that, in any conversation,

> I shall always see and know something that [my interlocutor], from his place outside and over against me, cannot see himself: parts of his body that are inaccessible to his own gaze (his head, his face and its expression), the world behind his back, and a whole series of objects and relations, which in any of our mutual relations are accessible to me but not to him.[9]

Woolf's androgynous mind and Bakhtin's "excess of seeing" provide us with models for imagining the productive interaction of print-based and digital literary scholarship. If a rift exists between the two approaches at present, it is helpful to imagine them as two distinct hemispheres of a single mind or as interlocutors in dialogue. Each participant in this conversation, each hemisphere of this linked mind, is able to see something that the other cannot. This means that, for each side to be able share its insights with the other, both must learn to speak the other's language.

This book argues that both print and digital literary traditions have something to tell us about each other. Their encounter presents an enormous opportunity to revisit and revise our received methods of reading, interpreting, and teaching literature – as well as an occasion to adapt traditional literary approaches to the task of explaining and coming to terms with the digital world. Most fundamentally, the encounter of print and the digital presents us with the opportunity to sharpen our sense of what literature is, what it is becoming, and what it is for. But to make the most of this productive encounter, scholars and students trained in print-based approaches need to be able to talk to those steeped in the digital. This book exists to facilitate this conversation.

Although this book is occasioned by the rise of Digital Humanities, my aim is not to provide a comprehensive overview of DH or an assessment of the ways it is reshaping the humanities as a whole. The field of DH and the variety of approaches it encompasses are simply too vast for that, and my own specialized training as a literary scholar prevents me from venturing too far into digital work in history, philosophy, art history, or religion. Nor do I attempt to provide a systematic critique of the state of digital literary studies today, an exhaustive list of literary DH projects, or a particular intervention in this subfield.[10] My intention is much broader: it is to explore what is at stake for literature and literary studies in the transition from print to digital forms. This is a book for anyone interested in literature and its future: undergraduates, graduate students, faculty in literature departments, and readers of all kinds. It assumes interest in and commitment to literature but no expertise in digital literary studies. For those interested in taking the plunge into DH, this book will serve as a gateway drug, providing a way into more specialized work and introducing some key texts and resources. (It will not, however, single-handedly turn such readers into Digital Humanists.) For all other readers, this book will serve as an accessible introduction to the major questions that digital approaches and digital technologies are raising for the study of literature. My hope is that such readers will put down this book convinced of the importance of attending to and respecting the digital world.

This book is arranged in three parts. The first, "Is Literature Dying in the Digital Age?," introduces the volume's main themes. It provides an intellectual context for current anxieties and enthusiasms for the digital and argues that periods of technological transition like our own have historically presented, and present today, fruitful opportunities for asking big literary questions.

Part II, "Digitization," investigates claims that the making-digital of originally print-based literary texts allows for unprecedented access, permits us to ask new questions of literary texts, and implies new models of scholarship. The chapters in this section argue that digital techniques and resources supplement, rather than supersede, traditional modes of literary analysis such as close reading, while also making the case that engaging with literary digitization often leads to a deepened understanding of print. Part III, "Born Digital," focuses on new digital literary forms that incorporate affordances such as digital distribution, interactivity, and multimodality. These chapters look at how digital self-publishing serves both to challenge and to reinforce the notion of individual authorship, how interactivity serves to reinvigorate traditional modes of literary analysis such as narratology, and how multimedia forms such as videogames force us to reconsider the boundaries of the literary. The concluding chapter, focused on contemporary print fiction, argues that the experience of print is today inescapably structured by the experience of the digital.

Each of these sections is focused on problems rather than solutions – on exploring the literary questions raised by the transition to digital forms rather than trying to answer them definitively. Individual chapters are organized around detailed case studies and close readings that seek to uncover complexity and ambivalence rather than to achieve comprehensive scope. I take this approach because knotty problems and interpretive cruxes are precisely what make our historical moment such an exciting time to study literature. Because digitization is happening around us and we do not have critical distance from it, we do not yet possess any settled sense of its ultimate significance or where it is taking us. In the midst of this turmoil, it is far more interesting to debate issues than to predict outcomes. This is true of the undergraduate classroom, where this book can be used as a starting point for exploring and unpacking the literary questions posed by digital forms – a critical activity for which close reading of representative texts and resources remains the most productive approach. It is true also of digital literary scholarship generally. Traditional scholars have long been suspicious of digital work based on their perception that it seeks hard-and-fast incontrovertible answers through the application of quantitative scientific approaches. As I seek to show throughout this volume, however, the best digital scholarship shares with the best traditional scholarship a commitment to uncovering new problems, new texts, and new approaches. Far from threatening to close it down prematurely, the best digital scholarship promises to enrich the humanities conversation and to keep it going.

Acknowledgments

This book grew out of "The Digital Text," the undergraduate class I taught in the English Department at the University of Toronto from 2011 to 2013. My first thanks are due to Nick Mount and Alan Bewell, who assigned the course to me, giving me one of the great opportunities of my life. Immense thanks are due to the students and teaching assistants of "The Digital Text," with whom this book developed in dialogue, and who suggested many of the ideas, interpretations, and texts that it explores. Although it is impossible to thank each of them individually, I would like to offer particular thanks to Matthew Schneider and Elisa Tersigni. I would also like to thank the students of "Literature in the Digital Age," a similar course I taught at the University of Guelph in 2014.

This book was conceived and written over a period spanning my doctoral studies at the University of Toronto, postdoctoral fellowships at the University of Victoria and the University of Guelph, and an assistant professorship at San Diego State University. I would like to thank the Social Sciences and Humanities Research Council of Canada, which funded my postdoctoral work at the University of Victoria, and the College of Arts and Library at the University of Guelph, which funded my Michael Ridley Postdoctoral Fellowship in the Digital Humanities. Of the many colleagues who provided feedback on drafts and outlines of this volume, I would like to offer particular thanks to Nicholas Bradley, Stephen Ross, Susan Brown, and Melba Cuddy-Keane. I am indebted to Julian Brooke and Graeme Hirst for their assistance with the sections on computational literary analysis. Thanks to Craig D. Adams, Nicholas Carr, Stephen Marche, and Dash Shaw for taking the time to discuss their work with me.

Thanks to Ray Ryan, my editor at Cambridge University Press, who saw promise in the volume and believed in it from start to finish; to my anonymous Cambridge reviewers, who offered truly invaluable feedback at every stage; to Caitlin Gallagher and Minaketan Dash, for making the publication process a smooth one; and to Gail Naron Chalew for her exceptional copyediting. They have collectively convinced me of the enduring merits of the collaborative venture called "print publication" (see Chapter 6).

Thanks to my good friends Reuven Ashtar and Jared Bland for their support and advice. Thanks to my mother Jill Rice for her unending and unvarying support, and to my father Daniel R. Hammond for encouraging my work in this field.

Finally, I would like to thank Marta Balcewicz, without whose encouragement and detailed feedback I could not have completed this book. It is dedicated to her.

Part I

Is Literature Dying in the Digital Age?

Chapter 1

The Digital Medium and Its Message

At the time of his death in 1980, Marshall McLuhan was principally famous for two things: for having said, "The medium is the message" and for having deeply confused an entire generation by doing so. When I was growing up in Ontario in the 1980s, I remember watching a government-sponsored commemorative TV advertisement about McLuhan, part of a series of sixty-second celebrations of eminent Canadians. In the ad, an actor portrays a tweedy, mustachioed McLuhan leading a seminar at the University of Toronto. Suddenly he has his Eureka moment: "No, no... The medium is not more *important* than the message it carries.... It – it's obvious. The medium *is* the message."[1] Students leave the class, excited by the power of the gnomic phrase, yet also utterly perplexed by it. Back in the classroom, the fictionalized McLuhan paces about, ranting madly in solitude. Unable to fit his rambling theories into the minute allotted, the advertisement cuts him off mid-sentence. McLuhan had undoubtedly come up with something important, the advertisement implied – but exactly what it was remained entirely unclear.

Today, McLuhan has come into focus. In part this is because the things he said about electronic media like radio and television turned out to be more applicable to digital media such as networked computers and smartphones. As *Wired* magazine recognized when it posthumously named McLuhan its "Patron Saint" in 1993, his theories only really began to make sense with the arrival of the internet. Since then, as the digital medium has extended further and further into our daily lives, we have come increasingly to feel the truth of McLuhan's statement, "The medium is the message." So much of what we consume online is just the old media fed to us in new ways: Netflix is mostly made up of old TV shows and movies; YouTube is replete with MTV-style music videos and commercials; the most popular podcasts are radio shows. As McLuhan said, "The content of the medium is never the message because the content is always the old medium."[2] The real change comes from the new medium itself, which "creates a new situation for human association and human perception."[3] Even when the content of digital media is identical to its analog predecessors, we can feel how the digital medium itself changes our

3

lives: all-night Netflix binges abetted by the ability to watch whatever we want, whenever we want; the comments section on an old music video from the early 1990s that connects us with diehard fans of a song we thought everyone had forgotten; the favorite weekly podcast on a topic so obscure it would not stand a chance on commercial radio. "*That,*" McLuhan contends, "is the effect the medium has – that total, pervasive effect – *that* is the message, the social change that is brought about."[4]

No group is more sensitive to the changes inherent in the shift to digital forms than readers of literature. What the digital age has accomplished, above all else, is to defamiliarize the act of reading. It has done so by offering us choices. We begin reading an article in a print magazine on the bus; when we get to work, we finish reading it on the magazine's website. In the living room, we read novels on our tablets; in bed, we thumb the pages of a paperback. Reading a photocopied scholarly article, we discover another article we would like to consult; opening our laptops, we head for the library website and download the PDF. As we shift back and forth between print and digital forms, reading becomes an increasingly self-conscious act. We study not only the words on the page or the screen but also the way that the medium itself seems to shape our reading. Is it harder to concentrate on a long novel on an iPad, where e-mail notifications and Twitter messages easily break the spell of narrative? Does an embedded video in an "enhanced e-book" enrich the reading experience or merely distract from it? If the ability to discuss a novel with an online reading community transforms a solitary experience into a social one, is this for the better or worse?

This chapter takes up the big questions that accompany the shift from printed to digital forms: how reading is changing in the digital age and how our shifting reading practices are reshaping our society and ourselves. It explores these issues through the debate initiated by Nicholas Carr's 2008 article, "Is Google Making Us Stupid?" – perhaps the most influential public account of the message of the digital medium. For Carr and his respondents Clay Shirky and Sven Birkerts, the debate turns on three key points: (1) the question of attention, of whether the printed book fostered the ability to concentrate in depth and at length and whether discontinuous reading habits promoted by digital forms are destroying this ability; (2) the question of whether print fostered individual consciousness and whether electronic media privilege group consciousness; and (3) the question of democracy, of whether the digital age – with its promises of unrestricted access to texts and new horizontal forms of association and collaboration – is inherently more democratic than the era of print. Because the debate between Carr, Shirky, and Birkerts unfolded online, it affords us the opportunity to test whether the characteristics of digital textuality themselves support one side of the argument or the other. And because the debate was later taken up in a series of printed book-length analyses in the popular and academic press, we can ask the same of the printed medium.

"Is Google Making Us Stupid?"

Nicholas Carr's 2008 *Atlantic* cover story "Is Google Making Us Stupid?" opens with a paradigmatic statement of the heightened media-consciousness characteristic of the digital age. "Over the past few years," he writes,

> I've had an uncomfortable sense that someone, or something, has been tinkering with my brain, remapping the neural circuitry, reprogramming the memory. My mind isn't going – so far as I can tell – but it's changing. I'm not thinking the way I used to think.[5]

The precise change that Carr perceives is a slackening in his ability to focus: "What the Net seems to be doing is chipping away my capacity for concentration and contemplation," he says: "My mind now expects to take in information the way the Net distributes it: in a swiftly moving stream of particles." One activity makes Carr feel these changes most acutely: reading. "Immersing myself in a book or a lengthy article used to be easy":

> My mind would get caught up in the narrative or the turns of the argument, and I'd spend hours strolling through long stretches of prose. That's rarely the case anymore. Now my concentration often starts to drift after two or three pages. I get fidgety, lose the thread, begin looking for something else to do. I feel as if I'm always dragging my wayward brain back to the text. The deep reading that used to come naturally has become a struggle.

As the article continues, it becomes clear that it is a specific type of reading – *literary* reading – that Carr believes is most threatened in the digital age. Polling some acquaintances – "literary types, most of them" – he hears from one friend, formerly a "voracious book reader" with an English Literature BA to prove it, who has stopped reading literature entirely; another friend reports, like a voice from a post-apocalyptic film, "I can't read *War and Peace* anymore. . . . I've lost the ability to do that. Even a blog post of more than three or four paragraphs is too much to absorb. I skim it." Carr himself, another English major, writes, "Once I was a scuba diver in the sea of words. Now I zip along the surface like a guy on a Jet Ski."

It's no coincidence, Carr argues, that we are most aware of the internet's cognitive effects while reading – nor is it coincidental that reading is the activity most affected by the spread of the digital. This is because reading *created* the very mindset that the digital age is now dismantling. In making this argument, Carr follows McLuhan very closely. In works such as *The Mechanical Bride* (1951) and *Understanding Media* (1964), McLuhan argued that Western thought was powerfully shaped by the development of the alphabet and its extension through the printing press. The repetition and uniformity that were made possible by the printing process, he postulated, served to promote the repetition and uniformity of Western linear logic, while the mass-produced book, read in private from the reader's fixed point of view, helped encourage the notion of individuality. Carr invokes McLuhan explicitly, elegantly summarizing his notion that "media are not just passive channels of information" but in fact "shape the process of thought" as they "supply the stuff of thought." Carr further accepts McLuhan's basic premise that the printing press was instrumental in shaping the Western mind. "The kind of deep reading that a sequence of printed pages promotes," Carr argues,

> is valuable not just for the knowledge we acquire from the author's words but for the intellectual vibrations those words set off within our own minds. In the quiet spaces opened up by the sustained, undistracted reading of a book... we make our own associations, draw our own inferences and analogies, foster our own ideas.

In the busy, noisy, frantic space of a digital text, by contrast, it is impossible to achieve the concentrated serenity that supports the literary mind. Even an identical text transferred from print into an electronic format enters into a chamber of digital disruptions:

> When the Net absorbs a medium, that medium is re-created in the Net's image. It injects the medium's content with hyperlinks, blinking ads, and other digital gewgaws, and it surrounds the content with the content of all the other media it has absorbed. . . . The result is to scatter our attention and diffuse our concentration.

The deep reading fostered by print is important not only because it is necessary for comprehension, Carr argues, but also because it supports a particular kind of subjectivity. Behind the fast, cheap, superficial, "Jet Ski" mode of internet skim reading "lies a different kind of thinking," Carr says, and "perhaps even a new sense of self." Literary reading is not only the most conspicuous victim of a new and widespread form of attention deficit disorder – it is also the linchpin of the cherished notion of the individual consciousness as active, engaged, and critical. If our ability to read literature is at stake in the digital age, Carr implies, so too is the very notion of the individual.

Clay Shirky and the Democratic Riposte

"Is Google Making Us Stupid?" quickly became a touchstone for arguments about the social and cognitive effects of the internet – and it was on the internet itself that this debate initially took place. At the same time as the hard copy appeared on newsstands, *The Atlantic* ran the full text of the article for free on its website. The digital version of the article spread quickly through links on social media and in personal e-mails, and it rapidly inspired a wide-ranging digital response, from the comments section of the *Atlantic* website to blogs, Facebook, and Twitter. One of the most fascinating venues for this digital debate was the website of the venerable *Encyclopedia Britannica*, which invited a distinguished group of thinkers to participate in a blog-based forum it named "Your Brain Online." The first to respond was Clay Shirky, a writer on the social effects of the internet who presented a forceful rebuttal of Carr's position. Shirky begins by accepting some of Carr's premises. He agrees with Carr's McLuhan-derived notion that "the mechanisms of media affect the nature of thought" and admits that the "unprecedented abundance" of information online has the power to steer our reading practices toward what he calls "interrupt-driven info-snacking."[6] Shirky recognizes that Carr's article, despite its expansive title, is "focused on a very particular kind of reading, literary reading, as a metonym for a whole way of life." Shirky is indeed willing to go so far as to accept that literature, literary reading, and the "whole way of life" that they supported, are dying.

His objections center on two points: first, Carr's insistence that the internet is responsible for the death of literature; and second, the notion that the death of literature should be lamented at all. "Here's the thing," Shirky writes: "no one reads *War and Peace*. It's too long, and not so interesting. . . . The reading public has increasingly decided that Tolstoy's sacred work isn't actually worth the time it takes to read it." But it was television, not the internet, that initiated this move away from literary reading, which by the time of the internet's popularization was already long underway. The only difference is that in the television age literature managed to retain some of its "cultural status." As Shirky writes, "*Litterateurs* . . . continued to reassure one another that *War and Peace* or *À La Recherche du Temps Perdu* were Very Important in some vague way." The internet, however, finally led the public to withdraw this empty veneration. Citing Carr's own remarks that "we may well be reading more today than we did in the 1970s or 1980s, when television was our medium of choice," Shirky argues that "the internet has brought reading back as an activity" – just not *literary* reading. "Because the return of reading has not brought about the return of the cultural icons we'd been emptily praising all these years," he says, "the enormity of the historical shift away from literary culture is now becoming clear."

For Shirky, the real thrust of the shift to digital textuality – the real cultural significance of the internet – is its expansion of democracy. In a follow-up to his original post on the *Encyclopedia Britannica* blog, Shirky describes the internet as "a medium that radically expands our ability to create and share written material," adding, "Every past technology I know of that has increased the number of producers and consumers of written material, from the alphabet and papyrus to the telegraph and the paperback, has been good for humanity."[7] If we are currently undergoing an initial bout of information overload, struggling to spot the pearls of wisdom as we zip along the surface of online reading, we need only give ourselves time to adjust. "Technologies that make writing abundant," Shirky says, "always require new social structures to accompany them." Rather than casting a wistful retrospective gaze on the passing of a literary culture tainted by snobbery and exclusivity, Shirky argues that we ought to focus our attention on the new artistic possibilities of a democratic, inclusive, post-literary digital age. "Getting networked society right," he writes, "will mean producing the work whose themes best resonate on the net, just as getting the printing press right meant perfecting printed forms." "Nostalgia for the accidental scarcity we've just emerged from is just a sideshow," he concludes; "the main event is trying to shape the greatest expansion of expressive capability the world has ever known."

The Gutenberg Elegies Revisited

Shirky's post, even more than Carr's original article, was geared to provoke a reaction. With haste and vehemence that would have made Tolstoy proud, nearly everyone who had ever finished *War and Peace* emerged to announce that fact and defend the cherished work. Larry Sanger, the co-founder of *Wikipedia*, temporarily laid down his arms against his natural enemy, *Encyclopedia Britannica*, and posted a long response on its website, entitled "A Defense of Tolstoy & the Individual Thinker": having "read *War and Peace* twice" and "*loved* it," Sanger accused Shirky of "plain old philistinism."[8] Nicholas Carr joined the conversation as well, responding to Shirky on the *Britannica* forum with charges of "techno-utopianism" and "a highbrow form of philistinism."[9] The most surprising figure to join in the debate on the *Britannica* forum, however, was Sven Birkerts.

In 1994 – nearly fifteen years before "Is Google Making Us Stupid?" and shortly before the internet had begun to make its widespread social impact – Birkerts published *The Gutenberg Elegies*, a remarkably prescient book that anticipated many of Carr's arguments. In a chapter titled "The Death of Literature," Birkerts invokes McLuhan to argue, "We are in the midst of an epoch-making transition": "the societal shift from print-based to electronic communications is as consequential for culture as was the shift instigated by Gutenberg's invention of movable type."[10] This transition is most readily perceived, Birkerts argues, in the act of literary reading: "Who among us," he asks, "can generate the stillness and concentration and will to read Henry James, or Joseph Conrad, or James Joyce, or Virginia Woolf as they were meant to be read?" Working from similar theoretical and anecdotal bases, Birkerts's chief worry – as with Carr – is that the new electronic regime will disrupt the model of subjectivity fostered by the printing press. The "circuit and screen," he writes, are "antithetical to inwardness,"[11] and the electronic era is thus one in which "the human individual fac[es] the prospect of the erasure of individual selfhood."[12] The rapid technological advances since the early 1990s have severely dated many of Birkerts's descriptions of electronic threats to individual subjectivity. The seriousness of his warning that we are, "appliance by appliance," "wiring ourselves into a gigantic hive"[13] is greatly undercut by the particular appliances he names: "Telephone, fax, computer-screen networks, e-mail, interactive television – these are the components out of which the hive is being built."[14] Yet if we set aside the CD-ROMs, the fax machines, and the "VCRs, with Nintendo capacities," Birkerts's account of a new form of technologically linked "hive mind" remains chillingly prophetic. Substitute his devices for ours, and his statement, "The idea of spending a day, never mind a week, out of the range of all our devices sounds bold, even risky," is truer today than in 1994.[15]

Birkerts's arguments in *The Gutenberg Elegies* indeed serve as effective preemptive counters against the kind of democratic "techno-utopianism" in which Shirky engaged in the 2008 debate. Contra Shirky, Birkerts sees the digital world as carrying an antidemocratic thrust "The techno-web and the democratic ideal are in opposition. Our whole economic and technological obsession with getting on-line is leading us away – not from democracy necessarily, but from the premise that individualism and circuited interconnection are, at a primary level, inimical notions."[16] If digital interconnection is leading us away from a notion of democracy premised on the plurality of strong, independent citizens, Birkerts proposes to use the printed book as a weapon against its incursions. Like Carr, Birkerts sees reading as a McLuhanian "counter-environment": a place outside the dominant media environment from which we can register and study its effects. "We hold in our hands a way to cut against the momentum of the times," Birkerts writes. "We can resist the skimming tendency and delve; we can restore, if only for a time, the vanishing assumption of coherence."[17] In a moment of rare optimism, he perceives "the possibility for a genuine resurgence of the arts, of literature in particular":

> The book . . . will be seen as a haven, a way of going off-line and into a space sanctified by subjectivity. So long as there is a natural inclination toward independent selfhood, so long will literature be able to prove the reports of its death exaggerated.[18]

In a rousing peroration, Birkerts ends *The Gutenberg Elegies* with a prescription for resisting the encroachment of the electronic: total abstinence. Echoing the words attributed to Satan in the hellfire sermon in James Joyce's *Portrait of the Artist as a Young Man*, "*non serviam*, I will not serve,"[19] Birkerts closes his volume with this statement: "From deep in the heart I hear the voice that says, 'Refuse it.'"[20]

Alas, the voice was not strong enough to keep Birkerts away from his computer in the summer of 2008. Incited by Shirky's blithe dismissal of *War and Peace* – not to mention his insulting characterization of Birkerts as a "know-nothing" – Birkerts emerged from digital hibernation to reiterate his elegiac theses. In a line delivered with all the polish of a car-commercial slogan, Birkerts asserts, "*War and Peace* has achieved – and for over a century represented – a certain standard of greatness"; its "value," as such, cannot be read as "a function of popularity."[21] As to Shirky's insistence that we must focus our attention on "trying to shape the greatest expansion of expressive capability the world has ever known," Birkerts argues that intimate familiarity with works like *War and Peace* is a prerequisite for such a project:

> Shaping needs not only shapers, but some consensus vision among those shapers of what our society and culture might be shaped toward. I don't know that we trust the commercial marketplace to tell us. So, some deep comprehension of our inheritance, including the work of the now-derided Leo Tolstoy, is essential.

Thus Birkerts's sense of the stakes of the shift to digital media had not changed since *The Gutenberg Elegies*. "I prize a sense of inhabiting my self-constituted boundaries as a distinct 'I,'" he wrote in a follow-up post: "I fear that the steady centrifugal pull of the internet blurs me in these respects, makes it harder for me to achieve the subjective distinctness I am after."[22] If this was so, he had reason to be concerned: it was his second post on the *Encyclopedia Britannica* blog that week, with another yet to come.

From Message to Medium: Adriaan van der Weel's "Salient Properties" of Digital Textuality

Beyond a general acceptance of McLuhan's thesis that "the medium is the message," there is little agreement between rival factions regarding the specific tendency of the digital medium. For Carr and Birkerts, the digital age in general and digital forms of textuality in particular make it more difficult to muster the concentration required to engage actively with literature, thereby challenging a notion of the individual fostered by a textual medium requiring deep, linear attention. For Shirky, the Carr-Birkerts line of argumentation is nostalgic at best and elitist at worst. The shift toward digital textuality should be celebrated, he argues, for ushering in a more democratic age of literary production in which greater access to texts makes for more readers, greater ease of publication makes for more writers, and the interactive nature of the medium challenges the very lines dividing readers from writers.

Because we find so little agreement between these rival factions in the content of their arguments, let us take a cue from McLuhan and shift our focus from message to medium. Given that the debate was not only *about* digital textuality but in fact also *occurred digitally*, let us investigate the nature of digital discussion itself to test the rival claims on which it turned. Do the characteristics of online conversation serve to justify Carr's pessimism or to validate Shirky's optimism? How would the debate have played out differently had it taken place entirely in print – if Shirky had responded to Carr in the Letters to the Editor pages of the September 2008 issue of *The Atlantic* or if Birkerts had expressed his support for Carr's arguments in a revised and enlarged print edition of *The Gutenberg Elegies*?

Before we can answer these questions, a better understanding of the specific characteristics of digital textuality is required. A useful starting point in our investigation is Adriaan van der Weel's *Changing Our Textual Minds* (2011). Looking at digital forms from the perspective of book history, van der Weel identifies the following "salient features" that distinguish digital texts from their print predecessors.[23]

1. *Textual instability.* Printed texts are static, unalterable, and permanent; this explains the cachet of first editions, as well as the seriousness with which errors and omissions are treated in printed books – wounds that inserted errata slips can never quite heal. The protean digital text, in contrast, is forever alterable. This "lack of closure" – the fact that a digital text is never truly finished, remaining always open to further visions and revisions – is, for van der Weel, one of the most marked differences between the digital and print.[24]

2. *Ease and low cost of copying.* The business model of book publishing is premised on the relatively high costs of printing and distributing physical books. Digital texts, however, are extremely cheap and easy to copy. For instance, to view a web page, your browser must copy all relevant data from the server on which the page resides. Such digital copies are not only extremely inexpensive but also perfect. The distinction between original and copy is thus troubled in the digital realm.

3. *Speed.* Crucial to the ease of copying is the speed at which it occurs. The speed of transmission on the internet is such that any point on the network can be reached almost immediately, regardless of physical distance. The relatively small size of entirely text-based files means that volumes that would take up many shelves in physical form can be transferred almost instantaneously.

4. *Two-way traffic.* While printed texts tend to travel on one-way streets, from publisher to printer to distributor to bookseller to reader, all traffic on the internet is bidirectional, based on the interaction of clients and servers. These roles, moreover, are necessarily reversible: every computer can be both a client and a server.

5. *Lack of hierarchy.* Because it was originally designed so that it would continue to function even if large parts of it were destroyed, the internet is architecturally "flat." Whereas the distribution of a given printed text could be interrupted, for example, by bombing the printing house where it is being produced or by destroying a truck delivering an edition, digital texts move across the internet in "packets" that will find new routes if their path is obstructed at any point. Because of this nonhierarchical, "flat" structure, the internet is effectively centerless.

6. *Convergence of modalities.* Whereas the printed page is limited in the modalities it can transmit (text, still images, and – in flip books – moving images) it is possible to combine many more modalities in the digital realm: text, still images, moving images, and sound. The digital medium thus makes possible the convergence of all other media, such as recorded music, television, newspapers, magazines, and books.

Modalities and media

Though I strive to avoid technical jargon in this book, a definitional digression is required for the terms **modality** and **medium**. For my purposes, a **modality** is a type of information that can be communicated through a medium. In the course of this book, we will deal with four artistic **modalities**: text, still images, moving images, and sound. A **medium**, by contrast, is a specific communication technology for recording and disseminating messages. Particular media (or mediums) are capable of transmitting particular combinations of modalities. The medium of print, for instance, usually records and transmits the modalities of text and still images; the medium of radio deals only with the modality of sound; and the digital medium is able to carry all four of these modalities.

---

7. *Access through content.* One of the main functions of print libraries is to organize books in such a way that readers can find the texts they need as quickly as possible. Digital texts, however, make it possible for readers to bypass such organizational machinery, along with whatever "gatekeeping" function it might serve. Rather than searching for a text by author, subject, or genre, readers can search the book's content directly, for instance looking for books that contain certain sentences or phrases.

These "salient properties" serve to clarify what is distinctly "digital" in the Carr/Shirky/Birkerts debate. First, it transpired much more rapidly than a print debate carried out in the pages of newspapers, magazines, or – slowest by far – books; interlocutors exchanged barbs in intervals of hours – not days, months, or years (*speed*). Digital publication also opened the debate to a much wider readership than would have been possible in print. Because argument and counterargument, post and counterpost, took place in a medium that distributes texts instantaneously (*speed*) throughout the entire globe at very low cost (*ease and low cost of copying*), there were few disincentives for interested readers to take in the whole of the debate. If they had not heard of the particular discussion, but were interested in the cognitive effects of the internet, a few moments' Googling would lead them to it (*access through content*). Perhaps the most distinctive feature of the digital medium, however, is the ability for these readers to participate in the debate themselves. Owing to their computers' ability to switch instantly from client to server (*two-way traffic*) and to the particular affordances of the platforms on which the debate took place, these readers had the ability to very easily post their comments and thus switch roles from reader to writer. Try doing that with a book.

With van der Weel's "salient properties" in mind, we are ready to ask which side of the debate they tend to support. Van der Weel himself takes Shirky's side. If we are witnessing the transition from the "Order of the Book" to some new "disorderly" digital world, he argues, it will ultimately be a gain for democracy. "The material form of the book," he writes,

> makes it an instrument that naturally favors the creation of lasting records of human thought, and that naturally imposes a hierarchical, orderly, and linear order on those records. Books are self-contained, unchangeable, authoritative: monuments of achievement. By extension, in a literate society like ours, an education system based on books favors a hierarchical, orderly, and linear way of thinking. In this manner the Order of the Book strongly influences – even determines – our way of conceptualizing the world.[25]

The digital realm, by contrast, "constitutes a more level form of cultural transmission":

> [It is] democratic, fluid, tending towards disorder, consisting of endless chunks of textual matter, connected actively and deliberately through links, and passively and potentially through search queries, allowing endless permutations and recombinations. Moreover, these text chunks also find themselves in the company of chunks of other modalities, in equally rich variety and quantities. The well governed and orderly textual world in which everything has its place is being confronted by a docuverse of text and other modalities that is decidedly disorderly, even anarchic.[26]

Van der Weel's arguments shed light on the Carr/Birkerts/Shirky debate. There is no doubting the democratic thrust of a digital medium that allowed this debate to occur in real time in searchable, freely accessible channels. The most powerful card in Shirky's hand, however, is the digital medium's affordances for reader participation: the opportunity that it extends for readers to become writers – for passive subjects to become active citizens. A close examination of the actual reader participation in this debate, however, reveals a more complicated picture.

Participation, Pro and Con: Reading Readers' Comments

As I write these words, the online version of "Is Google Making Us Stupid?" has received 23,000 Facebook shares, 2,000 tweets, and 466 comments. The comments system on the *Atlantic* website is anonymous, but requires users to be logged in. Registered users can comment and vote a post up or down by clicking on corresponding arrows. The comments are displayed in order of their voting rank (those with the most up-votes minus down-votes appear first) although the conversation is threaded, so that low-ranked replies to highly ranked comments appear near the top.

That these comments exist at all serves as a living argument in Shirky's favor: it is unquestionably "democratic" that the digital version of "Is Google Making Us Stupid" should allow readers to become writers and participate in the discussion – which they did, in large numbers. The way the comments are arranged on the *Atlantic* website – by user votes – is itself straightforwardly democratic. It is somewhat surprising, then, that given the opportunity to express their feelings on the social effects of the internet and to vote however they chose on other readers' comments on the subject, almost no one agreed with Shirky's line of argument. In fact, only 3 of the 466 commenters took his side: commonengineer noted that, as a nonsubscriber to *The Atlantic*, "Had it not been on-line, this article could not have come to my attention";[27] silverfox808 saw the fact that so many users had read and commented on Carr's lengthy article as "evidence contradicting [his] fundamental premise"; and Andrew Skeehan succinctly wrote, "If it weren't for the Internet, I would not have found your article, read it in its entirety, and enjoyed the lively discussion that followed" (Skeehan's comment received a single up-vote).

Most of the 466 comments instead relate to the issue of concentration. Recognizing a rare harmony of form and content – here was a long, dense online article about how difficult it is to read long, dense articles online – a great number of commenters treated the reading of Carr's article as an opportunity to test its thesis. Of these comments, the vast majority found that Carr's thesis was correct. By far the most common single response to Carr was "tl;dr," internet slang for "too long; didn't read." Forty-five comments (just under 10% of the total comments) belong to this category, most of which recognize the implicit humor in the situation. When RafaelR wrote, "I didn't read the article, can someone sum it up?", Javier Sanchez replied, "You just did! lol." Others were less sanguine. "I made it a point to read the whole thing without being distracted," wrote jpgram777. "It was hard. I wasn't able to do it. I found myself stopping to e-mail it to others. I was also interrupted by a few Instant Messages through iChat. Plus, I just found it hard to read 'on-screen.'" Although fngaz was drawn in by the "catchy" title and amusing illustration, "further down there was just a vast sea of words and nothing else to catch my attention. You mean I actually have to read all this?!?!"

As jpgram777's comment attests, it was not just the length and complexity of Carr's argument that made it difficult to follow but also the fact that it was published online. Some users tied this difficulty to the issue of media convergence – to the fact that because computers and smart phones are not dedicated reading devices, their other functions can interrupt the reading experience. Katrina Waldo wrote, "Even while I was reading this particular article, I was finding it difficult to concentrate . . . and ignore the fact that I had Facebook notifications, @-replies on Twitter, and available software updates. I can say," she concluded, "that I am legitimately frightened after reading this." Other readers blamed the particular presentation on the *Atlantic* website. AndyGCook noted that, while reading the article, he "came across 21 in-article hyperlinks." Preston said, "It's funny that there is an advertisement in the middle of this article. Or is that irony? Or is that just a bit sad?" It was enough to make more than one reader long for the still, linkless mono-media of the book. Evyrioclo astutely wrote,

> I think the idea that the internet and Google offers [sic] click after click after click is well-taken. When you have a book in hand, clicking is not an option. A book is weighty and 3-dimensional and leaves you with no other option. The irony of this is that by "having no option" in the area of clicking, the reader is "free" to simply dive deep, to read that particular piece.

While agreeing with many other readers that Carr's article was "way too long," Joyce proposed, "If it were in print, I wouldn't mind as long as I could hold [it] in my hand."

Further evidence in support of Carr's argument comes from those who missed its point entirely. A great many commenters clearly did not read past the article's misleading title. Among them was shancha, who began, "Ok let me explain, why I tell Nicolas an idiot," and continued irrelevantly, "If you are lost in the city, and Google Map, shows you the way, is it bad???????" Such fatally uninformed comments (to say nothing of the various trolls and spam bots that participated in the discussion) might seem a parody of democracy: evidence that although the internet *permits* these commenters to participate in a rational debate, it has, at the same time, paradoxically made them too stupid to contribute anything meaningful. Yet a democratic counterargument presents itself: perhaps these voices have always existed, but simply have not been heard.

Back to the Page: Debating the Digital in Print

Although digital debates like that on the *Encyclopedia Britannica* website were the first to take up "Is Google Making Us Stupid?," vigorous debates also took place in the pages of printed books – only a few years later, as dictated by the slower pace of print publication. 2010 saw the publication of both *The Shallows*, Carr's book-length expansion of his *Atlantic* article, and *Cognitive Surplus*, Shirky's response to digital pessimism of the Carr variety. Literary scholars took an active part in this stage of the debate as well. Two books by professors of literature – Cathy Davidson's *Now You See It* (2011) and Katherine Hayles's *How We Think* (2012) – are representative of the academic response to the Carr/Birkerts/Shirky debate. As printed books, *The Shallows*, *Cognitive Surplus*, *Now You See It*, and *How We Think* have much in common: they are physical objects whose words are static, unalterable, and permanent (~~textual instability~~); buying and reading them costs money (~~ease and low cost of copying~~); they took a relatively long time to write, edit, print, and distribute (~~speed~~); they were produced in the top-down, writer-to-reader world of print publication (~~two-way traffic, lack of hierarchy~~); they contain only modalities than can be printed in books, such as text and still images (~~convergence of modalities~~); and unless you obtain a digital copy, their content cannot be searched (~~access through content~~). Yet it did not necessarily follow that, because they were printed books, they should all take the side of print against the digital.

The Shallows not only continues Carr's argumentative line but also takes it to heart. As Carr relates in a digression near the end of the book, in order to write *The Shallows* he had to move to a remote mountain town with no cell phone connectivity or high-speed internet, deactivate his Twitter and Facebook accounts, "mothball" his blog, and go on a strict e-mail diet.[28] The book itself is a testament to the "salient properties" of print, most salient of which is the obverse of digital speed. Away from the rapid-fire exchanges of online debate, the argument that unfolds in *The Shallows* is similar to that of "Is Google Making Us Stupid?" – only longer, slower, more deliberate, and more clearly the work of a concentrated and isolated thinker. The principal difference is a deeper engagement with the relevant scientific studies in cognitive neuroscience. Carr's conclusions are similar but differently supported: now, when he argues, "The Net is, by design, an interruption system, a machine geared for dividing attention,"[29] he backs up his points with a study of the effects of digital reading on working memory that concludes "people who read linear text comprehend more, remember more, and learn more than those who read text peppered with links."[30] Although Carr's argument was well received in its print form – *The Shallows* was nominated for a Pulitzer Prize – it nonetheless clearly benefited from its rehearsal online. Most notably, Carr incorporates parts of the *Encyclopedia Britannica* exchange directly into *The Shallows*. He devotes several paragraphs to explaining, and refuting, the blog post in which Shirky claimed, "No one reads *War and Peace*," accusing

Shirky of supplying "the intellectual cover that allows thoughtful people to slip comfortably into the permanent state of distractedness that defines online life."[31]

Shirky's *Cognitive Surplus* appeared in print the week after *The Shallows*. Though it does not make any direct reference to the exchange on the *Encyclopedia Britannica* website, its arguments for the democratizing power of the internet are in the same spirit. What is truly new in the digital age, for Shirky, is that "the old choice between one-way public media (like books and movies) and two-way private media (like the phone) has now expanded to include a third option: two-way media that operates on a scale from private to public."[32] Whereas one-way media like TV and radio inspired a generation of "consumers and couch potatoes," the transformative aspect of the internet is "the inclusion of amateurs as producers, where we no longer need to ask for help or permission from professionals to say things in public."[33] All pre-digital media, Shirky argues, operated according to what he calls "Gutenberg economics": wherever it was expensive and difficult to own and operate the means of production, producers gained total control over what the audience would see. In the digital age, by contrast, when it is easy and cheap to produce and disseminate our own content, the distinction between audience and producer breaks down. For Shirky, any decrease in the average quality of artworks in a democratic media economy is more than compensated for by the more general distribution of the right to participate. "The stupidest possible creative act," he says, "is still a creative act." That Shirky should make these arguments in the pages of a printed book – a form of publication that remains very much closed to the average digital-age producer/consumer and continues to operate very literally within the world of "Gutenberg economics" – does, however, undermine them to a degree. If Shirky really believed what he was saying, why would he say it in a book?

We might ask a similar question in response to Davidson's *Now You See It: How the Brain Science of Attention Will Transform the Way We Live, Work, and Learn*. Though the interests of the book are as broad as its subtitle implies, Davidson, a literary scholar, presents a particularly pointed response to Carr's arguments about reading in the digital age. She lists *The Shallows* among "a spate of books with alarmist titles and subtitles" that claim that "technology destroys our brain."[34] In response to these books' insistence that "the contemporary era's distractions are bad for us," Davidson writes, "All we really know is that our digital age demands a different form of attention than we've needed before."[35] Drawing on her own reading in neuroscience, she suggests that "multitaskers [aren't] paying attention *worse*"; they are "paying attention *differently*."[36] Claiming that "what confuses the brain delights the brain," she presents "incongruity, disruption, and disorientation" as potentially "inspiring, creative, and productive forces" and argues that "new digital ways of thinking" might represent a "creative disruption of our usual thought patterns."[37] Davidson, however, holds little hope for literature in its traditional forms. She mocks Sven Birkerts's notion that "the real issue of the twenty-first century [is] that the Internet makes us so shallow we can no longer read long novels," suggesting we have far more pressing issues to confront first. The only form of narrative art she discusses at any length – the only form for which she sees a bright future – is the videogame. Arguing that digital distraction equals mental refreshment and presenting videogames as the most refreshing of the new digital forms, Davidson suggests that the diminishment of our capacity to enjoy old-fashioned "long novels" is a matter of secondary importance – truly a "sideshow," as Shirky had first proposed.

Hayles's *How We Think* picks up the thread of Davidson's argument, yet develops it in a more hopeful direction. Hayles, also a professor of literature, takes issue with some of Carr's analysis of his scientific sources.[38] Her main response, however, is to demand a more careful examination of the different *kinds* of reading that are emerging in the digital age and how they can best be made to interact. Hayles distinguishes between three types of reading: (1) *close reading*, the close analysis of complex texts that "correlates with deep attention, the cognitive mode traditionally associated with the humanities that prefers a single information stream, focuses on a single cultural object for a relatively long time, and has a high tolerance for boredom"; (2) *hyper reading*, the kind of reading that occurs most often online, which includes "skimming, scanning, fragmenting, and juxtaposing texts" and which Hayles associates with "hyper attention, a cognitive mode that has a low threshold for boredom, alternates flexibly between different information streams, and prefers a high level of stimulation"; and (3) *machine reading*, the analysis of text through the application of computer algorithms.[39] In Hayles's view, Carr is justified in worrying that "hyper reading" will cause changes in brain function that will in turn make "close reading" increasingly difficult. But Carr is wrong, Hayles argues, to position "hyper reading" as a totally malign parasite on close reading and to pit the two against one another in an either/or duality. "The problem," Hayles writes,

> lies not in hyper attention and hyper reading as such but rather in the challenges the situation presents for parents and educators to ensure that deep attention and close reading continue to be vibrant components of our reading cultures and interact synergistically with the kind of web and hyper reading in which our young people are increasingly immersed.[40]

Agreeing with Davidson that "hyper attention can be seen as a positive adaptation that makes young people better suited to live in the information-intensive environments that are becoming ever more pervasive," she nonetheless asserts, "I think deep attention is a precious social achievement" and "a heritage we cannot afford to lose."[41] Her own analysis in *How We Think* considers emerging forms of born-digital literature – works such as Steve Tomasula's multimodal digital novel *TOC*, a "remarkable literary work" that she presents as evidence of the rich "possibilities of the digital regime"[42] – while also investigating strategies for catalyzing the interactions of close, hyper, and machine reading on which the fate of our literary heritage depends.

Given the polarized nature of the debate between Carr and Shirky, Hayles's insistence on balance and hybridity is refreshing. It is also both sensible and appropriate, for ours is a mixed and hybrid moment. Although literature may be shifting into the digital medium, the fate of print is by no means sealed. Carr makes convincing arguments for print and against the digital, and Shirky makes convincing arguments for the digital and against print – yet print and the digital are too closely intertwined today to allow us to take either Carr's or Shirky's side absolutely. The complex interdependence of digital and printed text is indeed manifest in *The Shallows* and *Cognitive Surplus* themselves. Carr's book decries the fatal effects of the digital world on the literary mind – yet it incorporates key points from an online debate in which Carr participated. Shirky, after declaring *War and Peace* too long to read and attacking the "Gutenberg economics" of print publication as unethical and socially regressive, proceeds to expand these views in a 242-page print book published by one of the world's largest publishers. The situation is at least as complicated in *Now You See It*, in which a literary critic argues that we should not mind if young people are no longer able to read novels, yet presents her argument in a long printed book. It is not that Carr, Shirky, and Davidson are hypocrites; it is simply that they are living in a hybrid moment. Like so many of us, they have one foot in the print world and the other in the digital.

As we return to the three big questions with which we began this chapter, let us remain mindful of the paradoxical situation we find ourselves in and resist the urge to take a particular side. The digital world is harming our ability to concentrate on literature; yet the few moments of concentrated literary attention that we somehow manage to achieve can provide valuable means of understanding and even resisting the digital world. The digital medium is both strengthening democracy, by granting greater opportunities for access and participation, and weakening it, by making it more difficult to formulate individual opinions in solitude. Let us accept that, if the digital world is killing literature as we have come to know it, then this presents us with an immense opportunity to reevaluate and redefine literature. What is it? What is best about it and what is worst? What aspects of literature can we live without, and which aspects must survive? For literature to thrive, what must it become? In the digital age, each of these is an open question without a clear answer – which is why this is such an exciting time to study literature.

Chapter 2

Medium Shifts: Literary Thought in Media History

If we are indeed moving, as Adriaan van der Weel argues, from the "Order of the Book" – a society shaped by literary values of order, linearity, and reason – toward some new disorder of the digital, then the anxiety felt by many readers of literature is entirely understandable. Because it is *our* world and *our* values that are passing away, we can even be forgiven the occasional feeling of panic. Yet ours is not the first generation to experience a shift in literary technology or its attendant unease. Media historians speak of four ages of literature: the oral age, when literature was performed from memory for live audiences; the chirographic or manuscript age, when, after the development of the alphabet, literature attained its first written form; the print age, in which writing became subject to mechanical reproduction; and the digital age we are presently entering. We are indeed living through an epochal transition: the movement of literature from print to digital form is only the third such medium shift in history, and the first in more than five hundred years. But we can take some solace in the fact that, like us, those devoted to literature felt the ground shifting beneath their feet when knowledge passed from memory to written form, and from manuscript to print. Literary thinkers panicked in those moments of transition, and they panicked again when electronic media such as radio, film, and television challenged the supremacy of the written word. The history of literary technology is one that unfolds in cycles. We have been here before.

In this chapter, we look at the historical relationship between medium shifts and literary thought. In analyzing this dynamic interplay, three points emerge. First, transitions in literary technology tend to produce very similar anxieties. Second, periods of medium transition have tended to be productive moments for literary thinking, presenting opportunities to understand better what literature is and how it can be adapted to thrive in a new media environment. Finally, the field of literary studies itself experienced its greatest expansion in a period of medium transition, developing in response to the emergence of electronic media in the early twentieth century. To the question "Is literature dying in the digital age?," the historical record suggests a clear answer: no.

The Persistence of Pessimism: Reactions to the Invention of Writing and the Printing Press

Shortly after *The Shallows* appeared in print, Nicholas Carr directed readers of his *Rough Type* blog to a "fascinating" yet "disquieting" scientific study that seemed to provide definitive scientific grounding for his concerns about the damaging neurological effects of the internet.[1] "Google Effects on Memory: Cognitive Consequences of Having Information at Our Fingertips," published in the journal *Science* in 2011 by psychologists Betsy Sparrow, Jenny Liu, and Daniel M. Wegner, tests whether the availability of online information affects the way that we store information in our memory. Its main finding is that the internet is indeed becoming an increasingly important form of external or "transactive" memory – and that our access to vast stores of digital information online has materially affected the way we remember. In a series of experiments, the authors find that humans will not bother to remember information if they know it is available online, and they further note a shift in cognitive resources from remembering facts in themselves to remembering how and where to locate facts online. As they write in their dramatic conclusion,

> We are becoming symbiotic with our computer tools, growing into interconnected systems that remember less by knowing information than by knowing where the information can be found. This gives us the advantage of access to a vast range of information, although the disadvantages of being constantly "wired" are still being debated. It may be no more than nostalgia at this point, however, to wish we were less dependent on our gadgets. . . . The experience of losing our Internet connection becomes more and more like losing a friend. We must remain plugged in to know what Google knows.[2]

Reflecting on these sweeping statements, Carr wonders whether "we may be entering an era in history in which we will store fewer and fewer memories inside our own brains."[3] Then, referencing the Emersonian notion that "the essence of personal memory is not the discrete facts or experiences we store in our mind but 'the cohesion' which ties all those facts and experiences together," he characteristically raises the stakes: "As memory shifts from the individual mind to the machine's shared database," he asks, "what happens to that unique 'cohesion' that is the self?"

Carr interprets the article in *Science* as evidence that the internet is ushering in a new phase of human cognition. Yet before we follow him into such future-oriented speculations, we must note a striking parallel from the distant past: namely, that nearly everything Sparrow and her colleagues have to say about the internet's effects on memory was first said some 2,350 years before by Plato about writing. Plato's *Phaedrus* begins with Socrates walking outside the walls of Athens with a sophist named Phaedrus. The two engage in a competition to see who can deliver the best speech on love, and after each makes his attempt, the focus of the *Phaedrus* shifts from content to form: from the nature of love itself to the proper method for presenting one's thoughts on the subject. Here Socrates objects not only to the matter but also to the medium of Phaedrus's speech – for while Socrates recited his speech from memory, Phaedrus read his from a scroll. Socrates presents his objections to writing in the form of a historical parable. At the time of the invention of writing, Theuth, its inventor, boasted to the Egyptian king Thamus that writing would "make the Egyptians wiser and . . . improve their memory." Thamus responds to Theuth by arguing that writing will in fact weaken memory, forcing the mind to rely on external, objective, inhuman records. Writing, Thamus says, "will introduce forgetfulness into the soul of those who learn it": those who employ this dangerous technology "will put their trust in writing, which is external and depends on signs that belong to others, instead of trying to remember from the inside, completely on their own." In a literate society, Plato implies, it is not *people* who will be wise, but *books*. As Thamus tells Theuth, "You have not discovered a potion for remembering, but for reminding; you provide your students with the appearance of wisdom, not with its reality"; like the obnoxious dinner guest who turns to his smartphone's "transactive memory" to settle a debate, the literate "will be difficult to get along with, since they will merely appear to be wise instead of really being so."[4] Just as Carr worries that dependence on an internet-borne external memory will diminish our sense of self, Plato believes that writing will foster a more passive, less engaged subjectivity. In conversation, we can disagree with our interlocutor or ask for an elaboration; when we question an assertion in a written document, however, it remains "most solemnly silent" – if we attack it, "it can neither defend itself nor come to its own support."[5]

The similarities between the positions of Plato and Carr are indeed striking: for both, the new medium threatens to destroy the human memory, to weaken the human mind, and thereby to diminish our ability to reflect critically and engage actively as individuals. But Carr was not the first critic of the digital world to employ arguments closely resembling those of Plato. As early as 1982, when the digital computer was first entering public consciousness as a potential rival to writing and print, Walter Ong – who studied under McLuhan – noted the curious fact that "essentially the same objections commonly urged today against computers were urged by Plato in *The Phaedrus* . . . against writing."[6] Yet this peculiar congruence is not limited only to comparisons between orality and literacy, on the one hand, and print and digital media, on the other. As Alexander Nehamas and Paul Woodruff argue in their introduction to the *Phaedrus*, Plato's objections to writing are simply the first instance of a debate that has, in ensuing centuries, been repeated continually. Whenever *any* new medium presents itself, we tend to connect the older medium with rationality and stable subjectivity and to see the new one as threatening to both. Moreover, we tend to judge the new medium by the standards of the older medium, neglecting any positive potential that the former may possess. Plato is quite right to note that a written document is unable to respond to objections in the course of an oral debate, as a live speaker would, yet is apparently blind to the fact that his own complex and intricate philosophy is transmittable only in a form that is permanent and can be endlessly reread – in other words, in writing.[7] As Ong puts it, "Plato expresses serious reservations in the *Phaedrus*... about writing as a mechanical, inhuman way of processing knowledge, unresponsive to questions and destructive of memory" – yet "as we now know, the philosophical thinking Plato fought for depended entirely on writing."[8]

According to Nehamas and Woodruff, arguments like Carr's – however pressing and urgent they may seem – are in a sense inevitable, recurring in almost identical form every time a medium shift occurs. Their position is bolstered by the early reception of the printing press. Many early critics of printing focused on the aesthetic superiority of manuscripts, arguing that hand-copied books were more beautiful and more worthy of reverence. As John Donne (1572–1631) wrote, "What presses give birth to with sodden pangs is acceptable, but manuscripts are more venerated. A book dyed with the blood of the press departs to an open shelf where it is exposed to moths and ashes; but one written by the pen is held in reverence, and flies to the privileged shelf reserved for the ancient fathers."[9] In his essay "In Praise of Scribes," the Benedictine abbot Johannes Trithemius (1462–1516) lamented the obsolescence of monastic copying clerks on the grounds that the spiritual nature of their work, and their genuine love for the material they copied, would ensure greater accuracy than would the work of printers, who were motivated primarily by profit.[10]

The main objection to the printing press closely mirrored Plato's main objection to writing and strongly prefigured Carr's attitude toward digital text. In *Too Much to Know* (2010), book historian Ann Blair argues that the proliferation of printed books in Renaissance Europe prompted an experience of "information overload on an unprecedented scale."[11] In 1566, Jean Bodin complained that "the life of a man, however prolonged, is hardly sufficient to read" all the available material;[12] in 1581, Francisco Sanchez estimated that it would take ten million years to read every book in existence.[13] In 1477, Hieron-imo Squarciafico claimed "the abundance of books makes men less studious," weakening the memory and relieving the mind of necessary work.[14] In 1523, Erasmus attacked printers who "fill the world with pamphlets and books [that are] . . . foolish, ignorant, malignant, libelous, mad, impious and subversive." "Is there anywhere on earth exempt from these swarms of new books?" he asked, before asserting that, because "men's minds are easily glutted and hun-gry for something new," the "distractions" of ever-increasing numbers of books "call them away from the reading of ancient authors."[15] Many feared that the glut of books would distract readers from intensive study of The Book: John Calvin (1506–1564) derided the "confused forest of books,"[16] whereas Martin Luther (1483–1546) declared "the multitude of books . . . a great evil", adding, "The aggregation of large libraries tends to divert men's thoughts from the one great book, the Bible, which ought, day and night, to be in every one's hand."[17]

In the early era of print – when there was "too much to know" and too little time to process it, and when the volume of printed matter made quality control increasingly difficult – Plato's ideal of wisdom seemed increasingly at risk. Time did little to quell these concerns. In 1680, Gottfried Wilhelm Leibniz despaired of "that horrible mass of books which keeps on growing," arguing that "the indefinite multitude of authors will shortly expose them all to the danger of general oblivion."[18] Edgar Allan Poe (1809–1849) described "the enormous multiplication of books in every branch of knowledge" as "one of the greatest evils of this age": "it presents one of the most serious obstacles to the acquisition of correct information," he wrote, "by throwing in the reader's way piles of lumber, in which he must painfully grope for scraps of useful matter peradventure interspersed."[19] Yet a few were able to perceive the advantages of the new medium. For James Boswell (1740–1795), the democratic impact of printing was more than adequate compensation for its uneven quality. "It has been maintained that this superfoetation, this teeming of the press in modern times, is prejudicial to good literature," Boswell wrote. "But it must be considered that we now have more knowledge generally diffuse." "All our ladies read now, which is a great extension," he added, and "there is now a great deal more learning in the world than there was formerly; for it is universally diffused."[20] Even those unwilling to admit the advantages of print were able to profit from them. Despite its passionate arguments against printing and in favor of manuscripts, Johannes Trithemius had "In Praise of Scribes" printed. Without the printing press, we would not have the opinions of Bodin, Sanchez, Erasmus, Calvin, Luther, Leibniz, or Poe.

Thus, our fears and anxieties about the transition from printed to digital literature closely mirror those expressed by earlier generations of critics at crucial moments of media transition. The very technologies whose legacies we are seeking to protect – writing and the printing press – were greeted earlier by the same suspicion with which we are greeting the digital today. As Andrew Piper writes in *Book Was There: Reading in Electronic Times* (2012),

> Four hundred years ago in Spain people read too many romances (*Don Quixote*), three hundred years ago in London too many people wrote crap (Grub Street), two hundred years ago in Germany reading had turned into a madness (the so-called *Lesewut*), and one hundred years ago there was the telephone. We have worried that one day there would be more authors than readers (in 1788), that self-publishing would save, and kill, reading (1773), and that no one would have time to read books anymore (in 1855). Everything that has been said about life in an online world has already been said about books.[21]

Nicholas Carr very nearly recognizes as much in "Is Google Making Us Stupid?" when he cites Hieronimo Squarciafico and the *Phaedrus* in the course of his admission that we "should be skeptical of [his] skepticism."[22] Yet although he acknowledges the historical precedents, he ultimately decides to set them aside, arguing, in effect, "Yes, but it's *different* this time." "Perhaps those who dismiss critics of the Internet as Luddites or nostalgists will be proved correct," he writes, "and from our hyperactive, data-stoked minds will spring a golden age of intellectual discovery and universal wisdom":

> Then again, the Net isn't the alphabet, and although it may replace the printing press, it produces something altogether different. The kind of deep reading that a sequence of printed pages promotes is valuable not just for the knowledge we acquire from the author's words but for the intellectual vibrations those words set off within our own minds. In the quiet spaces opened up by the sustained, undistracted reading of a book, or by any other act of contemplation, for that matter, we make our own associations, draw our own inferences and analogies, foster our own ideas.

Carr simply leads us back to where we started: far from offering a convincing account of the unique challenges posed by digital textuality, he delivers yet another echo of Plato's argument that writing destroys memory by externalizing knowledge. Piper responds to writers like Carr by suggesting a different path and a different focus. "It is time to stop worrying and start thinking," he writes. "It is time to put an end to the digital utopias and print eulogies," to retire "tired binaries like deep versus shallow." Instead, Piper says, "Now is the time to understand the rich history of what we have thought books have done for us and what we think digital texts might do differently."[23] To focus on whether literature is dying in the digital age is to miss the enormous opportunity that a medium shift affords us. To repeat this book's central refrain, we ought instead to take several steps back and focus on more fundamental questions: What is literature? What was it? How is it changing? What is it for?

Literary Experimentation and the Challenge of New Media: The Case of Modernism

We can take some solace in the fact that Plato's response to writing and Erasmus's to print so closely mirror our anxieties about literature in the digital age. Yet another historical precedent – that of the modernist period – provides grounds not just for solace but also for genuine enthusiasm. The list of communication technologies invented and popularized in the decades around the turn of the twentieth century is truly staggering: wireless telegraphy was invented in the 1890s and eventually developed into commercial radio in the 1920s; the gramophone disc, the first technology for the mass reproduction of sound, was invented in the late nineteenth century and popularized in the first decades of the twentieth; the first silent films, shown around 1900, were followed by the first talkies in the late 1920s. Alongside the introduction of pure inventions such as radio, recorded music, and film, earlier inventions become part of everyday life with the standardization of the mechanical typewriter, the rapid expansion of electrical grids, the widespread adoption of the telephone, and the spread of personal photography with cameras like the Kodak Brownie.

Despite our own sense of the unparalleled mental upheaval that has been wrought by digitization and the spread of the internet, many media historians argue that the digital age merely extends and intensifies technologies that, to modernist eyes, truly had no precedent. Digital technology connects us more intimately than the telephone, the radio, or the telegraph ever did; yet, as Alan Liu writes, "modernism was the era that first lived with telepresence."[24] Skype and FaceTime put long-distance telephony to shame, but the very idea of a voice speaking from thousands of miles away was one that citizens of modernity were the first to confront. The mental reorientations required of them, moreover, extended beyond the everyday and into art. As Lev Manovich argues, the explosion in communications technology in the modernist period incited the formal innovations for which modernist art is best known. "Between the latter half of the 1910s and the end of the 1920s," he writes, "all the key modern visual communication techniques were developed: photo and film montage, collage, classical film language, surrealism, the use of sex appeal in advertising, modern graphic design, modern typography."[25] These innovations, he contends, were "all made in relation to what was then *new media*: photography, film, new architectural and new printing technologies."[26] For Manovich, digital-age artistic innovation pales in comparison to that of the modernist period: modernism "came up with new forms, new ways to represent reality and new ways to see the world," whereas the digital era has merely devised new ways of "accessing and using previously accumulated media."[27]

Many modernist literary thinkers understandably reacted with alarm to the rapid development of new communication technologies. Friedrich Kittler argues that before the development of electronic media, the book served as a kind of master medium: in an era when the gramophone and film did not yet exist, the book became a "surrogate of unstorable data flows"[28] – a way of evoking modalities whose mechanization was not yet possible. Kittler argues that the book owed its special "power and glory" to its ability to present not only words on the page but also to project sounds and images "in the imaginary of readers' souls."[29] The development of modernist media, however, challenged the cultural preeminence of literature for the first time. In an article on "The New Talking Machines" for *The Atlantic* in 1889, Philip G. Hubert Jr. expressed his worry that "many books and stories may not see the light of print at all," but would "go into the hands of their readers, or hearers rather, as phonograms."[30] In his ponderously titled 1894 *Scribner's* article, "The End of Books," Octave Uzanne similarly speculated that the book was "threatened with death by the various devices for registering sound which have lately been invented": he wrote, "I do not believe (and the progress of electricity and modern mechanism forbids me to believe) that Gutenberg's invention can do otherwise than sooner or later fall into desuetude as a means of current interpretation of our mental products."[31]

Yet not all modernist literary critics responded with despair to the rise of new media. For the most astute modernist critics, the development of new media such as film and radio served to clarify and sharpen their thoughts about literature. Precisely because new media threatened literature with extinction – precisely because they seemed to possess the ability to unseat it from its historical position of power – they prompted such critics into a productive reconsideration of what literature was, what it could offer that other media could not, and how it should adapt to changing technological and social conditions. Walter Benjamin was among the modernist critics to be thus inspired, and "The Work of Art in the Age of Its Technological Reproducibility" (1936) is perhaps his most significant essay on the shifting role of literature in the modernist media landscape. For Benjamin, the most fundamental change brought about by the new media is what he calls the "massification" of art: the extension of artistic experience beyond privileged social classes and into the general public – beyond the gallery wall and into the public sphere. A technology that allows for the mass reproduction of an oil painting, Benjamin famously argues, degrades the individual "aura" of the original work of art and "*substitutes a mass existence for a unique existence.*"[32] In the case of a technology like film, massification is inherent in the very technology of its production: a film is so expensive to produce that it would be economically unsustainable if not for the existence of a mass audience of theatergoers willing to pay to see it; as Benjamin writes, "an individual who could afford to buy a painting, for example, could not afford to buy a film."[33] As a committed socialist, Benjamin feels little nostalgia for the loss of "aura" implicit in the massification of art. His greatest enthusiasm for technologies like film, however, comes from their ability not only to reach mass *audiences* but also to facilitate mass *participation.* Because no specialized training is required in order to appear on camera, "*Any person today can lay claim to being filmed,*"[34] as genres like the newsreel made clear. The same was increasingly true of the written word. Whereas "for centuries it was in the nature of literature that a small number of writers confronted many thousands of readers," Benjamin notes that with the expansion of literacy and the growth of the press, "an increasing number of readers . . . turned into writers":

> It began with the space set aside for "letters to the editor" in the daily press, and has now reached a point where there is hardly a European engaged in the work process who could not, in principle, find an opportunity to publish somewhere or other an account of work experience, a complaint, a report, something of the kind. Thus, the distinction between author and public is about to lose its axiomatic character.[35]

In another essay of the same period, "The Author as Producer" (1934), Benjamin makes the case more forcefully: literature must learn from modernist new media and transform the passive reader into an active participant, as part of a larger effort to replace subjugation with independent citizenship. Benjamin begins the essay by arguing that the historical crises unfolding in the mid-1930s demand that his contemporaries reassess the nature and tendency of literature itself. "We have to rethink our conceptions of literary forms or genres" in the context of the rise of Fascism, he writes, and what is most important in this "mighty recasting of literary forms"[36] is the development of new modes of art that "induce other producers to produce." His dictum in the essay is "*An author who teaches writers nothing teaches no one*": the only socially impactful literary forms are those that inspire previously passive consumers to become part of the process of artistic production themselves. He proposes a rubric by which to evaluate all new literary forms: "this apparatus is better the more consumers it is able to turn into producers – that is, readers or spectators into collaborators."[37] Benjamin presents Bertolt Brecht as an exemplar. Brecht's famous "alienation effect" prompts an active response by breaking the spell of illusion. "It arrests the action in its course, and thereby compels the listener to adopt an attitude vis-à-vis the process"; "it is concerned less with filling the public with feelings, even seditious ones, than with alienating it in an enduring way, through thinking, from the conditions in which it lives."[38] The resemblance of Brecht's epic theater to film – which also engages a mass audience and opens avenues for audience participation – is not incidental. Indeed, Benjamin sees the "alienation effect" as the direct appropriation of a technique from modernist new media. "Epic Theatre," he writes, "takes up a procedure that has become familiar... in recent years from film and radio": "montage," by which "the superimposed element disrupts the context in which it is inserted."[39] Far from serving in an antagonistic relation to literature, then, emerging artistic forms like film indeed suggest to Benjamin the very techniques by which literature can attain a renewed social relevance.

Like Benjamin, Virginia Woolf was inspired by the advent of electronic media to imagine new forms and new social roles for literature. In her essay "Poetry, Fiction, and the Future" (1927), Woolf argues that new media have created a paradox of connectedness in the daily lives of citizens of modernity, linking them over vast distances through the technology of "telepresence" yet alienating them from their immediate neighbors. Taking a walk on a London street, she observes,

> The long avenue of brick is cut up into boxes, each of which is inhabited by a different human being who has put locks on his doors and bolts on his windows to ensure some privacy, yet is linked to his fellows by wires which pass overhead, by waves of sound which pour through the roof and speak aloud to him of battles and murders and strikes and revolutions all over the world.[40]

Technologies like the radio and telephone have instilled their incongruous logic into the modern mind itself: "Feelings which used to come simple and separate do so no longer. Beauty is part ugliness; amusement part disgust; pleasure part pain."[41] As a result, the old genres of literature no longer serve, and they require updating. "When we ask poetry to express this discord, this incongruity, this contrast, this curiosity, the quick, queer emotions which are bred in small separate rooms," it "cannot move quickly enough, or broadly enough to do it."[42] As with Benjamin, Woolf's response to the challenges of modernist media is not to despair but to innovate. If the spatial paradoxes of radio and telephone have helped create a "mind . . . full of monstrous, hybrid, unmanageable emotions,"[43] then writers must develop matching new hybrid genres to capture and describe this new mentality. Woolf's prescription for the "future of fiction" is a form "written in prose, but in prose which has many of the characteristics of poetry" – a new genre having "something of the exaltation of poetry, but much of the ordinariness of prose":

> It will give the relations of man to Nature, to fate; his imagination; his dreams. But it will also give the sneer, the contrast, the question, the closeness and complexity of life. It will take the mould of that queer conglomeration of incongruous things – the modern mind. Therefore it will clasp to its breast the precious prerogatives of the democratic art of prose; its freedom, its fearlessness, its flexibility.[44]

The hybrid form that Woolf envisioned in "Poetry, Fiction, and the Future" was one that she was herself developing in poetic novels such as *To the Lighthouse* (1927) and *The Waves* (1930). If radio and the telephone had unbalanced the mind in such a manner that the old literary forms no longer "served," Woolf's response was not to abandon literature itself, but to make new forms for a new historical situation and a new generation of readers.

Woolf's contemporary T. S. Eliot shows that even a violent dislike for new modernist media could prove fruitful in spurring literary innovation. In "Marie Lloyd" (1922), a memorial for the recently departed star of the British music hall, the specific target of Eliot's ire is the cinema. For Eliot, Lloyd was not only a peerless performer but in fact also possessed a "moral superiority" due to her ability to engage members of her working-class audience as co-creators. "The working man who went to the music-hall and saw Marie Lloyd joined in the chorus and was himself performing part of the act," Eliot argues: "he was engaged in that collaboration of the audience with the artist which is necessary in all art."[45] In an essay that serves as much as an obituary for the music hall as for Lloyd herself, Eliot laments the rise of the cinema, a medium that in his view destroys this element of audience/performer collaboration:

> With the decay of the music-hall, with the encroachment of the cheap and rapid-breeding cinema, the lower classes will tend to drop into the same state of protoplasm as the bourgeoisie. . . . [The working man] will now go to the cinema, where his mind is lulled by continuous senseless music and continuous action too rapid for the brain to act upon, and will receive, without giving, in that same listless apathy with which the middle and upper classes regard any entertainment of the nature of art.[46]

The elegiac tone of "Marie Lloyd" is, however, entirely misleading, because at the same time that Eliot was mourning the death of the music hall, he was also actively developing new literary forms to counteract the psychic effects of the cinema. In "The Possibility of a Poetic Drama" (1920), Eliot proposes the music hall as a way forward for modernist poetry, encouraging his peers "to take a form of entertainment and subject it to the process which would leave it a form of art."[47] More than a decade later, Eliot continues to argue in *The Use of Poetry and the Use of Criticism* (1933) that theater and the music hall must be hybridized with poetry: if poets could achieve a more intimate relationship with a wider audience in the theater, he writes, they "could at least have the satisfaction of having a part to play in society as worthy as that of the music-hall comedian."[48] Between writing these two essays, Eliot was working to develop forms that combined music hall, drama, and poetry in works such as *The Waste Land* (1922), the unfinished *Wanna Go Home, Baby* (mid-1920s), and *The Rock* (1934). Like Benjamin, Eliot pursued a career-long interest in developing a new literary form that would engage a broad audience and turn spectators into performers, and like both Benjamin and Woolf, his quest to renovate literature was directly inspired by the advent of new media technologies.

Literary Studies and/as Media Studies

Modernist new media spurred innovations on both the creative and the critical side of literature, as we have seen. Yet the field of literary studies itself would not have developed as it did if not for the challenge of new media such as radio and film. Consider the example of New Criticism, the methodology that supported the great expansion and institutionalization of academic literary studies in the late 1930s and early 1940s. New Criticism was founded on the belief that literary language was distinct from other forms of written language, such as scientific reports, historical accounts, or office memos – and that, because of this distinctiveness, literary language itself was the proper focus of literary studies. To this end, the New Critics promoted "close reading," a procedure that examines the literary work as an intricately crafted object whose words cohere in an "organic" structure supported by precise connotations and perfectly counterbalancing irony. The New Critical doctrine was formed, in part, in response to the philological and biographical criticism that dominated literary studies in the late nineteenth and early twentieth centuries; to focus on the internal structure of a poem was to shift attention from its sources or the life and opinions of its author. Yet New Criticism was shaped just as powerfully by the advent of new media. It was no coincidence that a methodology focused on all that was unique to literary language should develop at a historical moment in which the supremacy of the written word was being challenged by electronic media.

The fruitful push-and-pull between new media innovation and literary thought is clearly at work in I. A. Richards's *Principles of Literary Criticism* (1924), one of the founding texts of New Criticism. The starting point of Richards's inquiry is comparative. Accepting that "the arts are the supreme form of the communicative activity,"[49] he seeks to discover the properties that distinguish one art from another: "What gives the experience of reading a certain poem its value? How is this experience better than another?"[50] The traits peculiar to literary language come into clearest focus for Richards when he compares literature with the new medium of film. Following Eliot's characterization of the "cheap and rapid-breeding cinema" in "Marie Lloyd," Richards presents speed and passivity as film's defining features. Cinemagoers, he argues, "tend . . . to develop stock attitudes and stereotyped ideas, the attitudes of the producers: attitudes and ideas which can be 'put across' *quickly* through a medium that lends itself to crude rather than sensitive handling."[51] Complaining of the psychic effects of cinema on the viewer, Richards continues, "No one can intensely and whole-heartedly enjoy and enter into experiences whose fabric is as crude as that of the average super-film without a disorganization which has its effects in everyday life."[52] In Richards, we see the New Critical doctrine of literature spring negatively from the analysis of the competing medium of film. If the structure of a film is crude, disorganized, and inchoate, then that of literature is intricate, carefully balanced, and fully realized. Where a film weakens the mind by flashing images more quickly than they can be processed, literature requires a slow, careful, active reading.

After Richards, a central argument for the institutionalization of literary study was the notion that it might serve as a bulwark against the incursions of new media. F. R. Leavis and Denys Thompson open *Culture and Environment* (1933) – another foundational text of New Criticism – by stating,

> Many teachers of English who have become interested in the possibilities
> of training taste and sensibility must have been troubled by
> accompanying doubts. What effect can such training have against the
> multitudinous counter-influences – films, newspapers, advertising –
> indeed, the whole world outside the classroom?[53]

Yet, as they continue, "the very conditions that make literary education look so desperate are those which make it more important than ever before."[54] For Leavis and Thompson, what was needed was a curriculum that would "train awareness" of the ways that our cultural environment "tends to affect taste, habit, preconception, attitude to life and quality of living": "We cannot leave the citizen to be formed unconsciously by his environment; if anything like a worthy idea of satisfactory living is to be saved, he must be trained to discriminate and to resist."[55] The solution was literary reading: slow, concentrated, independent analysis that placed the student outside the dominant media environment in order to prompt critical reflection on it.

By distinguishing literature from other new media, the New Critics and their predecessors were not only able to identify the properties peculiar to literary language but also to formulate a social mission for literary studies that tied a sense of moral urgency to its expansion as a discipline. Historically speaking, then, the particular brand of literary studies that accompanied New Criticism's institutionalization in the mid-twentieth century can be seen as a form of comparative media studies that sought to carve out a place for literature in a shifting media landscape. Yet this historical argument works the other way around as well: though often considered an entirely separate academic field, the discipline of media studies – including digital media studies and digital media theory – can be understood as a specific development and expansion of the methods of literary studies that emerged in the early twentieth century.

The birth of literary studies from the challenge of new media and the subsequent development of media studies from literary studies are best demonstrated by the career of Marshall McLuhan. McLuhan's central importance to present-day digital media theory is unquestionable. Looking only at critics discussed in Chapter 1, McLuhan's influence is equally palpable on both sides of the optimism-pessimism divide and equally prominent among scholars and public intellectuals. The first name mentioned both in Nicholas Carr's *The Shallows* and in Katherine Hayles's *How We Think* is Marshall McLuhan. Sven Birkerts's *Gutenberg Elegies* contains eight separate discussions of McLuhan; Adriaan van der Weel's *Changing Our Textual Minds* mentions him fourteen times. Perhaps the only theorist who can rival McLuhan's influence in current discussions of the digital world is Friedrich Kittler, whose famous dictum, "Media determine our situation,"[56] is a near restatement of McLuhan's "All media work us over completely"[57] and whose work has been described as "a merger of Foucault, Lacan, and McLuhan."[58]

Although McLuhan's thought is central to the discussion of the digital present, it is unquestionably literary in origin. Jessica Pressman calls McLuhan "the father of media studies."[59] Yet McLuhan also serves as the "missing link" connecting literary criticism to digital media theory, for his analysis of electronic media emerged directly from his training as a literary critic. From the late 1930s until his death in 1980, McLuhan was employed as a professor of

English literature. He began his career, moreover, as a card-carrying New Critic: he studied under Richards and Leavis at Cambridge in the 1930s and, after returning to North America, published alongside American New Critics such as Allen Tate, John Crowe Ransom, Cleanth Brooks, and Robert Penn Warren in journals like the *Sewanee Review* and *Kenyon Review*. As Pressman and Philip Marchand have demonstrated, his time at Cambridge established the intellectual foundations for his subsequent media theory. Marchand argues that if Richards's insight was that a poem is "a far-reaching arrangement and clarification of impulses in the reader's head," then McLuhan's breakthrough was that "one could examine a machine as a far-reaching arrangement produced in the lives of its users":

> One did not understand a photocopier by grasping that it reproduced documents. One began to understand it when one grasped the sum of its effects, which included the destruction of government secrecy (by making it easy to leak documents) and the conversion of writers into publishers.[60]

McLuhan's comparative method can be described as that of Richards turned on its head: rather than seeking to understand literature through close observation of nonliterary new media, McLuhan sought to understand these same nonliterary media based on his thorough understanding of literature. If Richards's conception of poetry sprung negatively from his analysis of media like film, McLuhan's conception of electronic media sprung negatively from his analysis of print. Beyond the general notion that media shape thought, three of McLuhan's observations about electronic media have been especially influential for contemporary digital theorists: that electronic media would lessen the Western emphasis on logic and linearity; that they would promote group consciousness over individuality; and that they would break down the division between author and reader, performer and spectator. In each of these three facets, McLuhan argues that electronic media serve to *reverse* a condition initially established by the printing press. It was the repetition and uniformity of the printing process, he contends, that promoted the repetition and uniformity of Western linear logic; it was the mass-produced book, read in private from the reader's fixed point of view, that encouraged the notion of individuality; and it was the notion of the book-as-commodity, along with the related notion of copyright, that established individual authorship over collaborative production.

Leading critics of contemporary digital media have followed McLuhan's example not only by citing him en masse but also by seeking to understand the digital through the lens of literary scholarship. Matthew Kirschenbaum's

Mechanisms: New Media and the Forensic Imagination (2008) presents a particularly compelling example. Kirschenbaum pursues a seemingly nonliterary aim – to investigate the physical, material traces of computer data on hard drives and diskettes – yet does so by employing the deeply traditional literary discipline of bibliography.[61] We will encounter many such unexpected hybrids of analog and digital literary studies in this volume: for example, Jerome McGann's approach to digital text encoding through the "bibliographic codes" of a printed book (Ch. 5); Jay David Bolter's reading of hypertext fiction through the critical theory of Roland Barthes and Jacques Derrida (Ch. 7); and Jessica Pressman's investigation of Flash poetry through the lens of Poundian imagism (Ch. 8). Together such critics serve to justify Kirschenbaum's counterintuitive claim that "textual studies should be recognized as among the most sophisticated branches of media studies we have evolved."[62]

Powerful as the urge may be to submit to digital-age literary ennui, there is ample historical evidence to suggest we are entering a golden age of literature. The grounds of our anxiety are just as plausibly grounds for enthusiasm. The contemporaneous reactions to writing and print show us that we are seldom able to see the merits of a new textual medium until long after it has emerged; instead, we go about judging the new medium by the standards of the old, blind to the new possibilities it entails. The example of modernism shows us that existential threats can serve as productive spurs to literary innovation, sharpening our sense of what is special to literature, why it ought to survive, and how it can be adapted to thrive. The development of New Criticism in reaction to modernist new media shows us that alternatives help us better understand literature, and the case of Marshall McLuhan illustrates how immensely useful existing techniques of literary studies will prove in coming to terms with the digital medium.

The conditions are in place for a digital literary renaissance – but this is not to say that literature's transition into the digital will be smooth, easy, or pleasant. The strength of our collective unease suggests that it will be a long time before we are at home in the world of digital text, effortless in our employment and enjoyment of its new capacities. The challenge that the digital medium poses to literature in its traditional forms suggests how much work will be required to adapt it to new conditions – what a truly "mighty recasting of literary forms" will be necessary, in Benjamin's words. In the midst of this turbulence, we would do well to emulate the example of critics such as Richards, Leavis, and McLuhan: to pay close attention and to read carefully.

Part II

Digitization

Chapter 3

The Universal Library

Every medium shift entails a conversion of the literary record. When the oral age gave way to the manuscript age, waves of sound and folds of human memory became marks on papyrus and parchment. With the invention of print, words were converted from handwriting into bits of type, inked and printed on paper. Now, with the advent of the digital, these tangible marks on physical pages are being converted into electrical impulses – ones and zeros stored on hard disks and flash drives. This last process, "digitization," is the focus of Part II of this book.

Every process of conversion entails gains as well as losses, and digitization is no exception. As we saw in the previous chapter, moving a text from oral to written form makes it less agile and even less human – no longer able to respond to counterarguments, no longer stored within the mind – though its permanence allows it to outlive its speaker and permits much greater argumentative sophistication. A text typeset from a manuscript original may be less beautiful and copied with less care, but the relative ease of reproducing it makes it far more accessible to a large audience. Though a digital file can accurately render the look of a printed page and the letters it contains, it cannot record the smell of a book or the texture of its pages; at present, there is no digital format that can express the weight of a book in our hands or the tactile sensation of leafing through pages with a finger marking an important spot. Yet the digitization of literary texts promises significant gains. Because of the "salient property" that Adriaan van der Weel names "ease and low cost of copying," a digitized literary text is far more reproducible than even a printed page; indeed, the advantage of bits over atoms is so great that a digital text can be copied almost for free and then distributed anywhere in the world instantaneously. The "convergence of modalities" achievable in digital formats forces us to reconsider our sense of the "literary" by making it possible to present text and image alongside modalities that are impossible to store on pages: sound, video, three-dimensional color images, and so on. Finally, because the digital medium expresses text in numerical binary code, we can perform advanced statistical calculations on digitized literary texts.

Each of these advantages is the subject of a chapter in Part II. In this chapter, we consider one of the most exciting and socially significant aspects of literary digitization: the possibility of creating a library that contains digital copies of all literary texts and that grants free and universal access to them. We begin by looking at pre-digital efforts to create digital libraries, in manuscript and on microfilm, and by paying particular attention to the political motivations of such projects. Next we consider major digital libraries – Project Gutenberg, JSTOR, Google Books, the Digital Public Library of America – and the challenge that copyright law presents to the creation of a genuinely universal collection. These topics are bookended by a pair of literary fables: the first, from Virginia Woolf's *A Room of One's Own*, expresses an implicit faith in the social significance of a universal library; and the second, Jorge Luis Borges's "The Library of Babel," presents a dystopian account of the unintended consequences that might follow.

The Social Politics of Universal Access in the Pre-Digital Period

A Room of One's Own begins with a story about the politics of literary access. Woolf's narrator, who has been asked to give a lecture about women and fiction, sits down by the bank of a river to think the matter through. She sits and thinks, thinks and sits, waiting for ideas to come – until finally one does. Excited by its sudden arrival, she gets up and walks quickly across a grass plot, not knowing precisely where she is headed. But this is not just any grass plot; Woolf's narrator is in the fictional university town of Oxbridge, where, as an angry college beadle informs her, women are forbidden from walking across the grass, a privilege restricted to Fellows and Scholars. Woolf's narrator, understandably upset, leaves the grass – only to find that in the altercation with the beadle, she has completely forgotten her idea. Eventually she manages to calm herself, and once again her mind begins to wander. Walking through the campus, she recalls an essay by Charles Lamb describing his own visit to Oxbridge some hundred years before, when he inspected the original manuscript of Milton's "Lycidas." It occurs to her that this very manuscript is in a library only a few steps away. And so she heads toward the library, begins a new chain of thought – until she is again interrupted by a college official, this one informing her that ladies are not allowed in the library unless accompanied by a Fellow or provided with a letter of introduction. "That a famous library has been cursed by a woman is a matter of complete indifference to a famous library," she concludes:

Venerable and calm, with all its treasures safe locked within its breast, it sleeps complacently and will, for far as I am concerned, so sleep for ever. Never will I wake those echoes, never will I ask for that hospitality, I vowed as I descended the steps in anger.[1]

Woolf's narrator is privileged in many respects: she is fortunate to belong to an educated class that knows and values writers like Milton and Lamb and lucky to live within striking distance of one of the great libraries that house their manuscripts. If she were a man, she would be welcomed inside the Oxbridge library. But she is a woman, she is barred from entering, and so she curses the library.

Woolf's fable illustrates an important point about the pre-digital concept of the universal library: in the eras of manuscript and print, universality of holdings was a far more achievable goal than universality of access. Indeed, universal access was seldom a conscious goal at all. The problem with the Oxbridge library is not that it contains an insufficient number of texts; rather, it is that it grants extremely selective access to its bounty and places so much emphasis on gatekeeping. The same was true of the world's first attempt at a universal library, the Library of Alexandria. Founded on less than benevolent principles around 300 BCE by the Ptolemies, the successors of Alexander the Great, the Library is estimated to have held as many as 500,000 scrolls – somewhere between 30% and 70% of all known texts at the time.[2] In an era long before printing, when individual copies of a text needed to be copied laboriously by scribes, information was extraordinarily scarce; as such, papyrus scrolls – the preeminent bearers of information in the ancient world – were both a source and a symbol of power. Though scholars working in the Library of Alexandria, such as Euclid and Archimedes, produced important research, the Library's main purpose was to showcase the wealth and power of Egypt and, more specifically, the Ptolemies. To this end, it was ruthless in its collection of texts. Although it acquired many scrolls legitimately, buying them at book fairs in Athens and Rhodes, the Library also resorted to more dubious measures. A policy existed, for example, whereby ships entering the port of Alexandria were required to submit all their scrolls to the Library for copying – though it was the copies, and not the originals, that the ships received in return.[3] Ptolemy III also arranged a deal with the Athenians whereby, with the security of a sizable deposit, the Library could borrow and copy their precious official editions of Sophocles, Euripides, and Aeschylus; the brazen Ptolemy III was perfectly content to forfeit his deposit by returning the copies and keeping the originals. As Andrew Erskine argues, the establishment of the Library served to establish the Ptolemies as cultural leaders, which in turn served to consolidate their power.[4]

The symbolic power of the Library of Alexandria rested on scarcity – on its possessing more original scrolls than the libraries of competing kingdoms. This connection between scarcity and prestige survived the invention of the codex and the printing press in the era of print. The most renowned libraries, such as the Bodleian on which Woolf's Oxbridge library is modeled, were still the ones with the rarest holdings, and their valuable collections were carefully guarded. It was only with the advent of photography and microfilm that universal access became a technological possibility and a conscious aim. As with the Library of Alexandria, the story of the first "open access movement" is one that turns on politics, originating in concerns about preserving the British cultural heritage in the midst of two world wars. In 1918, Sir William Osler of the British Bibliographical Society argued the need to identify the locations of rare early English books so that they could be rescued in the event of air raids. Thus motivated, the Bibliographical Society supported A. W. Pollard and G. R. Redgrave in compiling their monumental *Short-Title Catalogue of Books Printed in England, Scotland and Ireland and English Books Printed Abroad 1473–1640*, the first edition of which was published in 1926. In 1938, with Britain under immediate threat of German invasion, Eugene Powers founded University Microfilms International (UMI) with the aim of photographing all 26,500 books listed in Pollard and Redgrave's *Short-Title Catalogue* and thereby preserving a crucial slice of British culture. This project, still ongoing, became the Early English Books (EEB) microfilm collection, distributed to libraries around the world.

Although their impetus was cultural preservation in the face of war, microfilming operations like those of the UMI gave rise to utopian speculations about the social possibilities of universal access. The most famous is H. G. Wells's contribution to the *Encyclopédie française* of 1937, "World Brain: The Idea of a Permanent Encyclopedia," where he envisions the advent of microfilm technology as heralding a democratic, peaceful planet and a unified human race. Microfilm technology, Wells argues, has already made it possible for "the rarest and most intricate documents and articles" to "be studied . . . at first hand, simultaneously in a score of projection rooms." There is thus

> no practical obstacle whatever now to the creation of an efficient index to *all* human knowledge, ideas and achievements, to the creation, that is, of a complete planetary memory for all mankind. And not simply an index; the direct reproduction of the thing itself can be summoned to any properly prepared spot.[5]

For Wells, the development of a technology whereby "the whole human memory can be . . . made accessible to every individual . . . foreshadows a real intellectual unification of our [i.e., the human] race." Because this microfilmed "World Encyclopedia" could be reproduced at relatively low cost, it could be distributed very widely ("in Peru, China, Iceland, Central Africa") and could thus serve as "a unified, if not a centralized, world organ to 'pull the mind of the world together'" and indeed as "a way to world peace." As Wells writes in the immodest conclusion to his essay, "A common ideology based on this Permanent World Encyclopaedia is a possible means, to some it seems the only means, of dissolving human conflict into unity."[6]

Needless to say, microfilm did not achieve Wells's utopia. The EEB was distributed to many campuses across the world, giving scholars unprecedented access to exquisitely rare items whose examination would previously have required expensive research trips and possible run-ins with gatekeeping libraries. Yet the EEB contained only a small subset of a small corpus of texts, and it was hard to use. Matthew Steggle relates, "When I think of using the *S[hort] T[itle] C[atalogue]* microfilms, I think of perishing rubber bands, uncoiling films, the smell of toner, and headaches behind the eyes."[7] Tellingly, the EEB became far more accessible and far more influential when its microfilms were scanned digitally and made available – as EEBO, Early English Books Online – in a medium far better suited to universality, the internet.

Open Access in the Digital Age: Technical Possibilities and Legal Barriers

In the digital age, the curse that opens *A Room of One's Own* ought to ring hollow – to echo only as a reminder of a past in which the logic of print and manuscript made scarcity an unfortunate but inescapable aspect of access to information. The technical foundations exist today to remove *all* barriers to access: not only to make rare literary manuscripts accessible to female middle-class English writers but also to make all cultural materials of all kinds available instantly and for free to anyone anywhere in the world with access to an internet-connected device. The first attempt to exploit these capacities of the digital medium was Project Gutenberg, founded astonishingly early in the history of computing, in 1971, when Michael Hart was granted $100,000,000 worth of computer time on an underused Xerox Sigma V mainframe at the University of Illinois. Believing that "the greatest value created by computers would not be computing, but would be the storage, retrieval, and searching of what was stored in our libraries,"[8] Hart decided to spend his computer time entering texts, beginning with the Declaration of Independence. The collection on the main U.S. Project Gutenberg site currently stands at more than 50,000 texts in over fifty languages. Hart, in a Wellsian spirit, saw immense social promise in the new technology of electronic text. In a 1992 essay, "The History and Philosophy of Project Gutenberg," Hart recalls that it was spurred by the realization that "anything that can be entered into a computer can be reproduced indefinitely,"[9] because of the "salient property" Adriaan van der Weel names "ease and low cost of copying" and that Hart himself calls, via a Star Trek reference, "Replicator Technology." Project Gutenberg's stated mission, derived from the digital medium's incredible facility for copying, is "to make information, books and other materials available to the general public in forms a vast majority of the computers, programs and people can easily read, use, quote, and search."[10] From its inception, the politics of Project Gutenberg has been egalitarian, populist, anti-corporate, and anti-elitist. The texts are produced entirely by volunteers, distributed free of charge in non-proprietary formats (generally, plain text), and made available in as many languages as possible. Though Project Gutenberg's archive consists primarily of what it calls "light" and "heavy literature," texts are selected for inclusion based on their likely appeal to the "general reader"; in Hart's words, "We do not write for the reader who cares whether a certain phrase in Shakespeare has a ':' or a ';' between its clauses."[11] For Hart, however, the greatest barrier to Project Gutenberg's achieving its goal of creating a truly universal library is not cultural, financial, or technological. As he said in a 2005 interview, "We have been capable of bringing every word ever written to a wider audience than ever before for years, but . . . a movement to deny access to this information has been underway for even longer."[12] Project Gutenberg, the first attempt at a digital universal library, was also the first to encounter the great foe of all such attempts: copyright.

Though copyright laws vary greatly between countries, the history of copyright in the United States is both very representative and extremely influential internationally. The U.S. Constitution of 1787 includes this provision: "To promote the Progress of Science and useful Arts, by securing for limited Times to Authors and Inventors the exclusive Right to their respective Writings and Discoveries."[13] The Copyright Act of 1790 specifies a term for such exclusive rights: fourteen years, renewable for another fourteen years if the author is still alive, after which time such "writings and discoveries" pass into the public domain, to be used freely for any purpose.[14] The history of American copyright law is one of continual extensions of these limits, generally prompted by pending expirations of particularly valuable copyrights or the advent of new technologies of mass reproduction. With the enactment of the Copyright

Term Extension Act of 1998 – known as the "Mickey Mouse Protection Act," because its passage was encouraged by lobbying from Disney that sought to protect its immensely profitable and soon-to-expire copyright – copyright now lasts as long as the life of the author, plus seventy years, or 95 years from the date of first publication. In practice, this means that any text published after 1922 remains frozen in copyright status, including "orphan" works whose copyright holders cannot be located. The most current of Project Gutenberg's nearly 50,000 texts is thus nearly one hundred years old; its top downloads are not popular favorites such as *Fifty Shades of Grey* or *Game of Thrones* but *Pride and Prejudice, Adventures of Huckleberry Finn*, and that heaviest of "heavy" literary texts, James Joyce's *Ulysses*, which was first published in 1922, just before the copyright window closed.

Copyright plays a leading role in the story of another early digital library, JSTOR, founded in 1995 to address a problem faced by many research libraries: the difficulty of finding shelf space to accommodate the increasing number of academic journals they were expected to purchase. By digitizing these journals, storing them on their servers, and providing researchers with instant full-text access to journal articles encoded with rich metadata, JSTOR offered far more than a solution to the specific problem of shelving. Through its affordances for searching and sorting, JSTOR made it possible to locate journal articles in entirely novel ways. For instance, if one happened to be interested in references to Albert Einstein in nonscientific journals in the period between his publication of the special and general theory of relativity, JSTOR's Advanced Search made such an esoteric query possible. Because most of the content held by JSTOR is under copyright, however, JSTOR must pay the publishers that provide its journals and so in turn charges subscription fees to libraries that wish to use its service.

The spiraling costs of such subscriptions have become an increasing problem for libraries in the digital age. In 1970, for example, the average cost of a subscription to an academic chemistry journal was $33; by 2014, the average cost was $4,044, with a subscription to the *Journal of Comparative Neurology* alone costing more than $30,000.[15] This situation is particularly galling because it places academic institutions in the position of having to buy back the research they have paid their professors to produce; in the case of public institutions, tax revenue is used both to fund research and to access results. The scholars who produce the research and write articles, moreover, are not paid by the journals to do so, nor are they paid for the editing and peer-review services they provide to the production of the journals; the private publishers, meanwhile, often make massive profits. The so-called pay wall erected around for-profit academic journals limits the access of researchers in developing countries and at smaller institutions to cutting-edge research simply because they cannot afford it. This deeply problematic situation has led many scholars to publish their articles in open-access journals or, in the case of articles destined for publication in subscription journals, to place "preprints" in open-access depositories such as *arXiv* and *CSeARCH*.

JSTOR, as a not-for-profit organization, is far from the worst offender in this difficult situation. It rarely hosts current issues of periodicals, leaving the publishers themselves to extract the high subscription costs of the latest research; further, it scales its subscription costs to the size of the institution. Yet in 2010, JSTOR became the target of a major protest against pay walls in academic publishing. In December of that year, Aaron Swartz, an American programmer and open-access activist, tapped into the computer network at MIT and downloaded more than five million articles from JSTOR's database. In a 2008 "Guerilla Open Access Manifesto," Swartz had attacked the manner in which "the world's entire scientific and cultural heritage, published over centuries in books and journals" was "increasingly being digitized and locked up by a handful of private corporations." The fact that many scientific articles were available "to those at elite universities in the First World, but not to children in the Global South," he deemed both "outrageous and unacceptable." Swartz advocated a campaign of "Guerilla Open Access": "We need to take information, wherever it is stored, make our copies and share them with the world. We need to download scientific journals and upload them to file sharing networks."[16] JSTOR interrupted Swartz's 2010 download when it discovered it, and campus police arrested him after videotaping him retrieving a laptop connected to the MIT network from an unlocked closet. Swartz negotiated privately with JSTOR to return the downloaded files, and JSTOR chose not to pursue charges; federal prosecutors, however, charged Swartz with crimes carrying a maximum penalty of thirty-five years in prison and $1 million in fines. In January 2013, with the charges still pending, Swartz committed suicide.

JSTOR was not an ideal target for Swartz's protest. JSTOR is not a corporation, is not operated for profit, and by late 2010 had instituted programs such as the African Access Initiative to provide African institutions free access to archival journals. Yet the Aaron Swartz Incident, as it became known, pushed JSTOR even further toward open access. Whereas, before September 2011, subscriptions were required to access even public domain (pre-1923) materials in JSTOR archives, all public domain material is now freely accessible. JSTOR has also begun allowing limited access to visitors without subscriptions and has opened much of its collection to text mining. Copyright continues to stand in the way of universal access to JSTOR's rich collection, however. By its own estimates, JSTOR users accessed more than 113 million articles in

2012,[17] yet JSTOR turns away some 150 million requests for information from nonsubscribing users each year.[18] In his speech honoring Aaron Swartz's memory, "Aaron's Laws: Law and Justice in a Digital Age," Lawrence Lessig recalled a conversation with JSTOR staff in which he was told that it would cost $250 million to make its entire collection open access.[19] Like Project Gutenberg, JSTOR demonstrates both the immense promise and the monumental challenge of universal access in the digital library.

Universality at Any Cost: The Case of Google Books

Though it is not the first attempt to build a universal digital library, Google Books is undoubtedly the most audacious effort. Gary Hall has described the project as an attempt to build "a 'universal virtual library' of available knowledge to rival that constructed at Alexandria,"[20] yet Google's ambitions are in fact much greater than either its ancient or contemporary rivals. Unlike JSTOR or Project Gutenberg, Google Books seeks true comprehensiveness in its collection – and it has shown that it is prepared to challenge copyright law to achieve that goal. Beginning in 2004, Google Books sought to digitize not only what was in the public domain and not only what it had permission to digitize, but all printed books. Further, in keeping with Google's founding mission "to organize the world's information and make it universally accessible and useful,"[21] it sought not only universal holdings but also universal access. In a 2009 *New York Times* op-ed titled "A Library to Last Forever," Google co-founder Sergey Brin laid out the rationale for Google Books: it would serve to "unlock the wisdom" stored in the world's books by making digital copies instantly available to any reader; it would carry out this unlocking not only for books published before 1923 but also for "the vast majority of books ever written," including out-of-print works inaccessible to all but "tenacious researchers at premier academic libraries" – and, unlike the Library of Alexandria, it would not burn down. Indeed, as Brin argued, an exclusive library like Alexandria might as well burn down for all the good it does ordinary readers: "even if our cultural heritage stays intact in the world's foremost libraries, it is effectively lost if no one can access it easily."[22]

Google Books, then known as Google Print, was launched at the 2004 Frankfurt Book Fair. In rapid succession, many of the world's great libraries signed up as partners; the University of Michigan, Harvard, Stanford, the Bodleian at Oxford, and the New York Public Library shipped books to Google at their own expense, with Google covering the costs of scanning. These scanned books quickly began to appear in Google searches and on the Google Books site proper, where public-domain works could be searched full-text, browsed, and downloaded free of charge and where copyrighted works could be viewed in "snippets." The inclusion of copyrighted works even in snippet form brought swift legal action. In 2005, both the Authors Guild and the Association of American Publishers sued Google, claiming it did not have the right to scan copyrighted works without permission or to present any portion of these works online. In 2005, Jean-Noël Jeanneney, president of the National Library of France, published *Quand Google défie l'Europe*, in which he accused Google of building not a universal but an Anglocentric library; even in the rare cases when it did include foreign works, Jeanneney argued, it usually did so in violation of the national copyright laws operating in their place of publication.[23] Despite this very public controversy, however, libraries continued to sign on as partners, including the University of Texas-Austin, Columbia University, those in the University of California system, and in Spain, Germany, Switzerland, Belgium, and Japan.

In October 2008, by which point Google had scanned some seven million books, a $125 million settlement was announced between Google, the Authors Guild, and the Association of American Publishers. By the terms of the agreement, Google would be allowed to sell access to the copyrighted works it had scanned, offer subscription access to the entire collection, and allow visitors to see up to 20% of copyrighted works for free. Further, Google would be granted the exclusive right to sell orphan works. Although authors could "opt out" of having their works included in Google Books, they would be included by default, and Google would be exonerated for all prior illegal scanning. This set-tlement was met with widespread furor. Google was accused of having sought a monopoly: far from establishing a universal library open to all, Google seemed to have established a proprietary silo over which it had complete control and could charge whatever it wished to access. Partner libraries accused Google of betrayal – of borrowing their books, scanning them, and then forcing them into a situation in which they had to buy them back through subscriptions. Privacy experts warned of the dangers of Google knowing what you read, when you read it, and what other activities you engaged in while reading. Many questioned the right of the Authors Guild – an organization with only 8,000 members – to sign over the ownership of orphaned works unilaterally. Foreign authors continued to complain that their national copyright laws were not being respected. In October 2009, before the opening of that year's Frankfurt Book Fair, German Chancellor Angela Merkel marked the fifth anniversary of Google Books by warning of the "considerable dangers" of the proposed settlement.[24]

In March 2011 – by which time Google had scanned some fifteen million books – Judge Denny Chin rejected the settlement. He gave many reasons for his decision, but argued in particular that the status of orphan works should be decided by the U.S. Congress, not by a private suit. For many, the rejection of this settlement seemed to spell the end of Google Books; as Robert Darnton put it in 2014, "After the court's decision . . . Google's digital library was effectively dead."[25] But the scanning continued; by the time Darnton published his article, Google had scanned more than thirty million volumes. And as I write these words, the fate of Google Books remains far from determined. In November 2013, Judge Chin pronounced a ruling in the Authors Guild vs. Google case – not on the settlement, but on the suit itself. He sided with Google, deciding that it had not violated U.S. law by scanning copyrighted books without permission nor by making available "snippets" of this copyrighted material. Google Books remains, for now, in all its legal and ethical shades of gray, the closest thing we have to a universal library.

Toward a Digital Republic of Letters

For all its manifest shortcomings, Google Books must be credited with at least two significant achievements: it showed that massive-scale digitization of books was possible, and by doing so in a manner that so many found so deeply problematic, it prompted its critics to imagine alternative models. One such critic is Robert Darnton, director of the Harvard University Library from 2009 to 2015. In early 2009, a few months after the settlement between Google and the publishing industry was announced, Darnton published a scathing response in the *New York Review of Books* titled "Google & the Future of Books." In his eyes, the settlement amounted to nothing less than a betrayal of the democratic social potential of the internet. As a historian of the book and of the eighteenth century, Darnton invoked the Enlightenment notion of the "Republic of Letters," a "realm with no police, no boundaries, and no inequalities other than those determined by talent."[26] Yet for Darnton, the eighteenth-century Republic of Letters was little more than a mirage: though it presented an appealingly democratic vision of a conversation that "anyone could join . . . by exercising the two main attributes of citizenship, writing and reading," in practice it was "democratic only in principle" and "dominated by the wellborn and the rich . . . . Despite its principles, the Republic of Letters, as it actually operated, was a closed world, inaccessible to the underprivileged." For Darnton, however, the internet held the promise of finally bringing the Republic of Letters to life. Open-access resources like Project Gutenberg and Wikipedia have the power to create a "Republic of Learning" open to "amateurs in the best sense of the word, lovers of learning among the general citizenry." Surveying an internet where "openness is operating everywhere," Darnton commented, in a Wellsian moment of technologically inspired utopianism, "The democratization of knowledge now seems to be at our fingertips. We can make the Enlightenment ideal come to life in reality." Enterprises such as Google Books, however, stand in the way of this goal. Whereas "libraries exist to promote a public good" – "'the encouragement of learning,' learning 'Free to All'" – "businesses exist in order to make money for shareholders." As a public good, a universal library cannot be entrusted to private hands. "If we permit the commercialization of the content of our libraries," Darnton argued, "there is no getting around a fundamental contradiction. To digitize collections and sell the product in ways that fail to guarantee wide access would . . . turn the Internet into an instrument for privatizing knowledge that belongs in the public sphere."[27] Although he speculated on the potential to "democratize" as we "digitize" – to "[rewrite] the rules of the game, by subordinating private interests to the pubic good, and by taking inspiration from the early republic in order to create a Digital Republic of Learning" – Darnton ultimately ended his essay on a note of gloom. "We could have created a National Digital Library," he says: "the twenty-first century equivalent of the Library of Alexandria. It is too late now."[28]

As the courts continued to delay their decision on the Google Books settlement, however, Darnton began to wonder whether a public, nonprofit alternative was perhaps feasible after all. In a talk delivered at Harvard in October 2010, "Can We Create a National Digital Library?" he reiterated his belief that such an institution could "make our fellow citizens active members of an international Republic of Letters" and "strengthen the bonds of citizenship at home."[29] After Judge Chin rejected the settlement in 2011, Darnton wrote another essay in the *New York Review of Books*, this time trumpeting a slightly renamed "Digital Public Library of America (DPLA)" that he defined as "a collection of works in all formats that would make our cultural heritage available online and free of charge to everyone everywhere."[30] That year, Darnton assembled a Steering Committee and secured funding for the project. In April 2013, the DPLA was launched.

The DPLA envisions itself much as Wells imagined his "World Brain." It aims at a genuine, if U.S.-centered, universality; in the words of its "About" page, it "strives to contain the full breadth of human expression, from the written word, to works of art and culture, to records of America's heritage, to the efforts and data of science" – and it seeks to make these massive holdings "freely available to the world" as well as "more easily discovered and more widely usable and used."[31] It defines itself in opposition to the Google Books model in two important ways. First, it is an entirely noncommercial, public enterprise. Rather than seeking profits or being answerable to shareholders, it seeks the diffusion of knowledge and edification of the citizenry. Second, it is not a centralized repository of digitized documents, but rather a system for linking the disparate holdings of a variety of public or nonprofit collections such as the Library of Congress, the Internet Archive, HathiTrust, and the digitized collections of individual libraries. In a 2014 *New York Review of Books* article published under the triumphant headline "A World Digital Library Is Coming True!" Darnton argued that the DPLA's "distributed, horizontal" organization served as a literal embodiment of its political mission: whereas Google's proprietary and monopolistic aims are implicit in its "vertical organization erected on a database of its own," the "horizontality" of the DPLA "reinforces [its] democratizing impulse."

The DPLA, born out of Darnton's carefully considered objections to the Google Books project, presents an attractive alternative: an open-access, noncommercial digital library with an explicitly democratic social mission. Yet it too raises some troubling questions. One might, for example, accuse Darnton of taking what Marshall McLuhan calls a "rear-view mirror" approach. Darnton envisions the DPLA as a way of using a new communications medium – the internet – to realize the failed eighteenth-century dream of a Republic of Letters. If the creation of a Republic of Letters – an egalitarian space for the exchange of ideas through reading and writing – responded to the political needs of the eighteenth century, it is not clear whether it responds to the very different political needs of the present. In his 2012 article "The Library of Utopia," Nicholas Carr notes that the only significant difference between the DPLA and Google Books is that the DPLA makes accessible particularly rare books and manuscripts that libraries were unwilling to ship to Google for scanning – the same kinds of materials that Virginia Woolf's narrator seeks in the opening of *A Room of One's Own*.[32] For Woolf and for Darnton, unfettered access to these kinds of precious documents clearly benefits democracy and active citizenship. Carr, however, is less sure. The social reformers of today, he suggests, might not see access to the "Lycidas" manuscript as such a pressing concern, because such materials would likely interest "only a small group of scholars" – a social and intellectual elite – rather than the broad public to which the DPLA is pledged.[33] Darnton defends the value of such resources: thanks to the DPLA, he argues, "a ninth-grader in Dallas who is preparing a report on an episode of the American Revolution can download a manuscript from New York, a pamphlet from Chicago, and a map from San Francisco in order to study them side by side"; a high school English student reading an Emily Dickinson poem can access digitized versions of her manuscripts though the DPLA and, in comparing them to their printed versions, "develop closer, deeper readings."[34] Yet the question lingers: do today's attempts at producing digitized collections of all the world's printed materials – all the manuscripts, scrolls, books, newspapers, magazines, journals, and pamphlets ever printed – truly respond to a pressing contemporary social need, or do they use today's technology to solve yesterday's problems?

The Horrors of Universality: Jorge Luis Borges and "The Library of Babel"

Though they may agree on little else, the voices we have encountered in this chapter agree at least on one point: that the creation of a universally accessible universal library is a laudable aim. The criticisms we have considered thus far focus on the universality of particular resources. How will any library be able to call itself truly "universal" when copyright is so restrictive? How could such a library respond to the most pressing needs of its patrons if it contains almost nothing published in the last century? How could a digital universal library be truly "universal" when not everyone has access to the internet, when many digitized resources remain inaccessible to persons with disabilities,[35] when not everyone is able to read or write, or when so few are able to muster the concentration to make it through an online article in *The Atlantic,* much less a digitized copy of a poetic manuscript or an Enlightenment-era political tract? With so many barriers to universal access still in place, few have paused to question the desirability of universal access itself. What will happen if we do finally succeed in creating a truly universal library?

Though written before the digital age, Jorge Luis Borges's short story "The Library of Babel" (1941) suggests a nightmarish answer to this question. Borges's story imagines a universe composed entirely of an infinitely large library – an endless honeycomb structure of hexagonal rooms lined with shelves. Each room contains 640 books of 410 pages each, each page containing 40 lines of 80 characters each, with no two books in the library identical. The library, which has existed forever and extends infinitely in space, contains books with every possible combination of characters and thus, in addition to an unfathomable amount of nonsense, all books in all languages. As Borges's narrator relates,

> Everything is there: the minutely detailed history of the future, the
> archangels' autobiographies, the faithful catalogues of the Library,
> thousands and thousands of false catalogues, the demonstration of the

fallacy of those catalogues, the demonstration of the fallacy of the true catalogue, the Gnostic gospel of Basilides, the commentary on that gospel, the commentary on the commentary on that gospel, the true story of your death, the translation of every book in all languages, the interpolations of every book in all books.[36]

In the dizzying logic of the place, Borges's first-person narrator recognizes that even his own text – "The Library of Babel" – "already exists in one of the thirty volumes of the five shelves of one of the innumerable hexagons – and its refutation as well."[37] Robert Darnton has described Google Books as "a digital mega-library greater than anything ever imagined, except in the fiction of Jorge Luis Borges."[38] Borges's imagined library is indeed far "greater" in scope, containing not just every book ever printed but also every book that could ever exist.

"The Library of Babel" is primarily a story about the psychic effects of information overload. The weight of information in Borges's library crushes its inhabitants, who are particularly devastated by the fact that, because everything exists somewhere within its structure, creativity itself is a logical impossibility. As Borges's narrator writes, "The certitude that everything has been written nullifies or makes phantoms of us all."[39] As a result, residents of the Library do not possess the notion of creative expression; the narrator speaks at one point of a "blasphemous sect" that attempts to produce divine books not by actually composing them but by rolling dice and transcribing the results.[40] The people of the library are crushed also by the sheer weight of nonsense that surrounds them. They spend their lives searching for significant – or merely coherent – books, but find only meaningless strings of characters. Paradise, from their perspective, is an index to the proliferating contents of the library, and a superstition pervades the library about a shelf containing "a book which is the formula and perfect compendium of all the rest."[41] Borges's narrator prays that someone, somewhere, will find it: "May heaven exist, though my place be in hell."[42]

Heaven, in this scenario, might look something like the search function in Google Books. As Nicholas Carr suggests in *The Shallows*, without Google, "the Internet would have long ago become a Tower of Digital Babel,"[43] and what Borges's narrator craves is a way to make the library's limitless holdings "universally accessible and useful." With such a resource at our own fingertips, however, we might push Borges's nightmarish vision further still. Crushing as it is for the inhabitants of Borges's library to know that, as a matter of logical deduction, original thought is impossible, might it not be worse still to possess the ability to prove definitely, via search, that your seemingly original idea or turn of phrase has already been claimed? In "The Library of Babel," Borges's narrator speaks of those who leave their native hexagons in search of so-called "Vindications" – books that provide justification for an individual's every act. Yet would it not be better to search for such a book in vain than to find it? Today, it does not take us long, with Google's assistance, to find the arcane text that justifies our strangest belief or the corner of the internet where everyone thinks and feels exactly as we do. Wells imagined his World Encyclopaedia as an "organ to 'pull the mind of the world together.'" A limitless and instantly accessible library might just have the opposite effect, sending us each into our own comfortable, isolated niche.

In this chapter full of thought experiments, Borges's contribution is provocative but by no means definitive. Perhaps the dystopia he describes will come to be. Perhaps, in contrast, Virginia Woolf's implicit wish will be fulfilled, and we will come to live in a world where anyone can gain access to any information they wish – information originally stored in books or in any other form. Perhaps this world will bring about a Wellsian utopia or the Digital Republic of Letters that Darnton foresees. Or perhaps copyright's persistent grip will mean that we will only be able to access the information we can pay for. What is most likely is some impure mixture of these purified visions. Perhaps the digital age will produce something quite modest: a slightly more democratic society, in which we are able to access more books and more literature than we were able to in the age of print. Perhaps, even if that is all it achieves, digitization will have been worth the trouble.

Chapter 4

Digital Editions and the Complexity of Remediation

In *Radiant Textuality* (2001), Jerome McGann writes, "Whatever happens in the future, whatever new electronic poetry or fiction gets produced, the literature we inherit (to this date) is and will always be bookish."[1] Even if we come to rely entirely on digital editions of literary texts that originally appeared in print, accessing them from digital libraries of the kind described in the previous chapter, that will not change the fact that these texts were first circulated as bound sheets of paper in a literary economy premised on the notion of the book as a physical commodity. Even if all literature produced from this point on is born digital (the subject of Part III of this book) that will not change the fact that the bulk of literary history was transacted in print. To neglect the bookishness of literature in the pre-digital period would be to neglect a significant portion of literary history.

Valuable as McGann's comment is, it is also somewhat misleading. The book was not the only medium for literature in the pre-digital period – nor was it universally considered the *best* literary medium. The Early English Books microfilming project was launched as a means of addressing a serious shortcoming of rare books: if they burned, they were gone forever. The gramophone was celebrated by many as a way of returning literature to its oral roots – from inhuman marks on a page to a living voice. Perhaps the boldest of all pre-digital attempts at overcoming the shortcomings of the book belonged to Vannevar Bush and his "Memory Expander" or "Memex." In a 1945 *Atlantic Monthly* article titled "As We May Think," Bush imagined a futuristic desk mounted with numerous screens and containing hundreds of thousands of microfilms. Overcoming the high price of printed books, the physical limitations of shelf space, and the difficulty of indexing a large library, the operator of the Memex could instantly display any of her vast number of microfilmed volumes and then link these volumes together through a process Bush called "associative indexing."[2] The gramophone never caught on as a literary medium; EEB microfilms were so difficult to use that they found an audience only among dedicated scholars; the complex Memex was never manufactured. Yet each stands as evidence that, even in the pre-digital period, many believed that literature would be better off in forms other than the book.

Furthermore, just because most literary texts circulated in printed form in the pre-digital period, this is not to say that all literary texts were *happy* as books. Even among the giants of literary history, many examples of bookish dissatisfaction present themselves. Though most readers have come to know his work through printed editions, William Blake forcefully resisted the printed medium; so deep were his objections to the book that he felt compelled to invent his own publishing method, "illuminated printing." The works of Emily Dickinson have likewise become famous in printed editions, yet she too strongly resisted print publication, preferring to keep her poems in manuscript form, often writing them on scraps of paper such as envelopes. Even the works of T. S. Eliot were distorted through their dissemination in print. The reception of *The Waste Land* was detrimentally affected by pages of endnotes that would not have been inserted if not for the commodity logic of print publication; further, Eliot's is a poem that clearly longs for spoken expression and that clearly mourns its entombment in the medium of print as a written rather than an oral text.

In this chapter, we consider digital editions of texts that originally appeared in print, beginning with a detailed investigation of the cases of Blake, Dickinson, and Eliot. Evaluating their digital presentation, respectively, on the William Blake Archive, the Dickinson Electronic Archives and Emily Dickinson Archive, and Faber's *Waste Land* iPad app, we ask whether a digital edition can really be said to "rescue" print-era texts that were not suitable to printed presentation. Next, we deepen this investigation by considering Jay David Bolter and Richard Grusin's concept of "remediation," which proposes that all digital editions of originally nondigital literary texts must be considered as translations, with inherent gains as well as losses. We close by asking whether digital editions have the power to shift interpretive power away from authors, editors, and publishers and to place it in the hands of readers.

Illuminated Pixels: The Case of William Blake

In literary classrooms, we tend to think of William Blake as a poet. Even if we are aware that Blake painted and that his paintings hang in the great galleries of the world, we think of a work like "The Tyger" as a poem when we encounter its verse-like representation in the pages of a literary anthology. Yet any printed rendering of Blake's texts – including "The Tyger" – vastly distorts the original form, which was forcefully multimodal, combining poetry, calligraphy, illustration, printmaking, and watercolor painting. The deeply idiosyncratic method that Blake invented for himself – "illuminated printing" – worked as follows. First, he would write the words, backward, in decorative calligraphy in acid-resistant ink onto a copper plate. Then he would illustrate the text, also backward and also in acid-resistant ink. Next he would bathe the copper plate in acid, and the acid would eat away at everything except his acid-proofed calligraphic/illustrated design, leaving a relief that could be printed. He would then ink the relief and print it onto paper. This produced a monochrome design, which Blake proceeded to paint by hand in watercolors. Robert Essick has called the resultant text, paradoxically, a "printed manuscript," because it is repeatable, like a printed text, yet also unique, like a manuscript. All copies of a given work were made from an impression from the same copper plate, yet each individual copy used different ink, was colored differently, and often had unique features added in the finishing process. Individual copies of Plate 14 of Blake's *The Marriage of Heaven and Hell*, for example, differ substantially: all the words in Copy E are brown, but four colors are employed in the text of Copy H; some copies have inked frame lines and others not; in the illustration at the top of the plate, the female figure hovering above the male looks down in all copies except Copy I, where she gazes off the page, looking directly at the reader (Figures 4.1a–b).

Blake's idiosyncratic method grew out of a strongly held objection to the mechanical nature of printed reproductions. If *The Marriage of Heaven and Hell* has anything like a thesis, it is found on Plate 3, where Blake writes, "Without Contraries is no progression. Attraction and Repulsion, Reason and Energy, Love and Hate, are necessary to Human existence."[3] Blake's adoption of a printing method that incorporates aspects of the apparently incompatible alternatives of machine-made print and handmade manuscript aligns with this Bakhtinian conception of opposition as a mutually beneficial dialogue rather than a zero-sum rivalry (see Preface). Blake makes this point directly on Plate 14, where he describes his printing method as an integral aspect of his apocalyptic mission to explode perceived oppositions and usher in new modes of unconstrained, nonbinary perception:

> The ancient tradition that the world will be consumed in fire at the end of six thousand years is true. as I have heard from Hell.
>
> For the cherub with his flaming sword is hereby commanded to leave his guard at the tree of life, and when he does, the whole creation will be consumed, and appear infinite. and holy whereas it now appears finite & corrupt.

(a)

(b)

Figures 4.1a–b *Copies D and I of Plate 14 of William Blake's* The Marriage of Heaven and Hell, *showing the significant variations Blake often introduced at the coloring stage of "illuminated printing."*

This will come to pass by an improvement of sensual enjoyment.

But first the notion that man has a body distinct from his soul, is to be expunged; this I shall do, by printing in the infernal method, by corrosives, which in Hell are salutary and medicinal, melting apparent surfaces away, and displaying the infinite which was hid.

If the doors of perception were cleansed every thing would appear to man as it is: infinite.

For man has closed himself up, till he sees all things thro' narrow chinks of his cavern.[4]

Blake is not humble: this is a speech act in which his apocalyptic vision is "hereby commanded." Neither is he timid about the significance of his unique medium: he envisions his program of "cleansing" "the doors of perception" as a causal result ("this I shall do") of his method – "infernal printing" – that works by "corrosives" to "[melt] apparent surfaces away" and "[display] the infinite which was hid." How exactly this process would function in practice, Blake does not say. Nor does he explain how he hoped to usher in the apocalypse by means of a printing method so labor intensive that only twelve copies of his key prophetic text were produced in his lifetime. The cherub with his flaming sword may well have left his guard at the tree of life – if only he could have been able to get his hands on a copy.

Posthumous editions of *The Marriage of Heaven and Hell* solved the problem of distribution, but introduced several others. Some typeset versions of Blake's poetry circulated during his lifetime, but it was not until 1863 that they were collected in an accessible form. *The Life of William Blake, "Pictor Ignotus"* was begun by Alexander Gilchrist and completed, after Gilchrist's death, by his widow Anne with assistance from Dante Gabriel and William Michael Rossetti. *The Marriage of Heaven and Hell* made its first typeset appearance in the Gilchrist volume, though like many other works, it was reproduced in excerpts interspersed with commentary. "To this shortly succeeds a series of Proverbs or Aphorisms, fantastically called 'Proverbs of Hell,'" Gilchrist writes at one point; "these Proverbs we give almost entire."[5] Gilchrist's subtitle, *"Pictor Ignotus,"* "Unknown Artist," neatly expresses the consequences of Blake's chosen medium of illuminated printing; Blake's work was only rescued from that medium-induced obscurity by Gilchrist's printed work and the second volume that D. G. Rossetti published in 1880. Yet the consequences of the typographical rendering of Blake's texts were severe. In addition to his verses being chopped up and interspersed with commentary, his peculiar and deliberate spellings were regularized ("Tyger" changed to "Tiger," for instance). Further, having to decide on a single version of each poem to set in type, Blake's editors obscured the purposeful variations of coloration and punctuation that

Blake introduced between individual copies. Perhaps most seriously, the typographical rendering of his words isolated one of the modalities in which he worked – text – from all the others, so that the complex interplay between word, calligraphy, and illustration was lost.

The William Blake Archive, one of the earliest major electronic literary archives, was designed to remedy the shortcomings of typographical editions of Blake's work by making available faithful digital renderings of his original texts. Speaking for fellow editors Morris Eaves and Robert N. Essick shortly after the Blake Archive's launch in 1996, Joseph Viscomi explained, "We recognize the typographic translation [of Blake's illuminated books] as grossly *distorting* the original artifact": "Typographic transcriptions, which abstract texts from the artifacts in which they are versioned and embodied, [make] good economic but poor editorial sense."[6] The Archive thus presents Blake in fully embodied form, offering high-quality, high-resolution, full-color digital reproductions of the pages of Blake's illuminated books. Though printed color facsimiles had already brought readers closer to Blake's original texts than earlier typographic print editions, digital presentation has additional advantages. It brings Blake's works out of the archives in which the originals were stored, making facsimiles available to readers anywhere in the world, instantly and for free. It allows readers to perform specifically digital operations on the images, such as zooming in and other forms of photo manipulation. Most importantly, it presents many – often *all* – versions of each of Blake's plates. Today, visitors to the Blake Archive are afforded a view of Blake's work unavailable even to the jet-setting scholar of the print era: all of his plates, in one place, side by side. Preserving both the embodied and the multi-versioned form of Blake's unusual personal medium, the Blake Archive offers a strong case that some texts are indeed better suited to digital than to print publication – that certain works, like *The Marriage of Heaven and Hell*, may find their ideal medium, and work their long-intended effects, only in the digital age.

A Digital Circumstance: Representing Emily Dickinson's Manuscripts

Emily Dickinson presents an equally persuasive case for digital rescue. Though we have come to know her work through printed editions, all such typographical renderings fundamentally misrepresent Dickinson's poetry, because, like Blake, she chose very deliberately not to circulate her work in print. The numbered poems we encounter today in the pages of literary anthologies remained during her lifetime – when she was able to control their circulation – entirely in manuscript form. In the earlier part of her writing "career" (a word whose pecuniary connotations make it awkwardly suited to Dickinson) in approximately 1858–1864, she worked by first composing on paper and then copying her poems into hand-sewn bound packets of handwritten sheets we have come to call "fascicles." The end result was something resembling a notebook, yet vastly different: Dickinson could easily have chosen to write in ready-made blank notebooks, but deliberately chose this more difficult path. Until around 1870, she continued to write on similar sheets of paper, but became less inclined to bind them together into fascicles. Later, her method became truly idiosyncratic: she would write on seemingly random scraps of paper – paper bags, bills, flyers, food wrappers, cut-out margins of newspapers, envelopes – and make no further effort to copy or bind them.

After her death, Thomas Wentworth Higginson and Mabel Loomis Todd prepared their 1890 edition of Dickinson's *Poems* by selecting certain items from among the fascicles and loose papers Dickinson left behind. They typeset them, titled them, numbered them, and arranged them into thematic groupings such as "Life," "Love," and "Nature." In the memorable beginning of *Dickinson's Misery* (2005), Virginia Jackson asks us to place ourselves in the position of Dickinson's first editors. Imagine sorting through the personal effects of a deceased relative and coming across a small box filled with papers: some sewn together, some loose, torn into shards, pinned together, and so on. How would we even recognize this as poetry? If we selected a few examples, cleaned up the spelling, fiddled with the arrangement of words on the page, and typed out the results, these words might come to look like lyric poems. But would not our actions serve to *impose* this genre identity on the scattered items in the box? As Jackson provocatively asks, "What if Dickinson did not write lyric poems?"[7]

Whatever their genre, whatever their meaning, there is no question that Dickinson's writings acquire their meaning in relation to the manuscript paper space of their original forms. To move them out of this space and into typographic form is unquestionably to alter their meaning. Consider one of the curiosities Jackson lists in her opened-box thought experiment: "There is writing clustered around a three-cent postage stamp of a steam engine turned on its side, which secures two magazine clippings bearing the names 'GEORGE SAND' and 'Mauprat.'"[8] The item that Jackson describes is the manuscript of what became Dickinson's poem 1167, "Alone and in a Circumstance –" (Figure 4.2). Dickinson's editors were in no hurry to recognize this work as a lyric poem: composed in 1870, it was not published in print until 1945, in the volume *Bolts of Melody*, edited by Mabel Loomis Todd's daughter, Millicent Todd Bingham. As Mark van Doren notes in his foreword to *Bolts of Melody*,

Figure 4.2 *Detail of the first page of the manuscript of Emily Dickinson's "Alone and in a Circumstance –," showing pasted stamp and "legs."*

Bingham had her work cut out for her: "The breaking of lines, the dividing of stanzas, the working out of alternative phrases or words – these are but a few of the jobs to be done."[9] Bingham persevered, however, converting two pieces of paper containing messy, crossed-out handwriting and a bizarre collage into something that looks very much like a lyric poem. In manuscript, the first four lines read something like the following:

> Alone and in a Circumstance – ,
>   of
> Reluctant to be told
> A spider on my reticence
> Assiduously   crawled
> deliberately
> determinately
> impertinently[10]

In *Bolts of Melody*, these lines are rendered as a neat quatrain, complete with normalized punctuation and capitalization but with only one of Dickinson's four suggested choices for the adverbial modification of "crawled":

> Alone and in a circumstance
> Reluctant to be told,
> A spider on my reticence
> Deliberately crawled,[11]

In addition to these typographic distortions and conventional regularizations of Dickinson's text in *Bolts of Melody*, there is the still graver omission of the locomotive stamp and the two strips of paper. Jerome McGann argues that Dickinson's insertions, cut out from an *Atlantic Monthly* review of George Sand's *Mauprat*, "set up a kind of gravitational field" in the manuscript, powerfully affecting the poem's meaning.[12] David Porter argues that "Alone and in a Circumstance –" "chronicles... the visit of a spider to a privy and particularly to an unmentionable part of the occupant's anatomy,"[13] seeing the poem, as Jerrald Ranta has neatly described it, as a "high-toned 'Little Miss Muffett.'"[14] Jeanne Holland, picking up on this suggestion, reads the pasted matter as a figure of the speaker's violated anatomy: "The stamp and its 'legs' emblematize Dickinson's female body, with its 'omitted center.'"[15] Holland in turn connects this imagery of privacy violated to Dickinson's chosen medium. Illustrating "a transgression, an intimate wounding without redress," the very form of the poem, Holland argues, provides a kind of compensation: built from the "household detritus" available to her, fashioned from her own "domestic technologies of production," Dickinson's manuscript demonstrates its proud resistance to the invasions of privacy-destroying print publication.[16]

Compelling as her argument may be, it is somewhat beside the point whether Holland is right or wrong about Dickinson's stamp. (Virginia Jackson, who does not see any possibility of definite resolution, accuses Holland of trying "to domesticate the strangeness of the lines and their contingent circumstances.")[17] The crucial point is that any reading of Dickinson's poem based only on its words is bound to be incomplete. As Jerome McGann argues, "Whatever this poem 'means,' the meaning has been visually designed."[18] Until you have seen the manuscript page – the stamp, the "legs," the variants, the punctuation, the handwriting, the position of words on the page – you have not read "Alone and in a Circumstance – ." For most of its history, this meant that to access Dickinson's complete text, you would need to visit Amherst College Library in person and obtain permission to see firsthand MS 129. In 1981, Ralph Franklin published a facsimile edition of *Manuscript Books of Emily Dickinson*, declaring "the manuscripts of this poet resist translation into the conventions of print."[19] Yet his volume only included facsimiles of Dickinson's fascicles and sets, omitting worksheet oddities such as "Alone and in a Circumstance – ." In any case, monochrome reproduction would not have provided faithful access to the original. To complete what Virginia Jackson has called the "unediting" of Dickinson – to rescue her from meddling transcribers and inadequate print reproductions – an electronic edition was needed.

The first such attempt was the Dickinson Electronic Archives (DEA), launched in the very early days of the internet, in 1994. Executive Editor Martha Nell Smith argued that the DEA would undo the "dismembering representation" of print transcription by offering full-color, unedited electronic reproductions of Dickinson's handwritten work: "What constitutes a 'poem' and poetic meanings," Smith argued, would thus be "left up to the reader." Further, the DEA would collect into a single virtual environment all of Dickinson's scattered oeuvre, which had been "dismembered by property rights and by literary orders."[20] In such statements, as Virginia Jackson has argued, Smith cast "Web publication . . . as the liberation of Dickinson's writing from the policing gaze of the print public sphere."[21] Yet the same property rights that the DEA sought to overturn prevented the realization of its aims. Although the DEA offered color facsimiles of several manuscripts, and searchable transcriptions of certain of Dickinson's works, issues of copyright prevented the inclusion of items in private collections or edited work published after 1922. The DEA thus shifted its focus, archiving work by Dickinson's correspondents and presenting itself as a hub for scholarly collaboration. This left the way open for the Emily Dickinson Archive, launched in 2014 by Harvard's Houghton Library. As one of the major holders of Dickinson manuscripts, the Houghton was more mindful of protecting copyright and better able to negotiate with other collections to produce "a single site for access to images of all surviving Dickinson autograph manuscripts."[22] Though more modest in its rhetoric, the Emily Dickinson Archive nonetheless accomplishes much of what Smith originally envisioned for the DEA. It took more than a hundred years, but we now have a way of accessing Dickinson's oeuvre as she left it behind her. Search for "Alone and in a Circumstance – ," and there it is: a small blue stamp with two strange legs – a curious center of gravity restored to a curious work.

Selling Sense: Eliot's Notes to *The Waste Land* and the Commodity Logic of Print

T. S. Eliot's *The Waste Land* presents a rather different case for digital rescue. Where Blake and Dickinson resisted and rejected distribution in print, Eliot embraced it wholeheartedly; where neither Dickinson nor Blake were interested in profiting from their efforts, Eliot proved a skillful marketer of his wares. In 1922, Eliot was paid some $2,800 for publishing *The Waste Land*, a figure that translates to well over $100,000 in today's money.[23] He was able to effect this financial tour de force because he understood how best to exploit the salient features of the print commodity. Whereas electronic editions distributed on the internet are instantly and globally accessible, a printed document, made of atoms rather than bits, must be transported through a much slower, more cumbersome distribution network. Yet in this cumbersomeness lies the potential for profit: because the same edition is not easily accessible to all readers, one can sell the same work in multiple formats to publishers in multiple jurisdictions and thereby multiply one's advances. Few have exploited this possibility more intelligently than Eliot, who, in less than a year, published *The Waste Land* in two periodicals in two countries (*The Criterion* in England and *The Dial* in the United States, both in October 1922); then as a book with a major press, Boni and Liveright, in the United States (December 1922); and then again as a deluxe book in the United Kingdom (handset by Virginia Woolf for her Hogarth Press in September 1923).

My students are routinely astounded when I tell the story of *The Waste Land*'s financial success – astounded and *annoyed*. How could Eliot make so much money from a work that is not only "difficult" but that also seems to revel in its difficulty – a text that seems to use its immense learning, its tremendous range of reference, and its knowledge of so many languages and alphabets not to invite readers in, but to keep out all but the elect? They are particularly appalled by the notes that Eliot appended to *The Waste Land*. Why write a poem so complex that only the author can decode it? Why reduce poetic reading to source hunting? Why insist on particular interpretations? Why not trust your reader to make sense of the poem for herself? Yet my students' perception of *The Waste Land* as "difficult" is in fact directly tied to Eliot's adeptness in the business of publishing. The poem's notes are largely responsible for readers' perception of the poem's inaccessibility, but Eliot would not have added them in the first place if he had not worked in a literary economy premised on the commodity logic of print.

In early 1922, Eliot returned to Paris from a sanatorium stay in Lausanne with a manuscript of *The Waste Land* in hand. His friend Ezra Pound arranged for him to meet the American publisher Horace Liveright, who expressed strong interest in publishing the poem in book form. There was a problem, however: *The Waste Land* was too short to publish as a standalone book. Liveright wrote to Pound, complaining, "I'm disappointed that Eliot's material is so short. Can't he add anything?"[24] As it happened, he could. In a letter written the next month to another prospective publisher, Eliot revealed his strategy: "My poem is of 435 lines; with certain spacings essential to the sense, 475 book lines; furthermore, it consists of five parts, which would increase the space necessary; and with title pages, some notes that I intend to add, etc., I guess that it would run from 28 to 32 pages."[25] In a tactic known to undergraduates the world over, Eliot decided to fiddle with the margins, increase the line spacing, throw in some perfunctory section titles and a separate title page – and to add some notes.

Inspired by a financial-bibliographic rather than an artistic impetus, *The Waste Land*'s notes were never essential to Eliot's vision of the poem – but they have strongly influenced its reception. Three decades after *The Waste Land* was published, Eliot addressed the issue ("The notes to *The Waste Land!*") in a speech delivered to an audience of 14,000 poetry fans assembled in the University of Minnesota basketball stadium:

> When it came to print *The Waste Land* as a little book . . . it was discovered that the poem was inconveniently short, so I set to work to expand the notes, in order to provide a few more pages of printed matter, with the result that they became the remarkable exposition of bogus scholarship that is still on view today. I have sometimes thought of getting rid of these notes; but now they can never be unstuck. They have had almost greater popularity than the poem itself – anyone who bought my book of poems, and found that the notes to *The Waste Land* were not in it, would demand his money back.[26]

Provided initially to maximize print revenues, the notes then proved impossible to withdraw from the bargain-conscious book-buyer, however much they distorted the poem. "My notes stimulated the wrong kind of interest among the seekers of sources," Eliot concluded. "I regret having sent so many enquirers off on a wild goose chase after Tarot cards and the Holy Grail."[27] In the ensuing years, as *The Waste Land* has become canonized and endlessly anthologized, the situation has become increasingly dire: in most literary anthologies, Eliot's endnotes now appear as footnotes, which are in turn supplemented with numerous editors' footnotes. Today, the page of an average edition of *The Waste Land* looks very much like a page from the Babylonian Talmud, with text surrounded by many levels of commentary and meta-commentary. As *The Waste Land* has come increasingly to resemble a sacred text, it has seemed less and less like something readers would wish to dive into and explore for themselves.

In 2012, an electronic edition of *The Waste Land* was released that finally succeeded in "unsticking" the poem's notorious notes. That summer, Faber and

Faber and TouchPress released the *Waste Land* iPad app, which, in yet another display of the poem's unlikely profitability, quickly became an international best-seller. At one point, the *Waste Land* app stood as the worldwide best-selling book app in Apple's iTunes Store; despite its hefty $13.99 price tag and massive 1-gigabyte download size, it outpaced Angry Birds and iFart as the best-selling app of any kind in the United Kingdom. Many factors explain its success: TouchPress's elegant design; the easily accessible scans of Eliot's manuscript; the informative video essays by experts such as Seamus Heaney and Jeanette Winterson; the superb audio readings by Alec Guinness, Fiona Shaw, and Viggo Mortensen. Perhaps the most immediately inviting aspect of the app, however, is the way it handles the notes. Orient your iPad in the "landscape" position, and the notes appear on the left of the screen: Eliot's notes, editors' notes – as many notes as you could wish for. But switch to "portrait," the natural position for reading, and the notes disappear. All that remain in this orientation are Eliot's words, devoid of their explanatory machinery, against a pristine white background, inviting you in to explore them. On a printed page, the notes either are present or they are not; an editor has decided this for you before the edition comes into your possession. If the editor has decided to include them, they are "stuck" to the page for as long as it exists.[28] On the screen of an intelligently designed electronic edition, however, the question of their appearance or disappearance is entirely at your discretion. Ask them to disappear and *The Waste Land* becomes a much less forbidding text – unencumbered by its familiar paraphernalia of explanation, it seems to invite you to explore its mysteries on your own and to trust in your success. Without sacrificing the revenue that was as central to Eliot's authorial intentions as apocalyptic unveiling was to Blake, the electronic medium resolves the print-specific dilemma that pursued the poem for nearly a century.

The Complexities of Remediation

The William Blake Archive, the Dickinson Electronic Archives and the Emily Dickinson Archive, and the *Waste Land* app present some of the most compelling cases for the advantages of digital presentation of literary texts. Bringing readers closer to their respective author's intended vision, each could be said to rescue texts that were ill suited to dissemination in print. Yet each of these projects also demonstrates another crucial point: although digital editions may bring us closer than print to the original form of certain literary texts, they do not – and cannot – offer us the original text itself. Indeed, even these exemplary digital editions of Blake, Dickinson, and Eliot are best regarded as *translations,* for like the print editions they seek to improve on, they too serve to move literary texts from one medium into another. As in all translations, something is inevitably lost.

One might argue, for example, that in their haste to rescue Blake's work from the medium of print, the editors of the Blake Archive moved it into a medium that Blake would have found equally objectionable. Blake chose not to distribute *The Marriage of Heaven and Hell* in print because print exemplified for him the rational, mechanized, industrial processes his work sought to overturn. The texts Blake produced in "illuminated printing" were themselves deliberately resistant to any mechanical reproduction: it is simply not possible to imagine any printed book that could capture all of Blake's works in all their versions, and this is exactly as Blake wanted it. The digital medium, with its incredible capacities of electronic reproduction, makes such an edition possible; in so doing, it does not so much "rescue" Blake's chosen method of illuminated printing as render it obsolete. Where Blake sought to make each copy unique, handmade, and distinct, the Blake Archive allows for the instantaneous, perfect, infinite reproduction of each of his page images. Where Blake produced a deliberately unstable text, the Blake Archive seeks stability and completeness in high-quality, color-accurate facsimiles of every copy of every plate of all his texts. Where Blake sought a method that would counter the rationalist spirit of his age, the Blake Archive stores images of imaginative transcendence in the hyper-rational matrices of databases and digital image files. Where Blake advocated ecstatic transport and sought to evoke it through his illuminated works, the Blake Archive presents his texts like specimens under a microscope – like patients etherized upon a table – to the cool, calculating, scholarly gaze of its visitors.

In its effort to undo the "distortions" of the print medium, the Blake Archive introduces new distortions of its own. In *My Mother Was a Computer* (2005), Katherine Hayles presents the Blake Archive as the case in point of a pervasive blindness by which the digital medium is mistakenly seen as a "neutral" carrier of older media. The Blake Archive, she argues, "establishes the gold standard for literary Web sites," particularly in the way it recognizes individual copies as unique physical objects and seeks to present them with all their bibliographic codes intact.[29] Yet Hayles is stunned by the editors' lack of self-consciousness with respect to their own transformations of Blake's illuminated texts. "The simulation of visual accuracy," she argues, "which joins facsimile and other editions in rescuing Blake from text-only versions that suppress the crucial visual dimensions of his work, is nevertheless achieved at the cost of cybernetic difference."[30] Considering the "Compare" features, which could be (partially) replicated in print only with "access to rare books rooms, a great deal of page turning, and constant shifting of physical artifacts," Hayles argues that "a moment's thought suffices to show that changing the navigational apparatus of a work changes the work."[31] "Concentrating only on how the material differences of *print* texts affect meaning, as does the William Blake Archive," she concludes, "is like feeling slight texture differences on an elephant's tail while ignoring the ways in which the tail differs from the rest of the elephant."[32]

In *Remediation: Understanding New Media* (1999), Jay David Bolter and Richard Grusin present a useful framework for analyzing digital translations like those of the *Blake Archive*. Bolter and Grusin distinguish between two types of digital archives: those that advocate their "transparency" and those that extol their "hypermediacy." In the first case, "an older medium is highlighted and represented in digital form without apparent irony or critique": "the computer is offered as a new means of gaining access to these older materials, as if the content of the older media could simply be poured into the new one."[33] In the second case, creators emphasize the differences between analog and digital media, presenting digital surrogates as improvements over analog originals.[34] Bolter and Grusin argue, however, that any act of digitization involves *both* "transparency" and "hypermediacy." According to their theory of remediation, even the most faithful conversion of an analog object into digital form inevitably entails fundamental alteration. The Blake Archive may envision itself as a faithful re-presentation of Blake's illuminated manuscripts, yet in exploiting digital affordances for linking, comparing, zooming, transforming, and so on, it is far from a neutral window on Blake's originals.

The logic of remediation applies also to a site like the Emily Dickinson Archive, which likewise transforms Dickinson's work through the act of digitizing it. A high-quality scan of "Alone and in a Circumstance – " may look very much like the scraps of paper Dickinson left tucked away in a box; in every other respect, however, it differs fundamentally. As Virginia Jackson argues, the digitized text is an "abstraction" of the original: a complex array of bits, a highly convoluted signifier of the original readable only through the intervention of machines.[35] Digital representations also inevitably fail to capture distinctly Dickinsonian additions such as the leaves she folded into letter-poems, for although foldable three-dimensional images are possible in the digital realm, we are several technological leaps away from being able to make a real leaf fall off the screen and into your lap. The principal difference between an envelope tucked away in a box and a digital facsimile of that same envelope, however, is the latter's ready accessibility. On the Emily Dickinson Archive, "Alone and in a Circumstance – " can be called up instantly by anyone with internet access and sufficient curiosity. It can then be searched, zoomed in on (the locomotive stamp can fill your screen), and linked to other poems. However illuminating to the reader or scholar, to read the poem in this way is to violate the privacy Dickinson worked so hard to achieve by writing it on a scrap of paper and leaving it hidden away in a closet. Jeanne Holland argues that the poem's form – handwritten, cobbled together from domestic objects such as magazines and stamps – stands as an embodied rejection of the public world in favor of the private. Like Blake, Dickinson chose her medium precisely because it precluded distribution to a mass audience in the print economy of her time. On the Web, large-scale reproduction is achieved with a facility unimaginable even in print. In visiting the Emily Dickinson Archive and zooming in on the digital facsimile of "Alone and in a Circumstance – ," it is *we* who become the Web-crawling spiders. It is we who violate Dickinson's desired reticence – assiduously, deliberately, determinately, impertinently.

Poetry in the *Waste Land* App: A Case Study in Remediation

We can be confident, at least, that Eliot would have approved of the *Waste Land* app's toggle-able notes; he more or less asked for them. But another digital affordance of the *Waste Land* app, its audio readings, presents a far more ambiguous case. In its original incarnation, the *Waste Land* app shipped with six readings: two by Eliot himself, recorded in 1933 and 1947, and one each by Alec Guinness, Ted Hughes, Viggo Mortensen, and Fiona Shaw. Whereas Eliot's own readings are uniformly dreadful – monotonous and tone deaf – the others are often thrilling. Shaw is passionate and nimble, giving each of the poem's characters its own distinct voice. Guinness is urbane and dexterous, shifting with liquid ease between the poem's personae. Hughes's wild reading exposes buried energy and hidden danger. Mortensen reinvents the poem in an American tough-guy idiom; it is *The Waste Land* read from the seat of a Harley-Davidson. As in all good performances of verbal art, these readers bring the poem to life – they make us not just comprehend but also *feel* its meaning. The *Waste Land* app's audio readings are without doubt its most appealing feature. They also stand as a testament to the virtues of digital presentation and, in particular, to the digital medium's "convergence of modalities": for no printed book, however well designed, can read its content aloud for you, just as no audio book can show you the printed words as it performs them or allow you to switch instantly between reading voices. Yet the app's audio readings, sublime as they as are, also provide a thorough lesson in the dizzying logic of remediation.

Poetry is the literary form that has been most affected by medium shifts. In the oral age, all literature was poetic in form; in the ages of manuscript and print, poetry lost its cultural centrality and became an increasingly written form, rather than a spoken one; now, the digital age promises a return to poetry's oral roots. Poetry shows the word "literature" to be an etymological misnomer: "literature" is derived from the Latin *littera,* meaning a letter of the alphabet. Yet poetry, the original literary form, predates the invention of letters, alphabets, and writing. Many of the stylistic characteristics of poetry that we now regard primarily as aesthetic adornment – rhythm, assonance, and figurative language, for instance – served very practical purposes in the time before writing. As Walter Ong argues in *Orality and Literacy,* they functioned as mnemonic devices:

> In a primary oral culture, to solve effectively the problem of retaining and retrieving carefully articulated thought, you have to do your thinking in mnemonic patterns, shaped for ready oral recurrence. Your thought must come into being in heavily rhythmic, balanced patterns, in repetitions or antitheses, in alliterations and assonances, in epithetic and other formulary expressions, in standard thematic settings (the assembly, the meal, the duel, the hero's "helper," and so on), in proverbs which are constantly heard by everyone so that they come to mind readily and which themselves are patterned for retention and ready recall, or in other mnemonic form. Serious thought is intertwined with memory systems. Mnemonic needs determine even syntax.[36]

Poetic form in an oral society is not ornamentation, then, but a way of encoding information so as to ensure its survival. After writing and printing superseded poetry as the preeminent means of storing information, poetry became a hybrid form. Typographical conventions were developed for its transcription. In time, visual features such as stanza breaks, enjambments, and indented refrains – none of which necessarily register when read aloud – became crucial elements of poetic meaning. Many critics lamented poetry's slow drift from an oral to a written form. Samuel Johnson objected to Milton's blank verse on the grounds that it was "verse only to the eye"[37] – that it *looked* like poetry but did not always sound like it. For example, in Book III of *Paradise Lost,* Milton compares his own blindness to that of "Blind Thamyris, and blind Maeonides, / And Tiresias, and Phineus, prophets old," writing,

> Then feed on thoughts, that voluntary move
> Harmonious numbers; as the wakeful bird
> Sings darkling, and in shadiest covert hid
> Tunes her nocturnal note. Thus with the year

Seasons return; but not to me returns
Day, or the sweet approach of even or morn,
Or sight of vernal bloom, or summer's rose,
Or flocks, or herds, or human face divine.[38]

In these lines, Milton repeatedly calls attention to the visual rather than oral form of his verse. The deliberately clumsy – even "blind" – enjambment "returns / Day" paradoxically registers only visually, because, as Johnson complained, "There are only a few skilful and happy readers of Milton who enable their audience to perceive where the lines end or begin"[39] Punning on the meaning of "numbers" as poetic meter, Milton forces the reader to mispronounce "harmonious" if she wishes to maintain the iambic pentameter of his blank verse – hardly a harmonious situation, sonically speaking.

From the time of the invention of writing, and particularly since the time of Gutenberg, all poets have worked in a "remediated" form: the written form of poetry served as a prompt for oral performance ("transparency"), yet it also became an object of visual interest in itself ("hypermediacy"). The remediated nature of poetry is perhaps clearest in the genre of concrete poetry, in which the typographic arrangement of words on the page is as important to the poem's meaning as their sound. Concrete poems date to the third century BCE, though their best known post-Gutenberg form belongs to poems by George Herbert, such as "The Altar" and "Easter Wings," in which the words are arranged so as to make the poem resemble, respectively, an altar and an angel's wings. Concrete poetry became particularly widespread in the modernist period – around the time Eliot published *The Waste Land* – in poems such as Apollinaire's "Il pleut," where the words are arranged to resemble falling rain.

The period in which *The Waste Land* was published was a high-water mark in critical lamentations of the written remediation of poetry. Throughout the 1920s, a debate raged over the "Death of Poetry," in which writers such as Virginia Woolf, Robert Graves, and Herbert Read argued that poetry had become increasingly marginalized in the modern world because of its dissociation from its oral roots. R. C. Trevelyan spoke for a generation of modernist critics when he asked, in *Thamyris; or, Is There a Future for Poetry* (1925), whether "the gradual divorce of poetry from music and intoning meant...a progressive impoverishment and deterioration, through senility and second-childishness, towards an unlamented death in a bastard and graceless prose."[40] Trevelyan had a particular poet and a particular poem in mind: Eliot was for Trevelyan the leader of a new breed of typographic poets "whose idiom is not universal, but calculated for a cultured private coterie," and he saw *The Waste Land* as a case in point.[41] Eliot himself may even have agreed with this assessment. In a letter written to Richard Aldington on November 15, 1922 – a month after the poem first appeared in the United Kingdom, and the month of its U.S. appearance – Eliot wrote, "As for *The Waste Land,* that is a thing of the past so far as I am concerned and I am now feeling toward a new form and style."[42] The new form and style was dramatic verse, and from this point on in his career, Eliot increasingly wrote for the stage, where poetry is delivered not as words on the page but as a living voice.

Eliot's desire that his poetry be *heard* is clearly present in *The Waste Land* itself. The poem's third part, "The Fire Sermon," begins,

> The river's tent is broken; the last fingers of leaf
> Clutch and sink into the wet bank. The wind
> Crosses the brown land, unheard. The nymphs are departed.
> Sweet Thames, run softly, till I end my song.[43]

The picture Eliot paints is of a contemporary London in which poetry has died: the wind crosses unheard, just as the awkward enjambment "wind / Crosses" passes seen but not heard. In this music-less world in which the singing nymphs "are departed," Eliot's quotation of Spenser's *Epithalamion,* "Sweet Thames, run softly, till I end my song," can only be ironic, because this is not a "song" at all, given that the poem's audience is far more likely to read his poem silently than listen to it read aloud. When he later references Marvell's "To His Coy Mistress" in the lines "But at my back in a cold blast I hear / The rattle of bones, and chuckle spread from ear to ear,"[44] the effect is again ironic, because he knows that, in the soundless landscape of modernist poetry, even such a forcefully auditory rhyme as "hear" / "ear" is more likely to be picked up by his readers' eyes than by their ears, the similarity in word shape registering more strongly than the repeated sound.

The context of the modernist "Death of Poetry" debate highlights the significance of the *Waste Land* app's audio readings. On the one hand, there is clearly a case to be made that the digital edition "rescues" the poem from the soundless medium of print. In this app, one has only to touch a line of verse, and typographic text is transformed into performed speech, as if by magic. Touch "Sweet Thames, run softly, till I end my song," and miraculously, the words *do* become song; touch the line beginning "But at my back," and one hears the "hear" / "ear" rhyme with one's ears. These audio readings bring to life other buried aspects of *The Waste Land.* Listen to Alex Guinness's reading of the first stanza, for example, where he shifts between a detached prophetic tone and the slightly zany German-accented voice of an aristocratic woman, and one understands immediately that Eliot's poem is not a monologue but a tissue of voices, a crucial fact that easily escapes a silent reading.

Yet, following the double logic of remediation, the digital edition of *The Waste Land* introduces new problems just as it solves old ones. For although *The Waste Land* wants desperately to be read aloud, it does not expect to be. *The Waste Land* is, to some extent, *about* the arid sonic landscape of the modernist period; it is, in part, *about* the "Death of Poetry." This aspect of the poem depends on the "Sweet Thames" line *not* being heard aloud and on the "hear" / "ear" rhyme *not* being perceived aurally. Although the addition of audio readings responds to one of the poem's greatest implicit wishes, there is something uncanny, unsettling, and indeed unnatural in the poem's migration into a rich multimodal environment. One feels this most acutely in the audio readings of the poem's many onomatopoeias – conventionalized typographic renderings of sound. Eliot fills *The Waste Land* with awkward onomatopoeias such as "Jug jug," the Elizabethan shorthand for a nightingale's song, choosing them precisely for their crudeness, in order to mark the wide gulf separating oral poetry from its written transcription. In preparing audio readings, the creators of the *Waste Land* app could easily have replaced Eliot's crude onomatopoeias with human whistling or with recorded birdsong. Instead, they asked their performers to speak the words aloud. To listen to Viggo Mortensen's awkward deadpan reading of the lines "Twit twit twit / Jug jug jug jug jug jug"[45] is to come face to face with the tortured complexities of remediation: to hear a sound turned into writing turned back into sound, with all the artifacts of each conversion left intact. As the *Waste Land* app demonstrates, digital editions can give us new access to analog originals and provide new experiences of print-entombed texts, but they never do so neutrally. Every digital edition is a translation, and as with all translations, each stands in a unique relationship – often ambivalent – to its analog original.

The Reader as Editor: Social Editions and *IVANHOE*

To this point, I have referred to the William Blake Archive, the Emily Dickinson Archive, and the *Waste Land* app as "editions." Yet it would perhaps be more accurate to call them "un-editions" or "anti-editions," for each seeks in its own way to wrest power away from the privileged editor and to place interpretive control in the hands of its readers. Presenting Blake's and Dickinson's works in versions more closely resembling their original form, they allow readers access to facsimiles of the original texts from which print editors made their decisions: what to print, when to regularize spelling, when to group two lines as a couplet, which version to recognize as authoritative, and so on. The designers of such websites are not so much editors as arrangers, presenting the primary texts in such a way that the readers perform the real editorial work themselves.

Whereas sites like the William Blake Archive and the Emily Dickinson Archive suggest the digital capacity for distributing editorial functions and making editing a more inclusive process, "social editions" like that of *The Devonshire Manuscript* – a sixteenth-century court miscellany – go further still. The facilitators of this project, at the University of Victoria's Electronic Textual Cultures Lab, give two reasons for presenting it in a digital as opposed to a print form. First, working digitally allows them to make corrections without the need for an errata slip or a new edition. Second, a digital edition allows visitors to their site to actually *perform* such corrections. The primary goal of the project is to "use existing social media tools to change the role of the scholarly editor from the sole authority on the text to a facilitator who brings traditional and citizen scholars into collaboration through ongoing editorial conversation."[46] The project is built on the Wikibooks platform, which permits collaborative and open authorship in much the same way as the Wikipedia platform, and so allows for a genuinely "crowd-sourced" critical edition. Yet, at present, these capacities are not being fully exploited; only invited experts are allowed to participate in the editing process, and the prospect of opening the editorial base to include graduate students and the general public ("citizen scholars") remains controversial. As one advisor to the project remarks, "There are very few people qualified to read this manuscript and say anything I would want to read."[47] Conversely, very few members of the general public would likely have interest in participating in the editing of an obscure sixteenth-century manuscript. The "social edition," an appealingly democratic idea in theory, has proven difficult to realize in practice.

Conceived some ten years before *The Devonshire Manuscript*, IVANHOE was an even more ambitious project for empowering the literary reader. Initiated by Jerome McGann and Johanna Drucker at the University of Virginia, IVANHOE sought to reimagine literary interpretation in the form of an online game. The project was born of frustration with electronic editions of literary texts that sought simply to mimic the features of printed books in digital forms. As Drucker recalls in *SpecLab: Digital Aesthetics and Projects in Speculative Computing* (2009), she had grown weary of advertising copy for "electronic 'books'" that promised to "'supercede the limitations' and overcome the 'drawbacks' of their paper-based forebears,"[48] yet failed to take advantage of the particular affordances of digital textuality. In a criticism that still applies to e-reading applications such as Apple's iBooks and devices like the Amazon Kindle, Drucker complained, "We see simulacral page drape but little that indicates the capacity for such specifically electronic abilities as rapid refresh, time-stamped updates, or collaborative and aggregated work."[49] It is the digital capacity for collaboration – specifically, for collaborative literary interpretation – that IVANHOE sought to exploit. For Drucker and McGann, the literary text is always an unstable site of collaborative engagement, regardless of the medium in which it is delivered. In his theoretical elaborations on IVANHOE, McGann invokes Bakhtin's notion that all texts are necessarily "immersed in a complex 'discourse field' of conflicting, competing, and overlapping 'languages'"[50] and recalls the "shared understanding" of Roland Barthes and Galvano della Volpe that "interpretation makes an active move upon the textual inheritance."[51] The advantage of a digital environment like IVANHOE lies in its ability to record and recall the interpretive "moves" that make up any reading of any literary text. As Drucker puts it, "All those traces of reading, of exchange, or of new arrangements and relations of documents . . . in which a text is produced, altered, and received, can be made visible within an electronic space."[52] As it was originally conceived, IVANHOE thus sought to use the peculiar advantages of the digital medium to "provide self-conscious insight into the literary work and into the processes of interpretation constituted by any and every act of reading."[53]

IVANHOE is a game of literary interpretation played as follows. Beginning with a "discourse field" (which includes a literary work as well as its reception and transmission history), each player (the minimum is two) adopts a "role" and makes a series of "moves." In each move, the player rewrites some part of the discourse field and then records a justification for the specific "deformation" she has performed along with her rationale for the "role" she has chosen to adopt. "The agreement," McGann writes, "is that each person will try to reshape the given work so that it is understood or seen in a new way."[54] The first time the game was played, by McGann and Drucker via e-mail in 2000, it focused on the discourse field of Sir Walter Scott's *Ivanhoe*. Adopting the role of an undergraduate student, McGann transformed the text so as to make Rebecca and Bois-Guilbert end up together, an outcome, McGann argues, that "responds to codings that are clearly present, if unexploited and even resisted, in the *Ivanhoe* Scott published."[55] In a subsequent playing, focused on Henry James's *The Turn of the Screw*, Drucker adopted the role of "an Oulipo-inspired graduate student"; her "moves" reworked the novel at every mention of the character Flora as "a feminist protest of Henry James's conception of the girl's sexual imagination."[56]

The motivation for IVANHOE's game-like approach to literary interpretation is captured by Drucker's own reflections of her experience of playing the first round of the game, which stress the shift from passive reading to active writing:

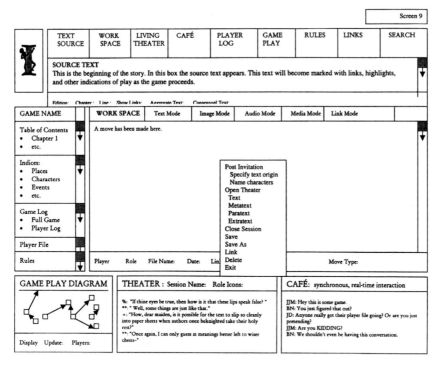

Figure 4.3 *Storyboard sketch by Johanna Drucker showing the intended functionality of the* IVANHOE *game.*

McGann had suggested that we see the book in terms of an opportunity for rewriting – for all of the possibilities within the book that it held out as potential tales. Tasked with the challenge of thinking about where and how we might change it, our relation to the text shifted radically. My own motivation as a reader suddenly spiked, fueled by an investment in finding the right place for an intervention. This realization of the power of shifting from passive to active reader, from spectator to participant in a project-based exercise became the basis of my commitment to Ivanhoe.[57]

Although the game could theoretically be played in an analog form using only pen and paper, Drucker set about designing an interface for playing IVANHOE on the web. In its fully realized state, IVANHOE consists of windows presenting the progressively "deformed" source text, logs of player moves, diaries of justifications for these moves, various visualizations of the unfolding game, and a "café" area for player discussions (Figure 4.3). "Created at the intersection of individual subjectivities in dialogue with each other through a work and its interpretive field," Drucker writes, "the interface was meant to permit the mapping of these interrelations, and emphasized the social nature of the production of imaginative work and the collaborative character of interpretive acts."[58]

Despite its innovative – even revolutionary – approach, IVANHOE has not had a significant impact on the way we read and interpret literature. In *SpecLab*, Drucker foresees that IVANHOE might "prove, ultimately, too esoteric in its aims and design for broad adaptation." Though insisting that the project's "virtue was that it was a toy and a tool, not packaged content, and its design was premised on a theoretically sophisticated set of premises," she notes that "the idea of a game of interpretation to save the humanities gained few converts."[59] Launched for the web in 2006, it is, at the time of writing, unavailable – incompatible with modern browsers and awaiting the funding necessary to make it so. One need not look far, however, to see that many of IVANHOE's best ideas have now been implemented in popular e-reading applications. For example, Goodreads provides a forum (much like IVANHOE's "café") in which readers can discuss and recommend books with other readers directly, without professional mediation. The Amazon Kindle's group-underlining feature makes interpretation a public, communal act, wresting power from editors and critics; when this option is enabled, Kindle readers can see the passages that mattered to other readers – not just those that experts and other literary "middlemen" considered important. Genius.com likewise provides an interface for crowd-sourced annotations of any text, from rap lyrics to Elizabethan poetry. Closest in spirit and interface to IVANHOE is SocialBook, developed by Bob Stein and the Institute for the Future of the Book, which provides a platform in which readers can not only underline but also make comments and carry out threaded conversations in the "margins" of digital books. Though less ambitious than IVANHOE, each of these projects participates in its mission of foregrounding literary interpretation as an active, transformative, communal endeavor.

We closed the previous chapter with a Borgesian thought experiment: imagine you have built the perfect digital library, and then imagine all that might go wrong. Let us now imagine that our universal digital library is populated with ideal digital editions of every literary text from the pre-digital era: searchable, zoomable, high-resolution, full-color digital representations of printed books, manuscripts, illuminated manuscripts, scraps of paper, and so on, in all their versions, with every one accompanied by oral readings by Alex Guinness, Fiona Shaw, and Viggo Mortensen. What could go wrong? Websites like the Blake Archive and the Emily Dickinson Archive show us one possible complication: that in our haste to undo the distortions of the printed medium, we might become blind to the new distortions introduced through our own acts of digital remediation. Editions like Faber's *Waste Land* app show us that moving a text out of its native medium, even when this shift manifestly "enhances" its content, can fundamentally alter its meaning. Digital editions that make reading a more active, communal process – "social editions" and game environments like that of IVANHOE – present complications of their own. In his article "Solitary Reading in an Age of Compulsory Sharing," Drew Nelles argues that such editions "run against the enclosed, solitary nature of reading" and "smack . . . of enforced sociality,"[60] serving as "symptom[s] of a culture that shares everything, even when there's very little to share."[61] In *Book Was There*, Andrew Piper worries that if a commercial distributor of electronic books begins recording our annotations and interpretations of digital literary texts, the individual reader will become "not an amateur or a connoisseur, one who loves or knows, but a test subject, someone who is constantly being measured."[62] As pessimistic as such reflections may be, they remind us of one of the most productive aspects of studying literature in the digital age: that the act of imagining alternatives to the printed form leads us not only to exciting new digital possibilities but also to a deeper understanding – and often a renewed appreciation – of print itself.

Chapter 5

Quantitative Approaches to the Literary

On my computer I have a plain text file of Charles Dickens's novel *Great Expectations*, an M4V video file of the 1998 film adaptation starring Ethan Hawke and Gwyneth Paltrow, and an MP3 copy of the film's soundtrack. The digital film takes up 1,133,953,365 bytes on my hard drive, the soundtrack 158,060,500 bytes, and the full text of the novel only 1,013,777 bytes. Why should a novel, which fills 476 pages in the edition on my bookshelf, occupy only 0.6% of the hard drive space taken up by a one-hour soundtrack? Why should an average-length film – it runs for one hour and forty-six minutes – take up more than one thousand times the space of a long novel?

The answer is simple: it is much easier to convert text into digital form than it is to convert any other modality. Despite the fact that digital video, music, and photography are now ubiquitous, whereas electronic books still have not entirely dislodged our affection for the printed book, text was in fact the first modality to "go digital." This is because text – whose basic unit is the letter, of which there are relatively few – is easily translated into binary code, the native language of computers. The first widely accepted standard for turning text into binary code was the American Standard Code for Information Interchange, or ASCII, which was formalized in the early 1960s and is still in wide use. Using seven bits (seven ones or zeros), the earliest version of ASCII included codes for lowercase letters a–z, uppercase letters A–Z, numbers 0–9, punctuation, and some special commands. In 7-bit ASCII, the phrase "Search me" becomes 1010011100101110000111100101100011110100001000001101101 1 100101, where

1010011 = S
1100101 = e
1100001 = a
1110010 = r
1100011 = c
1101000 = h
0100000 = (space)
1101101 = m
1100101 = e

Although confusing to a human eye, this relatively simple translation of human written language into the language of machines makes text a natural fit for computing. Not only are computer text files very small but they are also very easy to search: simply by seeking out a particular string of ones and zeros – child's play for even the slowest of machines – a computer can instantly identify any combination of words in a digital text. The language of sound and images, in contrast, is much more difficult to convert into digital form. Because the "alphabet" of music and visual art is much more complex (there are far more than twenty-six shapes, for instance, and the eye can perceive millions of colors), these files are larger and much harder to search. Asking a machine to find a thick red brushstroke over a light blue background in a digital image, or a jangly minor-chord guitar arpeggio during a middle-eight in an MP3, remains a challenging technological task. Indeed, given the relative ease of textual searching, the most common and efficient way to locate a song or photo online is to search adjacent text.

Thus text is the most "computable" of the modalities. It is the easiest to convert into machine language, it is the easiest to search, and it is also the most amenable to the most powerful capacity of the computer: namely, its incredible ability to perform mathematical operations. Once a literary text has been made machine readable – once the letters that compose it have been converted into ones and zeros – the number-crunching abilities of the computer are set free to perform quantitative analyses that shed light on the text's authorship, style, genre, theme, plot, and even ideology. Once we have enough digitized texts at hand – once we have begun to approach the condition of the universal library discussed in Chapter 3 – the computer's statistical capacities can be applied to vast numbers of texts at once. Such large-scale analysis can provide insight not only into individual texts but also into entire careers, genres, periods, centuries, and national literatures. The computer's ability to assist in literary analysis increases further still when we move beyond plain text – beyond literature as a collection of undifferentiated words – and begin to distinguish between types of words (stage directions, chapter titles, metaphors, nouns, foreign phrases, etc.) in a process known as text encoding.

Computing in the Humanities: A Brief History

Given the relative ease of turning text into machine-readable data, it is not surprising that the first work in what has come to be known as the Digital Humanities was textual in nature. It is generally agreed that the computational analysis of humanities materials began with Father Roberto Busa and his *Index*

Thomisticus project. In the early 1940s Busa, an Italian Jesuit priest, had written a doctoral dissertation on the notion of "presence" in the work of St. Thomas Aquinas. His work took a philological approach, centering heavily on word usage, yet Busa was interested not only in the more obvious words *praesens* and *praesentia* (present and presence) but also in Aquinas's use of the preposition *in* (in). Believing that "all functional or grammatical words . . . manifest the deepest logic of being which generated the basic structures of human discourse,"[1] Busa felt compelled to compile a list of all instances of *in* in Aquinas's oeuvre, a corpus of more than ten million words. Although Busa's patience was legendary, this task exceeded even its considerable limits.

What Busa began to imagine at this point, in 1946, was the first electronic concordance. The history of concordances – alphabetical lists of important words used in a text, with short citations of passages using the word – is a long one, extending far into the pre-digital past. But the sheer difficulty of compiling "analog" concordances (the first concordance to the Vulgate Bible, compiled by Hugo of St. Cher in the thirteenth century, reputedly required the aid of five hundred monks) meant that they were restricted to very important works such as holy books or Shakespeare's plays. Despite the importance of Aquinas's work and the ready availability of Jesuit priests willing to assist, the particulars of Busa's project made a traditional concordance impractical. First, there was the problem of ten million words. Then there was Busa's insistence on including all words, including seemingly insignificant ones, such as prepositions. Finally, there was Busa's requirement that words be listed not only alphabetically but also grouped by "lemma" – for instance, that related verb forms with markedly different spellings, such as *sum* and *es* ("I am" and "you are"), be listed together. "It was clear to me," Busa wrote, "that I needed some type of machinery."[2] But in a period before the first commercial computer, it took some time to determine exactly what machinery was called for. In 1949, Busa visited the chairman of IBM, Thomas J. Watson Sr., in his New York office. Watson convinced Busa of the merits of computers for his task and offered some support – though, because IBM's first fully digital computer remained several years away, he instructed Busa to enter the Thomist canon on paper punch cards. Busa promptly returned to Rome and began to assemble his team. After twenty-five years, several technological revolutions (including the move from punch cards to magnetized tape), many innovations (including the development by Busa and his associates of a program able to "lemmatize" 130,000 Latin forms), and a tremendous amount of human labor (Busa estimated more than a million hours), the first volumes of the Index Thomisticus began to appear in 1974. In 1992, the complete Index appeared in electronic form as a CD-ROM with hypertext features ("*cum hypertextibus*"). In 2005, it was published in a free online version.

In the meantime, in the 1960s, the first truly impressive work in computer-assisted text analysis began to appear. As with the concordance, quantitative approaches to literary criticism long predated the advent of the digital. In the late nineteenth century, for example, T. C. Mendenhall attempted to resolve the authorship of certain Shakespearean texts by counting the number of two-, three-, and four-letter words, and so on, in plays by Shakespeare, Marlowe, Bacon, and others. The advent of computers, however, made calculations of this kind far faster and more accurate than any human could achieve. A remarkable demonstration of the power of computational text analysis came in 1964, with the work of Charles Frederick Mosteller and David Wallace on the authorship of the Federalist Papers. Of the eighty-five Federalist Papers, fifteen are of disputed authorship, though each is known to have been written either by James Madison, Alexander Hamilton, or John Jay. Mosteller and Wallace, using what was in 1964 a vast amount of computing power, performed word-frequency calculations on the disputed texts and compared them to the data derived from works of known authorship. As in Busa's research, the most exciting results came from words unlikely to impress any human reader. Finding that Hamilton used "a" more than Madison and Jay, but "and" less than either – and that Hamilton preferred the infinitive "to be," whereas Madison and Jay tended to use "is" – Mosteller and Wallace concluded that Madison had in fact written all of the disputed papers. Their conclusion is widely accepted to this day.[3]

Quantitative Literary Analysis: A Long-Standing Controversy

The application of such quantitative approaches to literature has always been controversial. Although voices throughout history have called for the application of objective approaches to the study of literature, they have tended to be drowned out by those claiming that quantitative approaches are somehow unsuited to the inescapably human vagaries of literary expression. Once again, debates about the computability of literature long preceded the digital age. In 1873, Frederick Furnivall founded the New Shakspere Society. At a time when much remained to be settled about Shakespeare, as the society's strangely spelled name suggests, one of the group's principal aims was to establish definitively the chronological order in which Shakespeare wrote his plays. For this, Furnivall proposed a quantitative method based on "close study of the metrical and phraseological peculiarities of Shakespeare."[4] Frederick Gard Fleay, one of the loudest proponents of the society's numbers-based approach, argued, "Our analysis, which has hitherto been qualitative, must become quantitative," describing this quantitative turn as "the great step we have to take."[5] The advantages, he claimed, lay both in objective certainty and in the power of persuasion: though he acknowledged that "it may seem to some ludicrous to speak of the application of mathematics to such a subject," he insisted that "if you cannot weigh, measure, number your results, however you may be convinced yourself, you must not hope to convince others, or claim the position of an investigator; you are merely a guesser, a propounder of hypotheses."[6]

Many did, alas, find the society's mathematical approach "ludicrous." Chief among this faction was the poet and critic Charles Algernon Swinburne, who published a parody of the New Shakspere Society in *The Fortnightly Review* in 1875. Ridiculing the "purely arithmetical process" endorsed by the Society, Swinburne objected,

> For all the counting up of numbers and casting up of figures that a whole university – nay, a whole universe of pedants could accomplish, no teacher and no learner will ever be a whit the nearer to the haven where they would be. In spite of all tabulated statements and regulated summaries of research, the music which will not be dissected or defined, the "spirit of sense" which is one and indivisible from the body or the raiment of speech that clothes it, keeps safe the secret of its sound.[7]

For Swinburne, the putative advantages of quantitative criticism were erased by the fundamental disjuncture between literature and enumeration of any kind. What is peculiar to literary art, he claimed, is entirely irreducible to any mathematic schema: its "spirit of sense" cannot be modeled algorithmically, because it is too complex or too irregular. Quantitative literary criticism, in Swinburne's view, is founded on the flawed premise that literature can be treated as data.

This argument continues today in terms that are strikingly similar. In 2012, a paper appeared in the *Proceedings of the National Academy of Sciences of the United States of America* titled "Quantitative Patterns of Stylistic Influence in the Evolution of Literature." Authored by a team of mathematicians and computational linguists led by James M. Hughes, the paper analyzed literary texts mined from Project Gutenberg to determine whether contemporary writers were more or less influenced by what came before them than were writers of previous eras. Noting in their introduction that "quantitative methods have long been applied to literature, most notably in the analysis of style,"[8] the authors take for granted the usefulness of such an approach and move quickly toward a mathematical demonstration of their conclusion: that writers today are less influenced by their forebears than these forebears were by their own predecessors. This article created considerable controversy, though it was neither the authors' conclusions nor their specific methods that prompted the loudest objections. Rather, it was the very idea of performing quantitative literary analysis that most offended its detractors. Laura Miller, writing for *Salon*, called the study "an illustration of the dangers of empirical hubris." "Having a lot of numbers and equations," she warned, "is not the same as knowing what they mean, especially in such a complex and meaning-rich field as literature."[9] If Hughes's study, which focused on works in the public domain published before 1923, had dared to explore more contemporary materials, Miller proposed, these complex texts would have overwhelmed the study's simplistic approach: "For all we know, postmodernism might cause the math department's processors to melt down." With some apology, Miller concluded that qualitative information trumps the quantitative when it comes to understanding literature: "I realize that my evidence here is anecdotal," she says, "but I'm willing to bet that I know a lot more novelists than the Dartmouth math department does, and as a rule they read far more of the classics than the average civilian." In an *LA Review of Books* article tellingly titled "Literature Is Not Data: Against Digital Humanities," Stephen Marche repeated Miller's warnings in amplified form. Warning that "Big Data is coming for your books" – and declaring the algorithms that perform computational textual analysis "inherently fascistic" – Marche presented a slightly updated twenty-first-century iteration of the Swinburnian position:

> The algorithmic analysis of novels . . . is necessarily at the limit of reductivism. The process of turning literature into data removes distinction. . . . It removes taste. It removes all the refinement from criticism. It removes the history of the reception of works. *To the Lighthouse* is just another novel in a pile of novels.[10]

"Literature is irredeemably broken and messy," Marche concluded, and "its brokenness and its messiness are part of its humanness." Flawed, discontinuous, and imperfect, literature is best analyzed not by infallible machines but by humans of equally messy mind. "Insight," he insisted, "remains handmade."

From the New Shakspere Society to "Quantitative Patterns of Stylistic Influence in the Evolution of Literature," the two sides of the argument have remained largely unchanged. One the one hand, quantitative analysis has been welcomed as a means of freeing literary criticism from a reliance on qualitative speculation and anecdote – from "mere guessing and propounding of hypotheses," as Fleay called it. As Susan Hockey argues, the promise of quantitative analysis lies in bringing "the rigor and systematic unambiguous procedural methodologies characteristic of the sciences to address problems within the humanities that had hitherto been most often treated in a serendipitous fashion."[11] Still, even those literary critics most enthusiastic about the possible applications of computational analysis have tended to express reservations. In her 1989 preface to *Literary Computing and Literary Criticism*, Rosanne G. Potter begins boldly:

> Verification, though not a concept new to literary criticism, certainly represents a shift in focus away from brilliance of insight and assertion toward the detailed testing of scientific experimentation. . . . Objective treatments of texts frequently involve finding not only examples of features, but also counting them and comparing the results with known facts about language. Things counted produce sums; the existence of sums encourages comparison with other sums; statistical analysis follows almost inevitably.[12]

Before long, however, Potter shifts from Fleay's position to that of Swinburne, warning of the inherent risks in treating literature as matter for computation:

> Only the presence of critical judgment saves the research from veering off into number juggling. . . . The usual impact of numbers on texts is reductionist. All the beautiful specificity of figures of speech can get lost when each detail is represented by a number. A balance must be carefully maintained between acquired scientific methods and critical values.[13]

Distrust of "number juggling," the perceived disconnect between the "beautiful specificity" of literary language and its enumeration, the sense that "scientific methods" and "critical values" are in opposition, indeed competition – these are the attitudes that have kept the literary mind from a full embrace of quantitative analysis, even fifty years after Mosteller and Wallace demonstrated its power and its feasibility.

I propose the following way forward from this critical deadlock. Rather than regarding quantitative and qualitative analysis as mutually incompatible approaches that must be kept apart and carefully balanced against one another, let us test whether we can embrace *both*, remaining aware of the different perspectives that each offers while allowing each to illuminate the other. Stephen Ramsay recommends such a hybrid approach in his stirring conclusion to *Reading Machines* (2011), where he describes a vision of computer-assisted literary analysis that he calls "algorithmic criticism":

> It resists any approach to computationally assisted literary study that sees the positivistic claims of pure computationalism – the either/or of bare calculation – as the method by which humanistic inquiry may

finally, after centuries of insecurity, claim its rightful place as a form of knowledge. At the same time, it rejects the idea that computers, fundamentally incapable of participating fully in the most deeply humane of all scholarly reflections, can only offer "meaningful failure" or object lessons in the limits of computer science.[14]

For Ramsay, it is a logical error to regard the certainty and objectivity of computational analysis as a potential panacea for literary criticism, because in his view literary criticism is not about *answering* or *settling* questions; rather, literary criticism is about raising questions for debate and keeping meaningful conversations going. At the same time, Ramsay believes computational analysis can contribute to this conversation in meaningful ways. He imagines the main contribution of computer-assisted analysis as a form of what the Russian Formalists called *ostranenie* or "defamiliarization." In the words of Tanya Clement, a like-minded literary scholar, the chief advantage of quantitative methodologies is their ability to "defamiliarize texts, making them unrecognizable in a way (putting them at a distance) that helps scholars identify features they might not otherwise have seen, make hypotheses, generate research questions, and figure out prevalent patterns and how to read them."[15] Qualitative human reading and quantitative machine reading, in other words, are best viewed not as warring opposites but as mutually invigorating, productively distinct ways of seeing texts.

To this point, the Swinburnes and the Marches of literary history have carried the day. Most of what we know – or think we know – about literature has been gleaned through qualitative analysis and human-scale reading. So let us, in the following pages, give the Fleays and the Hughes a fair hearing. Let us see, following Ramsay and Clement, how quantitative approaches might defamiliarize our most cherished literary texts – what new visions they bring and what surprises they hold in store.

5.1 ANALYZING AN INDIVIDUAL TEXT

Word Frequency Lists and Word Clouds

Computers are prodigious counters. Feed a digital version of a literary text into the most modestly powered computer, and in a few milliseconds it will give you a set of figures more comprehensive and more accurate than a team of humans could produce in a week. Try the following, for instance. Go to the Project Gutenberg website, search for "pride and prejudice," and download

Summary: There are 6975 unique words , and there
are 121644 words in total. 2958 words occurred
once and 973 words occurred twice.

Words	Distribution	Counts
the	▮▮▮▮▮▮▮▮▮▮	4321
to	▮▮▮▮▮▮▮▮▮▮	4128
of	▮▮▮▮▮▮▮▮▮	3597
and	▮▮▮▮▮▮▮▮▮	3529
her	▮▮▮▮▮▮▮	2193
i		2047
a		1939
in		1862
was		1839
she		1688
that		1531
it		1522
not		1416
he		1320
you		1317
his		1254
be		1238
as		1179
had		1171
with		1051
for		1046
but		973
is		856
have		839

Figure 5.1 *TAPoRware List Words tool result for Jane Austen's* Pride and Prejudice, *all words.*

the top hit in plain text format (plain text being a barebones, ASCII-derived format for representing text digitally). Open the file in a text editor and strip out anything that is not part of the "text": the copyright notices from Project Gutenberg at the beginning and end, the note indicating that the digital edition was produced by an anonymous volunteer, and so on. (Is the title part of the text? Is the author's name? These are weighty decisions that I leave to you.) Now, save the file somewhere on your hard drive; navigate to the website of TAPoR, a suite of free text analysis tools hosted at the University of Alberta; and open the List Words tool for plain text.[16] Point the tool to the file, select "All words," and you will see a result similar to that in Figure 5.1. What it produces is a basic word frequency list, the starting point of most forms of computer-assisted textual analysis. At first, these results may seem disappointing: it is hardly revelatory, you may observe, that Austen frequently uses the words "the," "to," and "and," as all writers of English must. But take a moment to consider what has just happened. In a few minutes' time, you have accessed a digital file from a massive archive that has been developing since the late 1970s; you have edited this file, altering it to suit your particular needs; you have then sent this complete file, of more than 120,000 words, to a faraway computer server (in this case, in Edmonton, Alberta, Canada); and, then, in less than a second, this computer has counted every one of those 120,000 words, enumerated how often each of them occurs in the text, and returned a sorted list beginning with the most frequently used. The words at the top of the list may seem banal, but they reveal something profound about the differences between the way that humans read and the way that machines read. Not only do you or I not possess the patience or the time to count accurately every instance of "the" and "to" in *Pride and Prejudice*, but we barely even *notice* these words when reading. After reading *Pride and Prejudice*, we do not have the slightest clue whether "of" is used more often than "was," or "to" more frequently than "and." We are far too focused on words like "love" and "marriage," "Elizabeth" and "Mr. Darcy," to notice such details.

Seemingly insignificant function words, which we barely notice, can be profoundly revealing when analyzed by a computer. Mosteller and Wallace showed this in the 1960s when they proved Madison's authorship of certain disputed Federalist Papers. In his pioneering 1987 book *Computation into Criticism*, J. F. Burrows showed how important these words could be for literary analysis.[17] In fact, he did so by analyzing Jane Austen's novels. Rather than focusing on entire novels, Burrows performed counts of individual characters' most frequently used words and found that these differed sharply. He was able to isolate individual characters' distinctive speech patterns, or "idiolects," just by looking at their use of words such as "the," "of," "it," and "I." Burrows's work has been hugely influential on subsequent quantitative analyses of literary style, and his research demonstrates a crucial point: computers do not merely do things more quickly and accurately than humans but they also help us see things we could never see on our own. As Julia Flanders has argued, Burrows's research "foregrounds the computer not as a factual substantiator whose observations are different in kind from our own – because more trustworthy and objective – but as a device that extends the range of our perceptions to phenomena too minutely disseminated for our ordinary reading."[18] Not just a faster, more accurate vision, but a *different* vision.

Still, lists of most frequently used words require significant statistical analysis before they give up their secrets. For more immediately interpretable results, let us return to the TAPoR List Words tool and, rather than selecting "All words,"

Summary: There are 6640 unique words other than those in the stop list, there are 46847 words other than those in the stop list. There are 121644 words in total including the stop words.

Words	Distribution	Counts
mr	▃▂▁▁▁▁▁	782
elizabeth	▂▃▃▃▃▃	593
said	▃▃▂▁▁▂	401
darcy	▂▁▂▁▁▁	372
mrs	▃▂▂▂▂▂	343
bennet		294
miss		283
jane		260
bingley		257
know		236
soon		216
think		211
time		200
little		188
lady		183
good		181
sister		178
make		165
wickham		161
shall		161
dear		158
say		158
collins		156

Figure 5.2 *TAPoRware List Words tool result for* Pride and Prejudice, *stop words applied.*

apply a "stop words" list, which filters out the most common function words in the English language and returns a list like that in Figure 5.2. This result is much closer to something we can begin to interpret. Of the titles, names, and verbs that appear on this list, some are not terribly interesting: the prominence of "said" may only indicate that this is a novel, told in the past tense and with significant character speech. But the frequency of "know" and "think" may indicate a thematic interest in epistemology and the limits of human understanding, and the cluster of words concerned with temporal urgency and social obligations ("soon", "time," "family," "shall") may suggest undertones of tension and social repression in the novel's seemingly lighthearted marriage plot.

Figure 5.3 *Wordle.net word cloud for* Pride and Prejudice.

Before we become carried away in such speculations, however, let us move to a more useful method of visualizing stop-worded word frequency lists: word clouds. Go to the website of the Wordle tool (Wordle.net), paste your saved file of *Pride and Prejudice* into the text box, and you will see something like Figure 5.3.[19] Like the TAPoR list, the Wordle word cloud visualizes word frequency. Ignoring common words such as "and" and "of," it displays the text's most frequently occurring words. The more common the word, the larger it appears in the visualization, though the distribution of the words in the space is otherwise random. I like to think of word clouds as a kind of aerial photography for literary texts. Just as an aerial photograph can reveal features in the landscape that we might not notice passing through on foot – a slight ridge, a glacial moraine, a crop circle – a word cloud can reveal large-scale patterns that we might not perceive as we move from word to word and page to page, drawn by the narrative threads that compel us forward. One might look at the word cloud for *Pride and Prejudice* and see nothing more than reductive confirmation of what we already know about Jane Austen novels: a "Miss" meets a "Mr.," and he makes her a "Mrs." Yet, at this scale, we notice something odd about the personal names in the novel: why are all the male names surnames, and all the female names first names? Even if you had noticed this while reading, this "aerial" presentation might spur you to return to the text to probe more deeply the gender politics of the early nineteenth-century English gentry. The word cloud also confirms that family, of course, is a central theme, as the names and titles and words such as "sister" and "family" attest. Yet the sizing and arrangement of words in the word cloud might prompt us to a new interpretation of the theme. Consider the two words that Wordle has, entirely randomly, placed nearest to the word "family": "love" and "happiness." This is a perfectly comforting association – until we notice that "love" and "happiness" are so much smaller than "family," because they are used so much less frequently in the text. Indeed, in a novel about marriage, it is somewhat disturbing that love and happiness should figure seemingly as afterthoughts. Might family in fact be *opposed* to love and happiness in *Pride and Prejudice* – and, if so, does family triumph? Might some of the other frequently used words present in the Wordle visualization – "must," "might," "never," "now" – play into this opposition? A word cloud cannot answer any of these questions, but it can raise them. Like a word frequency list, a word cloud has the power to propose a new vision of the text: to defamiliarize it and, by presenting it from a point of view not accessible to our usual ways of reading, to spur us to further inquiry.

The Type-Token Ratio (TTR)

Word frequency lists also provide us with the means to perform our first literary calculations. Notice that the TAPoR word list in Figure 5.1 provides not only a tabulated list of the most frequently occurring words in *Pride and Prejudice* but also a count of the *total* words in the novel (121,633) and of the number of *unique* words (6,790). With these numbers, we can calculate what is called the "type-token ratio" or TTR, which is achieved by dividing the number of unique words (also called types) in a text by the total number of words (also called tokens). Consider the following very short text, the opening words of a transcript of the *Jerry Springer* TV talk show:

Jerry! Jerry! Jerry! Jerry! Jerry!

The TTR of this very simple text is 0.2: there is only one unique word ("Jerry"), and it is repeated five times: 1 divided by 5 is 0.2. The type-token ratio for the first six words of *Pride and Prejudice*, "It is a truth universally acknowledged," is 1: there are six unique words and six total words, and 6 divided by 6 is 1. So what does a TTR tell us? We might be tempted to see it as a measure of something like "language register" or even "literary quality," particularly given the contrast of Jane Austen with Jerry Springer. To do so, however, would be to read into the numbers. What TTRs measure, quite simply, is *lexical diversity* – a text's "wordiness." The principal application of TTRs is comparative: they allow us to sort texts with rich vocabularies from those with more restricted vocabularies. But in performing these comparisons, we must remain mindful

Table 5.1 *Unlike texts, ranked by TTR (sample size not standardized)*

	Types	Tokens	TTR
T. S. Eliot's *The Waste Land*	1,203	3,054	**0.394**
My blog post about bikes	836	2,374	**0.352**
Shakespeare's *Hamlet*	4,842	29,615	**0.163**
Episode of *Jerry Springer*	1,140	8,571	**0.133**
Virginia Woolf's *To the Lighthouse*	6,925	70,090	**0.099**
L. Frank Baum's *Wonderful Wizard of Oz*	2,937	39,252	**0.075**
E. L. James's *Fifty Shades of Grey*	10,418	155,819	**0.067**
Jane Austen's *Pride and Prejudice*	6,790	121,633	**0.056**

of what the numbers are telling us. Consider Table 5.1, which ranks a number of unlike texts according to TTR. Something, clearly, is "off" with these numbers, which give my blog post twice the lexical diversity of *Hamlet*, and the complete episode of *Jerry Springer* more than double that of *Pride and Prejudice*. The problem relates to length. The longer you write, the greater the likelihood that you will repeat a word; TTRs for longer texts thus tend to be lower. We can avoid this problem by standardizing our sample size. In this case, looking at only the first 2,374 words of each text – the total number of words in the shortest text – produces a valid comparison (see Table 5.2).

The numbers now begin to tell a story. That a notoriously wordy text like Eliot's *The Waste Land* should have a high TTR confirms our subjective impression. It might at first seem odd that my blog post should have a higher TTR than *Hamlet*, but several reasons present themselves. *Hamlet's* low TTR seems

Table 5.2 *Unlike texts, ranked by TTR (sample size standardized)*

	Types	Tokens	TTR
T. S. Eliot's *The Waste Land*	986	2,374	**0.415**
Virginia Woolf's *To the Lighthouse*	872	2,374	**0.367**
My blog post about bikes	836	2,374	**0.352**
Shakespeare's *Hamlet*	830	2,374	**0.349**
E. L. James's *Fifty Shades of Grey*	781	2,374	**0.329**
Jane Austen's *Pride and Prejudice*	694	2,374	**0.292**
L. Frank Baum's *Wonderful Wizard of Oz*	685	2,374	**0.289**
Episode of *Jerry Springer*	445	2,374	**0.187**

Table 5.3 *TTRs for individual chapters of James Joyce's* A Portrait of the Artist as a Young Man *(sample size standardized)*

	Types	Tokens	TTR
Chapter 1	1,680	9,566	**0.176**
Chapter 2	2,393	9,566	**0.250**
Chapter 3	2,295	9,566	**0.240**
Chapter 4	2,425	9,566	**0.256**
Chapter 5	2,540	9,566	**0.266**

to act as a genre marker: as a play, it chiefly reproduces oral rather than written speech, which tends to have lower TTRs; in addition, the convention of printing a character's name before every passage of his or her speech in a dramatic text leads to further repetition and a still lower TTR. Jane Austen finds herself toward the bottom of the table, which reflects her plain and unadorned style – slightly plainer than that of the best-selling erotic novelist E. L. James and slightly less plain than that of the children's novelist L. Frank Baum. At the bottom is the *Jerry Springer* episode: a transcription of oral language, in which dialogue is often interrupted by the lengthy repetition of the single word "Jerry!" If the comparison set is not especially revealing, it nonetheless demonstrates how quantitative elements can enliven literary discussion, leading us to reconsider basic distinctions between genres, to challenge our assumptions about particular writers or periods, and to suggest new lines of investigation and experiment.

TTR comparisons work best when one begins with a hypothesis to test. We might wish to test whether TTRs can be used to model a stylistic device within a single novel – for instance, the "progressive stylistic maturation" that is at work in James Joyce's *A Portrait of the Artist as a Young Man*. Reading the novel, we might notice how Joyce alters his style to mirror the maturation of his protagonist, Stephen Dedalus: in the section detailing Stephen's earliest childhood, the narrative voice is that of a child; in the section recounting his hyper-intellectual student days, the voice is that of a hyper-intellectual student. Let us see whether the progressive stylistic maturation of Joyce's narrator is reflected in an increasing TTR – whether an element of the increasingly complex narrative style is increasing lexical diversity. Standardizing for sample size and looking only at the first 9,566 words of each chapter (the total length of the shortest one, Chapter 4) yields the results shown in Table 5.3.

By and large these results confirm our hypothesis: as the narrator matures, his lexical diversity increases progressively, even if not at the steady rate that we might expect – especially in the abrupt shift from the first to second chapter.

Table 5.4 *TTRs for selected novels by Virginia Woolf (sample size standardized)*

	Types	Tokens	TTR
The Voyage Out (1915)	6,166	44,980	**0.137**
Night and Day (1919)	5,716	44,980	**0.127**
Jacob's Room (1922)	6,709	44,980	**0.149**
To the Lighthouse (1927)	5,280	44,980	**0.117**
Orlando (1928)	6,908	44,980	**0.154**
The Waves (1931)	6,490	44,980	**0.144**
The Years (1937)	5,066	44,980	**0.112**
Between the Acts (1941)	6,996	44,980	**0.156**

Looking back at the text, we see how much of Chapter 2 is composed of quotation – especially the voices of parents and priests, who themselves often quote Latin. This might in turn suggest ways of improving our experiment; for instance, by isolating the voice of the narrator from those of the characters he quotes.

In TTR experiments, the best results tend to be those that surprise us and upset our hypotheses. For example, having studied the novels of Virginia Woolf, but only ever qualitatively, I might describe the following trajectory for her career. In her first novels, her style is still relatively conventional, but becomes more experimental through the 1920s; this experimentation reaches an apex in *To the Lighthouse* and *The Waves*, but wanes with *The Years*, a best-seller in its day, before again increasing in her experimental final work, *Between the Acts*. Given this narrative, I would expect the TTR to be lowest in the early novels, higher in the 1920s and peaking with *To the Lighthouse* and *The Waves*, then decreasing in *The Years*, and perhaps experiencing a final increase in *Between the Acts*. This hypothesis is based on my assumption that "difficulty" – the challenge to concentration that certain Woolf novels pose for their readers – is related to lexical diversity, which is all that we can measure with TTRs. Table 5.4 displays the results for Woolf's novels, with sample size standardized to the length of Woolf's shortest novel, *Between the Acts*.

Some novels conform to expectations: subjectively "difficult" texts like *The Waves* and *Jacob's Room* have relatively high TTRs, whereas the "easier" *The Years* has the lowest TTR of her novels. On the other hand, the subjectively "easier" novel *The Voyage Out* has quite a high TTR, and *To the Lighthouse*, one of her most challenging novels, has a TTR that is only marginally higher than *The Years*. Vocabulary diversity, we might conclude, does not map onto subjective perception of "difficulty" in Woolf's novels.

Table 5.5 *TTRs for selected "difficult" modernist novels (sample size standardized)*

	Types	Tokens	TTR
James Joyce, *Ulysses*	11,441	70,090	**0.163**
Joseph Conrad, *Nostromo*	8,990	70,090	**0.128**
William Faulkner, *Absalom! Absalom!*	6,928	70,090	**0.099**
Virginia Woolf, *To the Lighthouse*	6,925	70,090	**0.099**

So we may ask this question: does lexical diversity map onto modernist literature's notorious "difficulty" more generally? Do subjectively difficult modernist novels have particularly high TTRs? Let us compare *To the Lighthouse* to a small but representative set of modernist novels, with TTR data standardized to the length of the shortest novel, *To the Lighthouse* (see Table 5.5).

The answer, from this small group of texts, is *no*: although the very high lexical diversity of *Ulysses* may explain its difficulty in the eyes of many readers, something else must produce that perception in readers of *To the Lighthouse* and *Absalom! Absalom!* But does lexical diversity separate reputedly "highbrow" modernists such as Woolf, Joyce, Conrad, and Faulkner from best-selling popular writers? To test this, let us compare TTR data for *To the Lighthouse* to three novels that appeared in the *Publisher's Weekly* list of the top-ten year-end best-selling novels for 1927, the year Woolf's novel was published. The results are shown in Table 5.6.

The answer, again, is *no*. Lexical diversity is not a marker of "mass appeal": works with relatively high TTRs can reach a wide audience, and works with comparatively low TTRs can present significant challenges to readers. Clearly some more sophisticated procedure is necessary to explain the perceived "difficulty" of works like *To the Lighthouse*. Indeed, it was this train of thought that led me to pursue my work on computational analysis of vocal differentiation

Table 5.6 *TTR of Woolf's* To the Lighthouse *compared to selected 1927 best sellers (sample size standardized)*

	Types	Tokens	TTR
Sinclair Lewis, *Elmer Gantry*	8,966	70,090	**0.126**
Edith Wharton, *Twilight Sleep*	7,955	70,090	**0.112**
Warwick Deeping, *Doomsday*	7,501	70,090	**0.106**
Virginia Woolf, *To the Lighthouse*	6,925	70,090	**0.099**

and free indirect discourse in modernist fiction, which I discuss at the end of this chapter.

TTRs in Literary Research

As the preceding experiments demonstrate, TTRs are a relatively blunt instrument. They are only useful for comparing texts: the actual value of a TTR means little, because it varies so drastically with a text's length. The texts compared must already be quite similar: comparing a play to a novel, for instance, will always tend to underestimate the real vocabulary diversity of the play unless one manually removes all speaker names. Because the texts must be of the same length to yield meaningful comparisons, we must lop off some part of a longer text to compare it to a shorter one – a troubling situation if the longer text is inconsistent stylistically, as is Joyce's *Portrait* or Faulkner's *The Sound and the Fury*, which has a different narrator for each of its sections. TTRs have some real advantages, however. Most evidently, the math is very simple: while humans would have a very hard time quickly counting the numbers of types and tokens in a novel, we are quite able to divide the one by the other, and it is not too much trouble to understand what the sum signifies. Although there are more useful statistical metrics of literary style, none is quite as easy to comprehend or to compute as the TTR.

This is not to dismiss the usefulness of TTRs in computational literary analysis. They were, for instance, an important part of the toolkit I developed with Julian Brooke and Graeme Hirst to detect vocal shifts automatically in T. S. Eliot's *The Waste Land*.[20] In seeking to identify those unmarked moments in the text where one voice "passes the mic" to the next, we looked at a variety of features. For instance, we rated each speaker's "readability" (how common are his or her words?), sentiment polarity (is s/he happy or sad?), sentiment extremity (*how* happy or sad is s/he?), and formality. We also looked at internal data such as word length, syllable count, punctuation frequency, the presence of line breaks, usage of particular parts of speech and pronouns, and verb tense. Finally, we looked at lexical diversity. TTRs were only one part of the analytic cocktail, but they were a useful part.

TTRs played a larger role in Tanya Clement's revelatory computational analysis of Gertrude Stein's *The Making of Americans*.[21] Any reader of Stein will be familiar with her famous repetitions. Any reader unfamiliar with Stein will be convinced by the following passage, chosen randomly (though fortuitously) from *The Making of Americans*, which both thematizes and instantiates repetition:

Every one then is an individual being. Every one then is like many others always living, there are many ways of thinking of every one, this is now a description of all of them. There must then be a whole history of each one of them. There must then now be a description of all repeating. Now I will tell all the meaning to me in repeating, the loving there is in me for repeating.[22]

Clement's hypothesis is that although Stein's "loving for repeating" has been universally noticed, it has been poorly understood, because human readers – lulled, perhaps, by Stein's soporific rhythms – struggle to notice the patterns that repetitions form. As Clement writes, "arguments scholars make about *The Making of Americans* are based on limited knowledge of the text's underlying structure because the patterns are difficult to discern with close reading." Using computational analysis, Clement was able to discover some startling patterns. Her analysis showed that repetitions are deployed with unexpected mathematical regularity: in each of the chapters in which the phrase "any such a thing" appears, for example, it appears exactly ten times. Clement also uncovered two spans of the text (on pages 444 and 480 of the Dalkey edition) that contain exactly the same 495 words – a discovery made more significant by the fact that the midpoint between these two sections, page 462, is the exact midway point of the book. Again, TTRs were an important part of Clement's approach. Clement was able to quantify (and visualize) what was unique about *The Making of Americans* by producing a graph comparing various features to a small sample of texts taken from Project Gutenberg (Figure 5.4). Among the clearest differentiating features (and one that particularly separates Stein from Joyce) is the low number of unique words in Stein's notoriously repetitive work. Another important phase of Clement's research was analysis of *The Making of Americans* with a tool called Vocabulary Management Profiles (VMP), which produces charts indicating the points in a text where stylistic shifts occur. VMP relies heavily on TTR data, assuming that the introduction of new episodes, settings, and characters will be signaled by increases in lexical diversity, whereas reflection on or description of previously introduced story elements will demonstrate lower TTRs. Although somewhat crude, TTRs provide an accessible first step in the quantitative analysis of literary style, as well as a powerful example of the new insights that such approaches can afford.

5.2 DISTANT READING: BEYOND THE INDIVIDUAL TEXT

Computational analysis of individual literary texts has the power to reorient our understanding by exposing patterns invisible to "analog," human

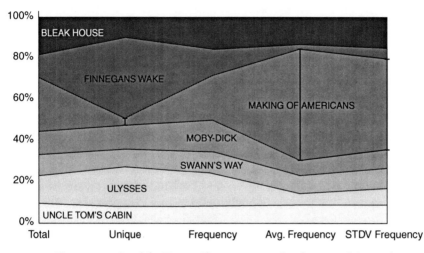

Figure 5.4 *Graph by Tanya Clement comparing features of Gertrude Stein's* The Making of Americans *to a sample of canonical literary texts.*

methods of reading. But the power of computational literary analysis increases exponentially when we move beyond single texts and begin to investigate large collections of texts. It does so for reasons of time and speed: we, human readers, are very capable of reading individual literary texts – but no human could read every literary text in Project Gutenberg or Google Books. As Franco Moretti has argued, the canon of nineteenth-century British novels – the novels on which scholars of the period focus their attention and might be expected to have read personally – numbers at most two hundred. Yet this figure represents less than 1% of the total number of novels actually published in Britain in the nineteenth century, which Moretti estimates at thirty thousand or more. In part, this critical myopia is due to an ideological commitment to the techniques of "close reading" – the careful, detailed analysis of a text considered as a discrete aesthetic unit. "You invest so much in individual texts," Moretti argues, "*only* if you think that very few of them really matter."[23] But the development of such a limited canon is also a practical matter: even assuming that a scholar was able to perform a "close reading" of one novel a day, for example, it would take a full century to read every novel published in Britain in the nineteenth century. It is here that computational analysis has the power to be truly transformative. For a computer, it is a matter of a few seconds' work to look through a 30,000-volume corpus and retrieve a particular set of features. This kind of analysis is not to be confused with close reading – Moretti calls it "distant reading" – nor should it be seen as a replacement for close reading, to which it is ideally a complement. But it does hold the power to affect the way we envision literary history. Most notably, it carries the promise to move literary criticism beyond a strictly delimited canon.

Searching the Archive in *Modernism: Keywords*

Consider, as a technologically modest example of the powers of distant reading, the case of *Modernism: Keywords*, a collaborative book I worked on from 2007–2013.[24] *Modernism: Keywords* is modeled on Raymond Williams's *Keywords* and shares with Williams's book a dauntingly simple aim: to identify words of crucial cultural importance – words so important that their precise meanings shifted frequently in the heat of public debate – and to explore the evolution of each of these keywords in short essays that cite particular usages of the words to capture specific instances of controversy. To perform research for his 1976 *Keywords*, which looked at the entire history of the English language, Williams relied on two primary resources: the *Oxford English Dictionary (OED)*, a towering monument of analog scholarship begun in the mid-nineteenth century and first published in a complete A–Z volume in 1928, and the breadth of his own personal reading. Impressive as both the *OED* and Williams's erudition undoubtedly were, and impressive as the results he achieved after twenty years of work, Williams was nevertheless haunted by his limited resources. In the introduction to *Keywords*, he complained, "The problems of information are severe," adding, "Any account is bound to be incomplete, in a serious sense, just as it is bound to be selective," before repeating, with added emphasis, "The problems of inadequate information are severe and sometimes crippling."[25]

Our task for *Modernism: Keywords* was somewhat less daunting than that of Williams. Whereas he looked at the entire history of the English language, our corpus was "written modernism in English": literature, literary criticism, and any textual materials relevant to either, written in English in the period 1880–1950. Even then, the problems of information were indeed severe: close reading all of the material would take several scholars several lifetimes. The keywords method of elucidating controversies in the period's salient vocabulary through the quotation of interesting examples meant that our approach was bound to be selective and "patchy"; we could certainly not include all modernist instances of every word. But to do our job properly, we needed to select usages not just from the obvious sources – not just from that tiny fraction of the cultural record that has been canonized, from "high culture," the texts normally accessed through close reading – but also from the whole culture and the full range of modernist expression. In this quest, we had an immense advantage over Williams: access to digitized archives of texts searchable by *keyword*. In 1976, the year that *Keywords* was published, much of the infrastructure for our own approach was already in place: the ASCII standard had been formalized for more than a decade, and Project Gutenberg had been in existence for five years. But the archives remained small and difficult to access. The cultural revolution that would profoundly change the meaning of the word "keyword" itself – that would make "keyword" a key-word of the digital age – was still several decades in the future. It was not until 1990 that Archie, the first search engine, was developed, and not until 1998 that Google was founded and the now-ubiquitous verb "to google" was introduced to the English language, meaning "to search vast stores of electronic texts by keyword." With the continuing expansion of archives such as Project Guten-berg and the founding of resources like JSTOR, the Internet Archive, and the Modernist Journals Project, the prospect of understanding a culture through its keywords was much more accessible in 2007 than in the 1950s when Williams began his work. We had the *OED*, we had our personal reading – and we had the treasure trove of all the texts of "written modernism" that had been digitized.

We did not immediately apprehend the bounty that lay before us. Indeed, we began the project in a very traditional, analog way: we gathered a large group of graduate students and scholars working on modernism together in a series of meetings, where we mooted various keywords and worked collectively to produce examples from "written modernism" that might contain interesting usages. One of the terms we collectively decided to pursue was "advertising." We thus organized a meeting to discuss "advertising" as a keyword, inviting anyone who felt they could offer useful examples. Among the chosen instances were Henry James's *The Ambassadors* (Chad Newsome's suggestion of a return to America and a career in advertising); F. Scott Fitzgerald's *The Great Gatsby* (the symbol-fraught billboard for oculist Doctor T. J. Eckleberg); Virginia Woolf's *Mrs. Dalloway* (the inscrutable skywriting scene); and James Joyce's *Ulysses* (Leopold Bloom, ad salesman). Although these turned out to be good examples – we used them all in the finished entry – they nevertheless reveal the limitations of the analog approach. When you leave the selection of keyword usages to human discussion and human memory, the examples tend to be canonical, as all these are, because humans reserve their finite resources of memory for what they deem most important. And because the human memory does not remember even the most important texts word for word, what you tend to get from discussion is not a pertinent phrase or sentence containing the word, but rather a character, a symbol, or a plot event connected with the word's underlying concept.

Recognizing these limitations and taking advantage of the salient property that Adriaan van der Weel names "access through content," we turned to digital searching in large archives with significant modernist holdings, such as Project Gutenberg, the Internet Archive, JSTOR, and the Modernist Journals Project.

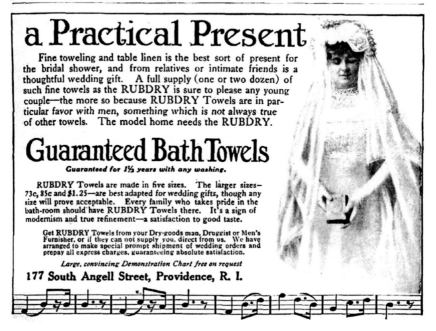

Figure 5.5 *Advertisement for Rubdry Towels from 1911 issue of* Cosmopolitan *(Modernist Journals Project).*

Although their holdings do not constitute anything like the full record of "written modernism," they massively exceed the limits of what we could collectively recall. Rather than searching within ourselves for texts whose actual word usage remained vague in our memories, we turned to searching archives of unlimited capacity whose contents could be instantly and precisely searched by keywords. One example suffices to demonstrate the effect this had on our work. Before beginning our research, we were aware that "modernism" was not a word that modernists often applied to themselves – that it was a label imposed retroactively by later critics seeking to define the period. Unable to recall many modernist usages of "modernism" ourselves, we were interested to see what the archive could provide for us. One of the most interesting and surprising results came from our search of the Modernist Journals Project, which returned an advertisement from a 1911 issue of *Cosmopolitan* for a product called "Rubdry Towels," billed as "a sign of modernism and true refinement – a satisfaction to good taste"[26] (Figure 5.5). This early cultural use of "modernism" – associating the word not with avant-garde iconoclasm but with a conventional, anodyne up-to-dateness – proved immensely useful to our research. We would never have come across it without digital searching, not

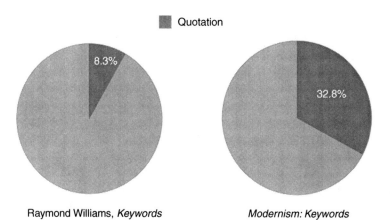

Figure 5.6 *Chart comparing the percentage of quotation in Raymond Williams's* Keywords *(1976) and* Modernism: Keywords *(2014).*

only because the advertising pages of a 1911 popular magazine are an unlikely target for a scholar's close reading but also because, even if a scholar had happened to open this particular issue to this particular page and to read the full text of this particular advertisement, it is extremely unlikely that she would have deemed it sufficiently important to store for future retrieval – in other words, to remember. The "Rubdry" example neatly demonstrates the "bottom-up" research model that a digital research environment implies. When our group met to discuss "advertising," we produced a list of canonical works that gave us insight into how a few well-known modernist writers engaged with this popular form; when we searched for "modernism," the archive surprised us with a popular, decidedly non-canonical text (an advertisement for towels in a women's magazine) that had something to tell us about modernism – not modernists telling us about advertising, but an advertisement telling us about modernism.

Once we had finished the manuscript for *Modernism: Keywords*, we did some basic digital analysis to see how a keywords book written in the era of "severe problems of information" might differ from one written in the age of digital archives. This analysis suggested a clear difference: a critical shift from "telling" to "showing." In Williams's text, 8.3% of the total words are quotations, whereas 91.7% are Williams's own. In *Modernism: Keywords*, 32.8% are quotation – nearly four times more than in Williams's work. Limited only by the extent of the holdings of keyword-searchable digital archives, we were able to find more quotations, and better quotations, from modernist writers and were able to allow these modernist writers to express themselves in their own words (Figure 5.6). These differences are clearer still in the Wordle word clouds we produced, respectively, from Williams's words and our own (i.e., all words *not* in quotation marks). Williams's are "telling" words: he explains the sense and the use of words through time. Ours are "showing" words: we introduce the words of others, relate what these individuals "argued" or "described," and balance their words against those of others ("however," "also") (Figures 5.7a–b). Two books are, of course, an extremely limited sample. Yet the example of *Modernism: Keywords* suggests a new direction for literary criticism in an era when it is able more easily to take in "the Great Unread": it may become more inclusive, more multi-voiced, and less fixated on the privileged 1% that has been the traditional focus of scholarship.

Word Frequency at the Scale of "Big Data"

Even at this relatively naïve level of technology – searching for text strings, something that has been possible since even before the standardization of ASCII in the 1960s – the existence of large literary databases has the power to change the way we understand and analyze the literary record. But if one moves beyond simple searching and begins to use the computer's immense capacity for statistical analysis, the transformative possibilities expand. As Matthew Jockers argues,

> Unless one knows what to look for . . . searching for research purposes, as a means of evidence gathering, is not terribly practical. More interesting, more exciting, than panning for nuggets in digital archives is the ability to go beyond the pan and exploit the trammel of computation to compress, condense, deform, and analyze the deeper strata from which these nuggets were born, to unearth, for the first time, what these corpora really contain.[27]

In 2011, while we were hard at work panning the digital archives for keyword nuggets, a remarkably accessible tool was released that promised to do precisely what Jockers suggests: not merely to allow *access* to selected archived materials – to serve them up to human readers for close reading – but also to *interpret* the entirety of the archive, all at once, and to present the results of this "distant reading." Introduced in an article in *Science* titled "Quantitative Analysis of Culture Using Millions of Digitized Books,"[28] the tool was called the Google Books Ngram Viewer. (An n-gram, in this context, is a phrase of *n* number of words: "Google" is a 1-gram, "Google Books Ngram Viewer" is a 4-gram.) Treating the Google Books archive not as an electronic library but as a linguistic corpus, it performs something simple but immensely

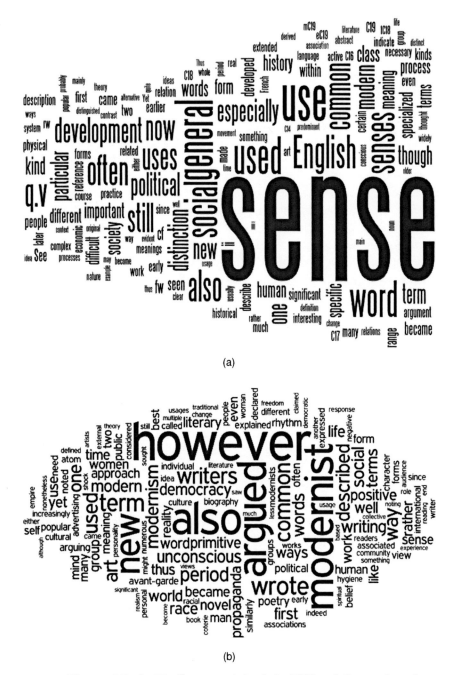

Figures 5.7a–b *Wordle.net word clouds for Williams's* Keywords *and* Modernism: Keywords, *quotation excluded.*

powerful: when you provide it with a phrase of up to five words and a date range, it produces a graph charting the relative usage frequency of that phrase over time.

For the *Modernism: Keywords* project, the prospect of the Ngram Viewer was initially as frightening as it was appealing. In the entries we had drafted to that point, we had made some bold generalizations about historical word use: "The word 'advertising' exploded in use in the modernist period"; "Modernists didn't often use the term 'avant-garde' to describe their work – nor, indeed, did they use 'modernist' or 'modernism.' These terms emerged much later, in retrospective accounts of the period." Here was a statistical means of proving – or disproving – our hypotheses. Thankfully for us, the Ngram Viewer generally provided us with data to back up our assertions (Figures 5.8 and 5.9). We became increasingly fascinated with the tool after Google added new features to subsequent releases of the Ngram Viewer, allowing searches by wildcard and part of speech – "*_ADJ genius" charting all phrases composed of an adjective and the word "genius," for example (Figure 5.10) – and incorporating more of the Google Books archive into its analyzable corpus.

Yet the more familiar we became with the tool, the more we began to notice its limitations. The data on which the Ngram Viewer relies are prone to two major types of errors: OCR errors (errors caused by the optical character recognition software Google uses to translate graphical marks on a page into machine-readable strings) and metadata errors (mistakes in the attribution of dates and places of publication to scanned books.) The Ngram Viewer chart for the F-word (Figure 5.11) provides one of the best examples of a result distorted by an OCR error. Although the chart would suggest the F-word's use was rampant before 1800, it is not the case at all that pre-1800 authors swore more than we do; rather, it is that OCR programs are not able to distinguish the English "long S" (which fell out of use around the turn of the nineteenth century) from an "F" and thus fail to recognize that these authors were actually writing "suck." As an example of a metadata error, consider a 1910 edition of Luther's *Open Letter to the Christian Nobility* (1520) in which the editor's additions are not distinguished from Luther's own words; thus "capitalism," present in the editor's footnote, appears on the Ngram Viewer chart in 1520. The Ngram Viewer provides both a compelling example of the power of distant reading and a reminder of how mindful we must be in performing this kind of research, where the validity of our conclusions is tied directly to the quality of our data.

Given its limitations, the most common use of Google's Ngram Viewer has been to provide quantitative verification of qualitative conclusions, which is

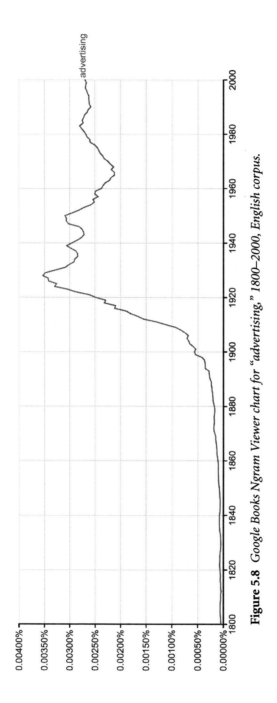

Figure 5.8 *Google Books Ngram Viewer chart for "advertising," 1800–2000, English corpus.*

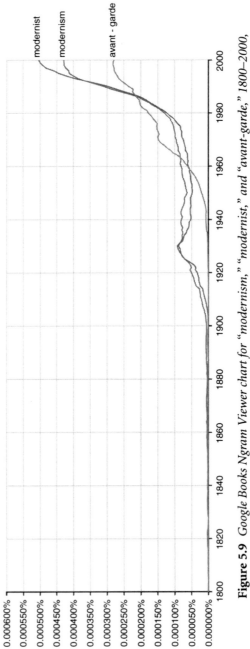

Figure 5.9 *Google Books Ngram Viewer chart for "modernism," "modernist," and "avant-garde," 1800–2000, English corpus.*

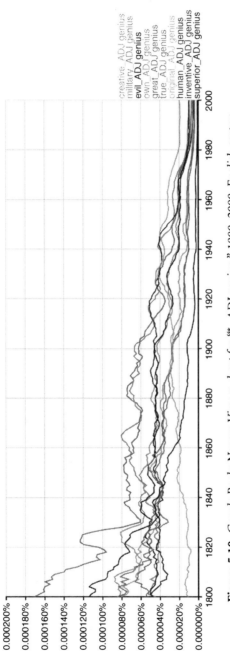

Figure 5.10 *Google Books Ngram Viewer chart for "*_ADJ genius," 1800–2000, English corpus.*

creative_ADJ genius
military_ADJ genius
evil_ADJ genius
own_ADJ genius
great_ADJ genius
true_ADJ genius
original_ADJ genius
human_ADJ genius
inventive_ADJ genius
superior_ADJ genius

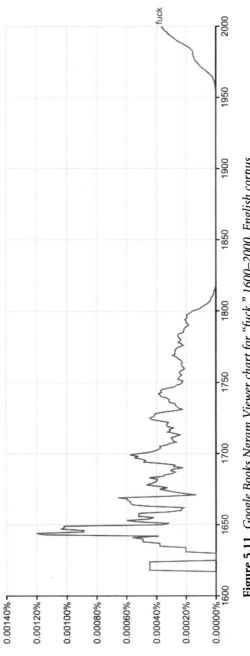

Figure 5.11 *Google Books Ngram Viewer chart for "fuck," 1600–2000, English corpus.*

how we used it for *Modernism: Keywords*. With a more reliable corpus in place, however, similar approaches focused on trends in relative word frequency can be used to yield genuine discoveries, rather than simply to support them. Ryan Heuser and Long Le-Khac's *A Quantitative Literary History of 2,958 Nineteenth-Century British Novels* (2012)[29] presents a persuasive example. Heuser and Le-Khac assembled a large corpus of novels published between 1785 and 1900 – a number significantly larger than the canon, yet small enough that the accuracy of each individual text and its metadata could be verified manually. Their method centers on a program called Correlator. When you type a given word into Correlator, you receive not a chart of that word's relative frequency in the corpus, as in the Ngram Viewer, but instead a list of all the other words in the corpus with similar frequency trends. Finding that groups of statistically correlated words tend to have similar meanings, the authors call such groups "semantic cohorts." For example, entering the word "gentle" in Correlator yields a list including "sensible," "vanity," "elegant," "reserved," "subdued," "mild," "restraint" – a semantic cohort the authors label "social restraint." Other semantic cohorts with similar trends to "social restraint" include "moral valuation" ("shame," "virtue," "sin," "moral"), "partiality" ("correct," "prejudice," "disinterested," "bias"), and "sentiment" ("heart," "feeling," "emotion," "callous"). Given their broad semantic and quantitative similarity, the authors group these cohorts together as "abstract values." Collectively, they find that these "abstract values" cohorts trend downward in their corpus, representing about 1% of all words in 1800–1810 but falling to about 0.44% (1 word in every 225) by 1900, a decrease of about 55% (Figure 5.12).

Heuser and Le-Khac's next task was to find a group of semantic cohorts that exhibited an opposite trend: one that increased in a similar proportion over the course of the century. Given that the "abstract values" so prevalent in the first half of the nineteenth century map neatly onto existing critical frameworks of the Romantic period, widely understood to be preoccupied with emotion and the immaterial, the authors expected to find upward-trending semantic cohorts typically "Victorian" in character: perhaps ones that were morally prudish or concerned politically with matters of empire. Instead, they discovered their first semantic cohort with an inverse trend only when they searched for a word with no clear semantic connection to any of the "abstract value" words: "hard." Entering this word into Correlator produces a massive list of some two hundred words (collectively representing as much as 6% of all words in the corpus) with extremely similar upward-trending relative frequencies. Among the top twenty words in the semantic cohort

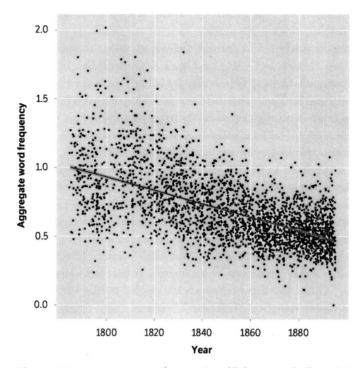

Figure 5.12 *Aggregate term frequencies of "abstract value" words in novels, 1785–1900 (Heuser and Le-Khac,* A Quantitative Literary History of 2,958 Nineteenth-Century British Novels*).*

(which they labeled "hard seed" words) are "smoke," "go," "look," "rough," and "liquid" (Figure 5.13). "We may not have found the expected shift toward Victorian values," the authors write, "but we found something even more interesting, a massive group of words categorically different from the abstract values fields that contextualizes and frames their decline within an even broader movement."[30] This movement, they argue, is a turn in novelistic language from "telling" to "showing": "a shift away from explicit comment, judgment, and placement within a value system to a more indirect mode of presenting bodies, appearances, details."[31] Insisting that they would never have come to their conclusions without the vantage point that quantitative analysis provides, they write, "When we were searching for semantic fields related to the decline in the abstract values fields, it did not and would not have occurred to us to look toward a group of 'hard seed' type words.... It took a computational method of finding language trends to discover this other group of words that,

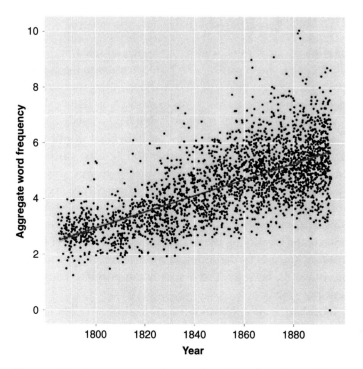

Figure 5.13 *Aggregate term frequencies of "hard seed" words in novels, 1785–1900 (Heuser and Le-Khac,* A Quantitative Literary History of 2,958 Nineteenth-Century British Novels*).*

while not semantically related to the abstract values words, are historically related."[32] Their experience carries an important lesson:

> If we required all data to make sense – that is, fit our established concepts – quantitative methods would never produce new knowledge. If the digital humanities are to be more than simply an efficient tool for confirming what we already know, if they are to be a method for making new discoveries and exploring the unexplored, then we need to check this tendency to seek validation.[33]

The distant readings performed by Heuser and Le-Khac do not replace close reading; indeed, without the insights already derived from a long history of scholarship premised on close readings, the results of these distant readings would have no context in which to surprise or challenge.

Topic Modeling

One limitation of the distant reading approach adopted by Heuser and Le-Khac is its focus on single words, with little attention to the context in which they appear. The greatest problem with working in this way is the difficulty in distinguishing between homonyms. For example, Correlator calls up the word "smoke" when the word "hard" is entered – but it does not distinguish between "smoke" as a verb or noun. Even when an individual word's part of speech is known, ambiguity often remains. Heuser and Le-Khac categorize the word "reserved" as belonging in the "social restraint" semantic cohort. Yet it only belongs to this cohort in one of its many senses; it might just as easily fit in with a group of "restaurant words" or "commercial transactions." We could resolve such ambiguities by returning to individual instances of the word, reading it in its context, and classifying the usage according to its local sense. Because distant reading operates by definition in massive corpora containing millions or billions of words, however, this is simply not possible. Thus the appeal of topic modeling.

Topic modeling – an application of an algorithm called latent Dirichlet allocation or LDA – is a method for automatically identifying words that tend to occur together in multiple places in multiple texts in large corpora. Rather than tracking how often a particular word occurs or tracking trends over time, topic modeling identifies the words that tend to cluster together. As critics such as Matthew Jockers have argued, topic modeling's focus on word *clusters* rather than individual words makes it particularly useful for analyzing literary themes. "If our goal is to understand the narrative subject and the recurrent themes and motifs that operate in the literary ecosystem," Jockers writes,

> then we must go beyond the study of individual n-grams, beyond the words . . . in order to capture what is at once more general and also more specific. Cultural memes and literary themes are not expressed in single words or even in single bigrams or trigrams. Themes are formed of bigger units and operate on a higher plane. If we may know the sense of a word by the company of words that surround it in a sentence, we may know a theme by the sentences, paragraphs, chapters, and even full books that express it.[34]

The mathematical process by which topic modeling provides insight into literary themes is extremely complicated. In layman's terms, it works roughly as follows. Begin with a corpus – a large body of texts unified in some way but whose themes are not immediately obvious: say, a few thousand nineteenth-century novels in English. Topic modeling assumes that every document in this corpus is made up of passages dealing with discrete topics. The algorithm's

preparations
block-house villages prophet
consultation surprise blankets
garrison expedition hunting-grounds
lynx captors medicine colour stream
dignity movement prairies forests red-skin prairie-bird
trader chippewa brothers bark allies squaws belt war-whoop
mouth ground arrows wilderness thicket squatter
deeds pale-faces river tree bee-hunter sign runner
manitou wampum tomahawk lakes red-men
shores sachem path whites tomahawk bushes pawnee
treaty game people council party knife squaw foes danger
serpent warfare band chiefs warriors scalps mountains
beasts paint skins skin yell language friends openings
tomahawks spot logs men chief war canoes french settlement
missionary hunters fire scout cover knives dogs
lenape prisoner nation scalp lodges mohawks
teton pine signs race fort indian spirit iroquois natives osage
paddle water manner circle food
snake venison indians tribes eye hut leaves feet
sioux direction land enemies buffalo customs
whoop fires prairie wolves limbs
scouts pale-face blanket savages warrior number peace
enemy rifle delaware nations cabin
region village children signal
yonder women valley captive braves captives log devils
war-path companions wigwam ears mohawk earth
tradition meat prisoners rifles march fathers parties red-skins
youth hawk-eye encampment females centre panther feathers
leather-stocking settlements moccasins bodies
wisdom movements interpreter wigwams
red-man traditions bones brethren captivity
powder distance
woodsman civilization

Figure 5.14 *Word cloud visualization of "Native Americans" topic (Matthew Jockers).*

job is to read every text and decide what proportion of each text addresses a particular topic. (It might decide that 30% of *Moby-Dick* deals with the topic of "whaling," for instance, compared to only 0.0001% of *Pride and Prejudice*.) The precise number of "topics" is up to the individual researcher to decide and is to some extent a matter of guesswork, depending on the size and diversity of the particular corpus. Let us say that we believe there are five hundred "topics" in our group of nineteenth-century novels. The algorithm then scans the corpus, examining each word in its context and comparing the context of each individual instance of the word to all the other contexts in which it appears; after much word juggling, it places each word in a "bag" along with the words that cluster with it most frequently in the corpus. For example, in Matthew Jockers's experiment using the Stanford Literary Lab's corpus of 3,346 books, topic 271 of 500 contained the "bag" of words represented in Figure 5.14, visualized with a word cloud for interpretive clarity. Topic modeling is an entirely "unsupervised" activity, meaning that the LDA algorithm knows nothing of the content of the archive or the way it has been interpreted by humans; it simply looks for words that tend to occur together. Not all topics will be interpretable by humans: of the 500 he generated, Jockers labeled 14 "uncertain" or "unclear."[35] But the cluster of words in Figure 5.14 – this "topic" – is readily legible as a theme: Jockers labels it "Native Americans." As Jockers points out, the fact that these words tend to co-occur eliminates certain problems of ambiguity: given the context of so many words about the natural environment, the word "stream" in the "Native Americans" topic clearly is not being used in a metaphorical sense, as in "stream of immigration," "jet stream," or "streaming media," but is used literally, denoting a small river.[36]

This technique is valuable in itself as a method of defamiliarization and discovery. Any number of research questions can be answered – and many more raised – by studying Jockers's list of the five hundred "themes" that emerge from his corpus.[37] But once these themes have been established, still more interesting interpretive possibilities arise. Because his corpus includes works not only from the United States but also from England, Ireland, and Scotland, Jockers was eager to discover which themes resonated most in particular national literatures. He found American writing to be characterized by its interest in themes of "wilderness," "the frontier," and "Native Americans"; English literature characterized by "royalty," "private education," and "shooting sports"; Scottish literature by "royalty" again, but also "religion" and, more strangely, "witches, wizards, and superstition"; and Irish literature by darker themes such as "doubt and fear" and "tears and sorrow." Because his corpus recorded information on the author's gender, he also asked which themes appeared most often in work by male and female authors. The stereotypes prevailed: female authorship was characterized by preoccupation with "female fashion" and "children," and male authorship by its enthusiasm for "pistols and other guns," "combat with enemies," and "moments of confusion in battle."[38]

Jockers's work on topic modeling in *Macroanalysis* has attracted its share of criticism. The most damning response has been to accuse Jockers of using a new technology to prove what we already know – or, worse, to reinforce stereotypes. The examples Jockers provides – the word cloud for the "Native Americans" topic or the topics that distinguish male and female authorship – raise the question of whether we need a complicated algorithm to reveal the drearily familiar racism and sexism of the nineteenth-century novel.[39] Jockers's reply to this question is sensible if not terribly satisfying. From his position, we may *think* we know certain things about literary history – that the nineteenth-century novel is racist or sexist, for example – but we have limited evidence to support our hypotheses; quantitative approaches, in his view, supply a new kind of evidence for verifying such critical commonplaces.[40] My own sense is that although Jockers's work is exemplary in uncovering promising new techniques for analyzing literature and demonstrating how they work, he does not go far enough in his applications of these techniques. It is up to other literary scholars, then, to extend methods like topic modeling – to go beyond the mere identification of themes or the correlation of such themes to gender or nationality and to use the advantages of computational techniques to probe the social forces underlying these facets of literary history. As I write these words, my own research is turning increasingly toward using topic modeling to gain new insight into the dynamics of literary history. Having assembled a large corpus of "written modernism in English," I am beginning my investigation of whether topic modeling might help us develop a new set of terms for a second volume of *Modernism: Keywords*. Though we relied to some extent on digital resources such as the Google Ngram Viewer, the process by which we selected our thirty-nine keywords for the first volume was still almost entirely "analog": it was the result of discussion, reflection, recollection, and close reading. What if we let LDA help us decide what the most important word clusters were for English-speaking modernists? How would the terms generated automatically differ from those arrived at in our previous, human manner? At this moment, I do not know – which is precisely the point.

5.3 LITERARY MARKUP

Encoding Literary Texts in TEI

We have now looked at many forms of computational textual analysis: word frequency lists, word clouds, type-token ratios, keyword searching in textual databases, statistical analysis of word frequency trends, and topic modeling of words that tend to occur together in massive corpora. Although the scale of analysis varies greatly in these techniques, from short individual texts to collections of millions of books, they nonetheless share something fundamental in their approach: each proceeds by considering every word in a text, never differentiating between the distinct *kinds* of words that it contains. Recall the type-token ratio for *Hamlet*: despite its status as a masterpiece of the English language, despite Shakespeare's reputation as an unrivaled wordsmith, *Hamlet*'s TTR was much lower than that of Woolf's *To the Lighthouse*, a novel of relatively low lexical diversity; was lower than that of a blog post I had written about bikes; and was only slightly higher than that for *Fifty Shades of Grey*. One reason for this is that *Hamlet* is composed mostly of dialogue, unlike a novel, which mixes dialogue and narration in more equal proportion. Because dialogue tends to be more repetitive than narration, the TTR of *Hamlet* – and of all plays – skews lower relative to other genres. Another factor in *Hamlet*'s low TTR is the redundancy introduced by the speaker names that precede every passage of dialogue: because they are repeated every time a character speaks, they drag the TTR down. Even though we compared them in equal sample sizes, then, we did not really perform an "apples-to-apples" comparison of *Hamlet* and *To the Lighthouse*. To do that, we would need, for example, to consider only the dialogue in both works and to throw out redundant character names when calculating the TTR of *Hamlet*'s dialogue. Rather than looking at all words in each text, we would need to consider only certain classes of words.

In practice, distinguishing between types of words is much easier said than done. Consider the opening lines of Act I of *Hamlet*, as the computer would see them, in a plain text file downloaded from Project Gutenberg:

```
ACT I.
Scene I. Elsinore. A platform before the Castle.
[Francisco at his post. Enter to him Bernardo.]
Ber. Who's there?
Fran. Nay, answer me: stand, and unfold yourself.
Ber. Long live the king!
Fran. Bernardo?
Ber. He.
Fran. You come most carefully upon your hour.
Ber. 'Tis now struck twelve. Get thee to bed,
    Francisco.
```

With our own years of experience reading plays, it is easy for us to distinguish between classes of words in this opening. The words "ACT I" indicate the beginning of an act; "Scene I" marks the beginning of a scene within that act. "A platform before the castle" indicates the setting of the scene; it is followed by a stage direction indicating the position of Francisco and the entrance of Bernardo. This is followed by a character speech: "Ber." indicates that the previously named Bernardo is speaking and is followed by his words. And so on. If we were asked to prepare a print edition of *Hamlet*, we would indicate the distinctions between these classes of words typographically by altering font size, weight, and italics – perhaps as follows:

ACT I.

Scene I. *Elsinore. A platform before the Castle.*

[Francisco at his post. Enter to him Bernardo.]

Ber. Who's there?

Fran. Nay, answer me: stand, and unfold yourself.

Ber. Long live the king!

FRAN. Bernardo?

BER. He.

FRAN. You come most carefully upon your hour.

BER. 'Tis now struck twelve. Get thee to bed, Francisco.

Though our familiarity with the conventions of drama leaves us with little doubt as to the distinctions between the words, these typographical markers – acts in large font, stage directions in italics, dialogue indented, speaker names in small caps and a smaller font than dialogue – resolve any ambiguities for a human reader and present a fully legible text. If we were asked to extract only the words of dialogue, or only the stage directions indicating entries and exits, or only dialogue by Bernardo in which Claudius is mentioned, we would have no difficulty whatsoever in performing the task.

A computer, in contrast, would find this task immensely challenging, even if provided with the typographical cues that we find so useful. I have, for example, marked stage directions here with italics. But not all plays indicate stage directions in italics nor are all italicized words stage directions. Indeed, even within a single text, italics might identify emphasis, titles, captions, or words in a foreign language. Because the conventions for the use of italics are so fluid, it is immensely difficult for a computer to be sure that "Elsinore. A platform before the castle" is not, for example, the title of Scene I rather than a description of setting. In this particular edition of *Hamlet*, entries and exits are indicated by italics contained in square brackets. But again, this is not a universal convention followed by all editions of all plays. And who, a computer might ask, is "Ber."? This name is equal neither to Francisco nor Bernardo, the text strings present in the portion between square brackets. Imagined from the perspective of a literal-minded machine reader, the typographical conventions that we use to mark distinctions are woefully inadequate. They are too fluid, too ambiguous, and too dependent on the reader's ability to decode implicit cues based on context to be suitable to machine processing. It is not that the computer lacks the capacity to do what we are asking – to extract all of Bernardo's dialogue from Act I, Scene I, for example. It is simply that it cannot do so without explicit instructions, and the sorts of typographic cues that work for humans do not make much sense to computers.

What computers need to perform these sorts of operations is a standardized, sharable, explicit, unambiguous, and unvarying method of distinguishing between types of words. The need for such a method – a way of representing the structural and semantic content of texts in a manner that can be understood both by humans *and* computers – has long been recognized, and led, in the late 1980s, to the development of the Text Encoding Initiative (TEI). What follows is a TEI rendering of that same passage from *Hamlet*:

```
<div type="act">
 <head>ACT I.</head>
 <div type="scene">
  <head>Scene I.</head>
  <set>Elsinore. A platform before
       the Castle.</set>
  <stage type="entrance">Francisco at his post. Enter
       to him Bernardo.</stage>
  <sp who="#bernardo">
   <speaker>Ber.</speaker>
   <l>Who's there?</l>
  </sp>
  <sp who="#francisco">
   <speaker>Fran.</speaker>
   <l>Nay, answer me: stand, and unfold yourself.</l>
  </sp>
  <sp who="#bernardo">
   <speaker>Ber.</speaker>
   <l>Long live the <rs who="#claudius">king</rs>!</l>
  </sp>
  <sp who="#francisco">
   <speaker>Fran.</speaker>
   <l><persName who="#bernardo">Bernardo</persName>?</l>
  </sp>
  <sp who="#bernardo">
   <speaker>Ber.</speaker>
   <l>He.</l>
  </sp>
  <sp who="#francisco">
   <speaker>Fran.</speaker>
   <l>You come most carefully upon your hour.</l>
  </sp>
  <sp who="#bernardo">
   <speaker>Ber.</speaker>
   <l>'Tis now struck <time when="00:00:00">twelve
       </time>. Get thee to bed, <persName
       who="#francisco">Francisco</persName>.</l>
  </sp>
 [...]
 </div>
</div>
```

The basic vocabulary of TEI – all those pointy brackets and slashes – will look familiar to anyone who has fiddled with HTML code, the language of the World Wide Web. Indeed, this is no accident, because HTML and TEI belong to the same family of XML (eXtensible Markup) languages. Like HTML, a TEI document is structured by elements. Consider the TEI element for a line of verse:

```
<l>Nay, answer me: stand, and unfold yourself.</l>
```

This element is made up of three parts: a start-tag, `<l>`, and an end-tag, `</l>`, which surround the element content, "Nay, answer me: stand, and unfold yourself." The start-tag and end-tag add what is called "metadata": they tell us something about what they contain. In this case, they tell us that the words they contain represent a line of verse, for which `l` is the agreed-on TEI element name. Start-tags can also contain what are called "attributes," which add even more metadata. For instance, in

```
<stage type="entrance">Francisco at his post.
Enter to him Bernardo.</stage>
```

the `stage` element is modified with a `type` attribute, which is given the value `entrance`, using the standard `<element attribute="value">` start-tag syntax. This tells us that "Francisco at his post. Enter to him Bernardo" is a stage direction (the TEI element for which is `stage`) of a type indicating entrances. (Other `type` attribute values include `technical`, for lighting effects, for example, and `gesture`, for a stage direction indicating a character's physical movements.)

TEI documents organize texts in what is called an "ordered hierarchy of content objects" or OHCO. Notice in the *Hamlet* encoding that the `<div type="act">` (Act division) element contains the `<div type="scene">` (Scene division) element, which in turn contains the `<sp>` (character speech) element, which contains `<l>`; the `</sp>` end-tag only comes after `</l>`, `</div>` only after `</sp>`, and so on. This structure tells the machine that our portion of text is made up of a hierarchy as indicated in Figure 5.15. As with all XML languages, TEI is insistent that elements be properly "nested" in an ordered hierarchy. If we tried to indicate that a scene both contained and was contained within a particular act, for example, a machine reading our TEI file would treat it as an error and either ignore it or crash.

A major difference between HTML and TEI is that whereas HTML is almost entirely concerned with telling web browsers how to *display* items, TEI is almost exclusively concerned with capturing structural and semantic information. An HTML rendering of Bernardo's speech might look like this:

```
<p><i>Ber</i>.'Tis now struck twelve. Get thee
to bed, Francisco.</p>
```

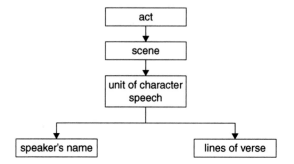

Figure 5.15 *Ordered hierarchy of content objects (OHCO) in the TEI representation of drama.*

This would instruct a web browser to render this unit of speech in whatever way it normally displays paragraphs (p elements) and to italicize "Ber." (this is indicated by the HTML i element). Our TEI encoding of this passage is considerably more elaborate:

```
<sp who="#bernardo">
  <speaker>Ber.</speaker>
  <l>'Tis now struck <time when="00:00:00">
     twelve</time>. Get thee to bed,
     <persName who="#francisco">Francisco
     </persName>.</l>
</sp>
```

TEI is, first of all, much more precise than HTML regarding the basic unit of text: this is not a "paragraph," something more proper to prose than drama, but rather a "character speech." Moreover, this is a speech by the character named Bernardo: the who="#bernardo" portion of the sp start-tag removes any ambiguity as to who is speaking by giving him a unique identifier (bernardo); this way, there is no possible confusion as to whom "Ber." might refer. The TEI encoding also adds explicit semantic information about Bernardo's use of the word "twelve": it is not just any number, the time element tells us, but a time of day; more specifically, it refers to midnight (when="00:00:00"), not noon, which in the officially sanctioned TEI formatting would be indicated as when="12:00:00". When Bernardo says "Francisco," finally, he means the person indicated elsewhere in the TEI document by the unique ID francisco – and if he had called him "Fran" or "Franny" or "fellow Dane," we would be able to determine who was indicated by these expressions.

The Applications of TEI

TEI becomes much less dry and forbidding when we move from the details of its syntax to the immense possibilities it opens up for literary analysis. One has only to imagine all the advanced operations we could perform on a document encoded in this way. "Generate a word cloud of all Hamlet's words, then a word cloud of only Ophelia's words, then one for all members of Claudius's court." "Show me all the lines in which Hamlet mentions Ophelia; then, every time a character mentions a place not in Denmark; then every speech that includes a reference to a philosophical text written in Latin before the ninth century." "Calculate the TTR for all upper class characters in *Hamlet*, and compare this with the TTR for all characters of lower class; then show me what percentage of upper class characters' speech is in verse as opposed to prose." "Show me Hamlet's lexical diversity before he puts on his 'antic disposition,' and compare that with his lexical diversity afterward." Exciting as such operations may be, the interpretive possibilities become truly fascinating when we scale this up and imagine that every literary text ever written were encoded in this manner. "Show me every novel by an English author, published between 1850 and 1890, set in India, with a first-person narrator, which includes a passage of translated Sanskrit somewhere in its first half and an untranslated passage of Sanskrit in its second half." "Call up every non-canonical poem published in French before 1600 that includes an extended metaphor, ranging over at least fifty lines, involving astronomical equipment; then perform a statistical analysis showing the main stylistic divergence between these poems and canonical poems including similar extended metaphors."

The mind boggles at the research opportunities of a universal library that is universally encoded in TEI. Yet the creation of such a resource will be immensely difficult, if not impossible. The greatest barrier is that text encoding in TEI is extremely labor intensive. The process of text encoding is premised on the notion that we, humans, understand things about texts that it, the computer, cannot understand without our help. As such, most text encoding is done by humans. It took me about a half hour to prepare the sample TEI of the beginning of *Hamlet*, and that is seven lines of a single play. Moreover my tag set was relatively simple: I was not tagging metaphors; I was not noting textual variants; I recorded nothing about performance history; I was not entering explanatory notes; I was not encoding geographical information, and so on. This means that, until we can teach machines to understand everything that we understand about texts, without our having to hold their hands, only the most canonical of writers – only writers whose work we, and the funding agencies that support it, regard as unquestionably important – will receive the minute attention and massive human labor required to build a robustly encoded archive.[41] Given that one of the main advantages of large-scale digital analysis is its ability to move us beyond the canon, this is a decidedly vexing situation.

Fantasy searches of the kind described earlier *are* feasible, however, in the limited number of archives built on robust implementations of TEI. Among the most impressive are the Rossetti Archive and the Whitman Archive. Visiting either website, it will not be immediately obvious that it is built from texts encoded in TEI. If you navigate to a particular document – say, *The Blessed Damozel* or the 1855 *Leaves of Grass* – you will see something resembling a Project Gutenberg HTML rendering of a literary text: one geared for display in a web browser, following the typographical conventions to which we are accustomed. The TEI tags function here something like a subcutaneous tracking tag attached to an animal in the wild: they are not obviously visible from the surface, but do their work away from plain sight. The fact that a TEI logic of explicit markup underlies the Rossetti Archive becomes apparent, however, when accessing the range of options available in its Advanced Search feature. The fact that you can search for text in very specific genres (canzonettas, colophons, and couplets), for example, shows that someone has taken the time to encode these features, which would otherwise remain opaque to the most advanced genre algorithm. The extent of the encoding on the Rossetti Archive is only fully apparent, however, when you download the freely available source TEI files. Here you see septets distinguished from quatrains, foreign languages and sources of allusions identified, rhyme schemes noted, and precise bibliographic information such as indentations and page signatures carefully indexed. Dante Gabriel Rossetti's images, too, are made searchable and discoverable through extensive TEI encoding, which provides standardized prose descriptions of each image along with its frame, size, medium, relevant dates, costs, the names of the subjects of the images, links to other relevant images and texts in the archive, and so on. Whereas the Rossetti Archive focuses primarily on bibliographic and visual information, the TEI source of the Whitman Archive focuses on textual variants and the manuscript as a physical object: additions, deletions, overwriting, pasting, illegible text, doodles in the margin, and so on. The search options provided on the sites themselves only hint at the range of machine processing and analysis that they make possible. If you were to download the TEI source and hire a programmer, you could track Whitman's tendency over time to cross out his words or to doodle, or you might invent a method for correlating Rossetti's relative fondness for painting female subjects in oil to his fondness for writing in quatrains rhyming *abab* where the terminal *b* rhyme is indented. Yet you would be out of luck if you wanted to perform such analyses beyond Whitman or Rossetti, or beyond the very few and very canonical writers who have received the laborious homage of TEI encoding. Until techniques of artificial intelligence advance to the point where machines can encode literary texts with the same fabulous precision as human annotators, Moretti's dream of "distant reading" in the "Great Unread" will remain incompatible with the dream of universal TEI encoding.

Literature as Data: The Limits of TEI

Even supposing that artificial intelligence were able to advance to this point, several intractable problems would nonetheless remain. For example, no TEI encoding of a literary text could ever hope to capture all its subtle nuances of meaning or all the differences that exist between individual readers' interpretations. Using a germane example, Katherine Hayles writes,

> To undertake the complete bibliographic coding of a book into digital media would be to imagine the digital equivalent of Borges's Library of Babel, for it would have to include an unimaginable number of codes accounting for the staggering multiplicity of ways in which we process books as sensory phenomena.[42]

Another major stumbling block is TEI's basic assumption that every document can be structured as an ordered hierarchy of content objects. As Jerome McGann, general editor of the Rossetti Archive, has argued,

> Poems, for example, are inherently non-hierarchical structures that promote attention to varying and overlapping sets of textual designs, both linguistic and bibliographical. But the computerized structures being imagined for studying these complex forms approach them as if they were expository, as if their "information" were indexable, as if the works were *not* made from zeugmas and puns, metaphors and intertexts, as if the textual structure were composed of self-identical elements. Some textual information in poems is indexable, but nearly everything most salient about them is polyvalent.[43]

These limitations of the TEI standard would intrude even in the relatively simple experiment we imagined earlier: a comparison of the type-token ratios of dialogue in *Hamlet* and *To the Lighthouse*. The sort of TEI encoding I performed on *Hamlet* is adequate to the task: if carried out throughout the whole text, it would easily facilitate the separation of dialogue from stage directions and act headers, for instance, and also make it possible to separate all of Hamlet's dialogue from Horatio's. TEI encoding would not work nearly as well for *To the Lighthouse*, however. Consider these three short paragraphs:

> The stocking was too short by half an inch at least, making allowance for the fact that Sorley's little boy would be less well grown than James.
> "It's too short," she said, "ever so much too short."
> Never did anybody look so sad. Bitter and black, half-way down, in the darkness, in the shaft which ran from the sunlight to the depths, perhaps a tear formed; a tear fell; the waters swayed this way and that, received it, and were at rest. Never did anybody look so sad.[44]

The second paragraph is a simple matter. Using the TEI element `said` – which indicates character speech and is thus more precise than the typographical quotation mark, which can also indicate words in "scare quotes" or titles – and a unique ID for Mrs. Ramsay, we can easily separate her words from those of the narrator:

```
<said who="#mrsramsay">It's too short,</said>
    she said, <said who="#mrsramsay">ever so much
    too short</said>.
```

But what of the first paragraph? No quotation marks are used, and the third-person pronouns and the use of the past tense suggest that these words belong to the narrator. Yet some words seem to come from Mrs. Ramsay ("half an inch *at least*"; "Sorley's little boy"), and the sentence structure seems to mirror a subjective process of thought that leads Mrs. Ramsay to speak the words in the next paragraph. In other words, this seems to be an instance of what narratologists call "free indirect discourse," a peculiar and uncertain mixture of narration and character speech. Even if we created a special TEI tag for free indirect discourse (none exists in the guidelines), it would not help with our task, because all that such a tag might hope to achieve is to indicate a span in which we cannot be sure who exactly is speaking. Even if we could conceive a way of tagging each of the different possibilities, it would be very difficult to do so without overlapping our tags and thus violating the TEI's OHCO. The final paragraph presents a still graver problem. As Erich Auerbach famously asked of this passage, "Who is speaking in this paragraph? Who is looking at Mrs. Ramsay here, who concludes that never did anybody look so sad?"[45] Auerbach himself was baffled, but concluded that such bafflement is crucial to Woolf's artistic method. It is entirely, significantly, delightfully unclear who is speaking here. The identity of the speaker, whether it is a narrator, or a character, or a group of characters together, or the author, remains forcefully unresolved. The possibilities overlap; the salient literary meaning is polyvalent, as McGann argues, and indeed non-indexable.

Somewhat paradoxically, TEI itself can be useful in exploring the peculiar non-indexability of literary language. In 2012–2013, in a project called *The Brown Stocking*, I led a team that used TEI to uncover uncertainty of voice in *To the Lighthouse*.[46] We asked 360 undergraduates at the University of Toronto to read a short, 250- to 500-word passage of Woolf's novel. Using a customized TEI tag set, each student encoded his or her best interpretation of who was speaking in the passage and which voices were introduced through free indirect discourse. For many students, this was a difficult process: it meant formalizing not *the correct* interpretation, because so many possibilities were present, but simply *their own* interpretation. We assigned each passage to several different students, and once we had aggregated all their TEI encoding, we produced what we called a "reader's map" of *To the Lighthouse*: an edition of the text that shows just how much individual variation is present in different readers' interpretations of a question as simple as "who is speaking?" If type-token ratios were not adequate to explaining what is "difficult" in *To the Lighthouse*, our "reader's map" suggests a likelier source: the novel's complexity of voice.

For Jerome McGann, the very inadequacy of TEI has something profound to teach us about how literary texts work. The difficulty that he and his team encountered in attempting to fit non-hierarchical, non-informational imaginative works into the informational structures of the Rossetti Archive's implementation of TEI paradoxically "[brought] a series of clarities not only about our digital tools but even more about the works those tools were trying to reconstitute":

> We realized that we were making inadequate assumptions about such works, and that we were using tools designed through those assumptions. That realization turned us back to reconsider the logical and ontological status of the original works.[47]

McGann regards text encoding as a form of human-computer dialogue: "We begin by implementing what we think we know about the rules of bibliographical codes. The conversation should force us to see – finally, to imagine – what we don't know that we know about texts and textuality."[48] It is the story of literature in the digital age in miniature. The encounter with the digital is, at its most productive, a scene of creative defamiliarization. We begin with what we think we know; then, by transposing it into a new form, we realize we did not know it nearly so well as we imagined. Digital analysis, as we have seen, has much to tell us about literature: it can help us perceive hidden patterns, allow us to venture beyond canonical works, and permit us to organize and retrieve literary texts in ways previously impossible. Yet literature, in its very resistance to the logical structures on which computational models depend, in turn has much to teach us about the digital.

Part III

Born Digital

Chapter 6

Short-Circuiting the Publication Process

Parts II and III of this book are distinguished by their respective focus on *digitized* and *born-digital* texts. A digitized work is one that begins its life in an analog form – on paper or parchment – and is made digital through a process of conversion. A born-digital work, in contrast, remains digital at every step of its production, transmission, and consumption: it is one that is composed, edited, and laid out on a digital device; that reaches its readership via the digital medium; and that is designed from the outset to be read and experienced on a screen, not a page. A purely digital signal path can radically alter the nature of the literary text: it can allow for an "interactivity" whereby the reader can directly influence the shape and outcome of the narrative, or it can allow the author to incorporate modalities not available on the page, such as sound, music, animation, and video. These new possibilities, and the ways they force us to rethink what we call "literature," are the focus of the next two chapters in this section. But even when born-digital literature eschews medium-specific elements such as interactivity and multimodality – even when it sticks to what is already possible in a printed book – the effects can be transformative. That is the focus of this chapter.

Most literature produced today is digital in almost every stage of its production. Most authors write on a computer, in a word processor; most of them submit their work to their editors in the form of a digital file; most editors enter their corrections into the same digital file; most edited texts are then laid out in desktop publishing programs; and these texts are then generally sent to printers as a digital file. If a book becomes analog at all, today, it generally does so at the output stage: at the printing house, where an object that has existed digitally from its inception is converted into an analog book. Most successful writers still choose to make this final conversion and do so for several reasons: because writers and readers are accustomed to thinking of literature as existing in book form, because many readers prefer the experience of reading from printed pages rather than screens, because printed books make for better commodities than vaporish electronic files, because a far more mature system exists for selling books and bringing revenue to their writers. Yet many writers – an ever-increasing number – choose *not* to make that final conversion into the analog, preferring to keep their texts digital in every form of production and distribution. Some do so to exploit digital-specific affordances of interactivity and multimodality, as we see in the following chapters. Others are attracted to the digital for more down-to-earth reasons.

Practical factors have always governed the adoption of new textual media. The abandonment of the scroll in favour of the codex was due, for instance, to a series of concrete advantages: because you could write on both sides of a codex page, you could save considerable parchment or papyrus; codices were smaller than scrolls and thus easier to transport, as well as to hide; and where it might take hours to locate a particular passage in a miles-long scroll, codices were considerably easier to navigate. In the transition from manuscript to print, practical factors likewise carried the day: manuscripts may have been more beautiful and more worthy of admiration, as John Donne and Johannes Trithemius argued (see Ch. 2), but printed books were cheaper and more uniform, reached much larger audiences, and held the potential to make sizable profits for authors, publishers, and booksellers. Technical facts about digital text – the still greater ease of copying, distributing, and commenting, for example – entail major changes from the traditional process of print publication. Although these features may in some cases make it more difficult to profit from publication, they nonetheless hold many attractions for authors, such as the ability to self-publish, work without censorship or interference from an editor or publisher, and reach one's audience directly. These changes, however, may not only make literary authorship more fluid and flexible but may also transform it fundamentally, encouraging collaborative production and deemphasizing originality as a criterion of literary excellence. Even when the product of digital authorship is no different from what could be contained in a printed book – text and static images – the material differences between analog and digital production call for powerful changes in the most fundamental aspects of the literary text: new subjects, new styles, and new conceptions of the author.

Censorship in the Communication Circuit

We began the "Digitization" section with a fable from Virginia Woolf's *A Room of One's Own*, in which she attacks the gendered barriers to access in the information economy of the early twentieth century. If access was a challenge for Woolf, however, production was not: *A Room of One's Own*, like most of her books, was published by the Hogarth Press, which she owned and operated with her husband Leonard. Hogarth was formed on a shoestring budget in 1917, principally as a source of diversion for the Woolfs. But hand-setting type and operating the press machines quickly became something more than a means of relaxation. Running their own press allowed them, as Leonard explained in his autobiography *Beginning Again*, to bring into circulation unconventional volumes that "the commercial publisher would not look at":[1] translations of as yet unheralded Russian writers such as Dostoevsky and Ivan Bunin, the first English translations of Freud's writings on psychoanalysis, and modernist literature by writers like Katherine Mansfield and T. S. Eliot (Virginia Woolf hand-set the first English edition of *The Waste Land*, published by Hogarth Press in 1922). Hogarth Press eventually provided the Woolfs with a living; ten years after its founding, its revenues were sufficient to support them entirely. Long before it brought then financial independence, however, the Press offered the Woolfs artistic independence. Virginia Woolf knew of what she spoke when she argued for the freedom provided by "a room of one's own": Hogarth Press provided just such a room, allowing her to compose and edit a book such as *A Room of One's Own* and then to oversee (if not perform herself) its typesetting, printing, distribution, and marketing. J. H. Willis has argued that Woolf's style and particular genius "developed as it did . . . because she was free from editorial pressures, real or imagined, and needed to please only herself."[2] It was a freedom known to very few writers in the age of print.

For writers not in possession of their own printing house, the process of print publication presents numerous frustrations. First, and often most difficult, is the matter of convincing someone else – an editor or publisher – to spend the time and money to bring one's work into print. Jack London's *Martin Eden* (1909) captures this deeply alienating experience in its famous vision of the "inhuman editorial machine"[3] of print publication: Martin, the eponymous hero of the novel, sends so many stories, articles, and poems for publication and is so consistently rejected that he becomes convinced that there is "no human editor at the other end, but a mere cunning arrangement of cogs that changed the manuscript from one envelope to another and stuck on the stamps."[4] Even after a work has been accepted, an editorial process governed by financial considerations can be deeply frustrating to writers of strong aesthetic and artistic commitments. One such writer, George Bernard Shaw, complained in an intemperate letter of 1895 that most publishers combined "commercial rascality" with "artistic touchiness and pettishness," concluding, "All that is necessary in the production of a book is an author and a bookseller, without any intermediate parasite."[5]

If ever there was a writer fully justified in holding such a low opinion of the "intermediary parasites" of the process of print publication, it was James

Joyce. Born in the same year as Virginia Woolf and, like her, one of the boldest experimenters in modernist fiction, Joyce enjoyed none of her privileged access to publication. Woolf freed herself to write as she liked by founding Hogarth Press; Joyce, every bit as uncompromising but lacking Woolf's entrepreneurial spirit, remained throughout his career at the mercy of the "inhuman editorial machine." Joyce's first major work, the short collection *Dubliners*, took nearly a decade to bring into print. After sending the manuscript to several publishers in 1905, Joyce appeared to have found a willing publisher in Grant Richards of London. Publication was halted, however, when the printers refused to print the book on grounds that it violated British obscenity laws, containing, for instance, several instances of the word "bloody." Joyce agreed to remove all obscenities, but his revised manuscript was nonetheless rejected. After more rejections, the manuscript was accepted in 1909 by the Dublin firm Maunsel & Co. – but publication was again scuppered, this time by the publisher's concerns regarding potentially slanderous references to the recently deceased English king. Finally, in 1914, *Dubliners* was published by Grant Richards, the firm that had first contracted it some nine years before.

The story was much the same for what came to be widely considered the greatest novel of the twentieth century, *Ulysses*. Joyce began looking for a publisher following the serialization of its initial chapters in the American periodical *The Little Review* in 1918. Among the first to receive the manuscript was Hogarth Press, which declined to publish it because the novel was too long for the Woolfs to typeset themselves (they estimated the task would take them two years) and because the commercial printers they contacted advised them that publication would lead to prosecution for obscenity. (Virginia Woolf, for her part, admitted that the "directness of the language" in *Ulysses* "raised a blush" on her cheek.)[6] In 1921, after the "Nausicaa" episode was serialized in *The Little Review*, *Ulysses* was declared obscene in the United States and banned from publication. Harriet Shaw Weaver – who had serialized sections in *The Egoist* – attempted to publish an English edition of *Ulysses*, but could not find a willing printer. Finally, in 1922, *Ulysses* was published in an edition of one thousand copies by the Parisian bookshop Shakespeare and Company; set by a French-speaking printer, however, the edition was riddled with errors. It was not until 1934, when the American ban was lifted, that *Ulysses* first became legally available in an English-speaking country.

We are accustomed to thinking of authors as solitary figures solely respon-sible for the works they produce yet the case of Joyce suggests otherwise. Between the writer and the reader of a printed work lies a vast machinery of independent actors, each with its own social, financial, and legal pressures and motivations – and each of these actors tangibly affects the text that reaches us as readers. The sense of the dynamic interplay and mutual dependence in the publishing process underlies Robert Darnton's well-known diagram of the "communications circuit"[7] (Figure 6.1). According to Darnton's schema, the author does not merely hand over her manuscript to a publisher, but is required to make revisions – often significant, sometimes destructive of the text's artistic mission. Printers and compositors do not produce the text passively; they make demands of their own and often refuse to print it. In addition, printers introduce errors, commit omissions, and make layout decisions that powerfully affect the work's reception. Books do not reach booksellers of their own accord but must be shipped, and when banned, like *Ulysses*, they must be smuggled. Booksellers determine not only the books we see on their shelves but also – by reporting back on what sells and what does not – the sorts of books publishers might accept in the first place and that authors undertake to write. Readers do not merely receive the text like empty vessels; their demands for particular kinds of books motivate the movement of the entire circuit. Decisions at each of these stages, moreover, are driven by individual actors' sense of what might attract legal or political trouble, by what might bring a profit or achieve a particular social end, and by the general economic climate. The "communications circuit" is not necessarily a bad thing; every printed book that we possess, after all, emerged from its complex machinery. But from the perspective of an author possessed of an artistic vision, one can easily understand Shaw's desire to bypass the "intermediate parasite" and speak directly to his readers. One can understand as well Woolf's desire to "short circuit" the publication process by owning her own press. The sort of control she was able to exert over her work was the dream of most writers in the age of print: no gatekeeping, no censorship, no bowing to a publisher's sense of what will sell, no incompetent typesetters or book designers in the way.

In the digital age, by contrast, every writer has her own Hogarth Press; every writer can achieve Woolf's "short circuit." Writing on the web, on a blog or a dedicated fiction-writing platform, writers can compose, edit, and format their own words. Because digital text can be copied instantly and endlessly, writers need not worry about printers. Instantaneous global distribution eliminates the need for shippers. The low cost of the entire process obviates the need to recoup expenses and, with it, the need for a bookseller. In the digital age, every writer has a direct channel to readers, with no intermediaries and no one to appease but her own aesthetic conscience. Yet this unprecedented access to publication can be a mixed blessing. As Adriaan van der Weel argues in "The Communications Circuit Revisited," the possibility for direct writer-reader contact afforded by digital textuality holds the promise of "democratizing" literary production, "in the true sense of bringing to ordinary people the

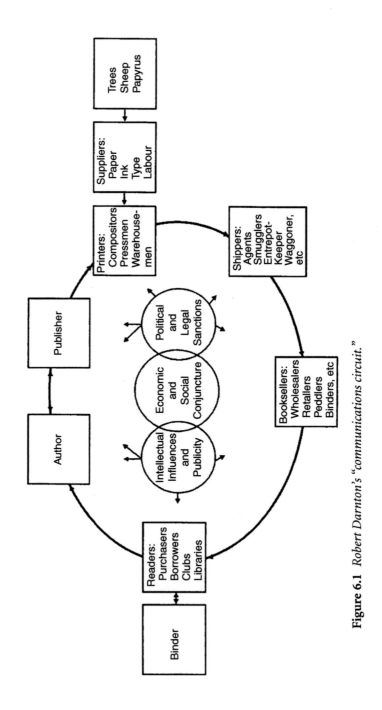

Figure 6.1 *Robert Darnton's "communications circuit."*

distribution of recorded text (and further democratizing production) by its low cost and easy access."[8] But by removing publishers and other actors from the literary loop, van der Weel argues, we lose something crucial. The print "communications circuit" implies many frustrations, compromises, and outright injustices, but it also adds value to the literary text – not only through editorial interventions or professional book design but also by whittling down the massive numbers of submitted texts into something manageable for readers. A publisher's reasons for selecting one text over another may not always be enlightened, but because every published text represents a financial risk, publication decisions are always based on a belief that the book will appeal to an audience. The writers who make it through this sometimes cruel process of sorting, selecting, and filtering at least stand a chance of reaching a large audience – and possibly making a living from it.

Every writer who self-publishes digitally, in contrast, finds herself in Borges's Library of Babel. In the world of digital self-publication, the challenge is no longer access to publication; almost everyone has that, free from meddling and censorship. The challenges are instead to find an audience among all the competing voices and to say something original worthy of such an audience. In the Library of Babel, where all possible texts already exist, no one even thinks of producing an original text, because everyone knows that everything has been said; "the certitude that everything has been written," Borges's narrator says, "nullifies or makes phantoms of us all."[9] Writers like Woolf, London, Shaw, and Joyce saw in the print publishing process a system that threatened to undermine their individual creativity and unique artistic vision. But in the digital age, when so many are so free to write whatever they like and we have unprecedented access to these proliferating texts, the very possibility of originality and individuality comes into question.

The Living Death of the Digital Author: Fan Fiction and Alt Lit

The privileged notion of the author is, historically speaking, relatively new, having grown up with the printing press. In the oral tradition, where every performance differed from every other, heavily modulated by the style and memory of the storyteller, notions of an originating author or a single definitive text were mostly nonexistent. The same was true of manuscript culture, where scribes altered, embellished, and annotated what they transcribed. This all changed when the printing press arrived with its fixed, unchangeable, identical copies. Whereas oral and manuscript models "created texts out of other texts, borrowing, adapting, sharing the common . . . formulas and themes," Walter Ong argues that print culture "gave birth to the romantic notions of 'originality' and 'creativity,' which set apart an individual work from other works . . . , seeing its origins and meaning as independent of outside influence."[10] The notion of copyright, developed in the eighteenth century along with Romanticism, enshrined in law this notion of the author as an original, creative figure whose distinctive creations merited legal protection.

The print-derived conception of original authorship was powerfully challenged in the twentieth century by the advent of structuralism and poststructuralism. In his 1967 essay "The Death of the Author," Roland Barthes argues that no act of authorship can be called truly "original," because the consciousness of the writing subject – the very consciousness wishing to express itself as "original" – is a construct of language. The text itself is not the unique expression of a creative mind, but the intersection point of numerous existing discourses – "not a line of words releasing a single 'theological' meaning (the 'message' of the Author-God) but a multidimensional space in which a variety of writings, none of them original, blend and clash."[11] If every text is, for Barthes, a mere "tissue of quotations," then the notion of an "Author" is a spurious means of imposing order and authority on literary texts, which ought to be left open to the free interpretations of readers. In his 1969 reply to Barthes, "What Is an Author?," Michel Foucault argues that we should replace the print-derived notion of the "author" with what he calls the "author function." The author, for Foucault, is not a "genial creator of a work in which he deposits, with infinite wealth and generosity, an inexhaustible world of significations" but rather a "functional principle by which . . . one limits, excludes, and chooses." The author does not precede the text at all, in fact, but is imposed retroactively as a convenience allowing readers to establish continuity of style, theme, and quality. The author, in Foucault's words, is "the principle of thrift in the proliferation of meaning";[12] in a world of too much information and too many voices, the author is a way of establishing a degree of order.

Although the ideas of Barthes and Foucault were widely circulated and vigorously debated in their own time, like those of McLuhan they achieved a new relevance with the advent of the digital medium. Mark Poster, heralding Barthes's and Foucault's "anticipation of digital authorship"[13] in *What's the Matter with the Internet?* (2001), argues that the shift to digital textuality "elicits a rearticulation of the author from the center of the text to its margins, from the source of meaning to an offering, a point in a sequence of a continuously transformed matrix of signification."[14] For Poster, the digital medium actively transforms the writing process in a manner that brings it more in line with poststructuralist notions of authorship. The ease with which digital text can be distributed, transformed, rewritten, and redistributed, Poster prophesies, "may function to extract the author from the text, to remove from its obvious meanings his or her intentions, styles, concepts, rhetoric, and mind" and thus "disrupt the analog circuit . . . through which the mechanisms of property solidify a link between creator and object."[15] If, as in the oral tradition, the digital medium makes it impossible to know for certain where a text originated, then perhaps, Poster speculates, we may simply stop asking who created a text and focus instead on the "links, associations, and dispersions of meaning" that it embodies.[16]

Fan fiction is the form of contemporary digital authorship that best demonstrates Poster's point. Fan fiction is not an invention of the digital age: in 1893, fans wrote new adventures for Sherlock Holmes after Conan Doyle tried to kill him off at Reichenbach Falls, and the term itself came into currency in the 1960s through homemade publications called fanzines. Yet it has nonetheless exploded in popularity in the age of the internet. On sites such as FanFiction.net, publication occurs according to a clear "short circuit" model. Writers post their stories, generally in short installments, at no cost and without the intervention of any editors or publishers. Given this circumvention of the model of print publication, fan fiction writers often come from culturally marginalized groups (they are overwhelmingly female, and queer authors are well represented) and to discuss taboo subjects (as in the popular "slash" genre, which imagines homosexual relationships between characters who are heterosexual in their canonical appearances).[17] Fan fiction authors speak directly to their readers, who on fan fiction sites are usually also writers and are at the very least *fans* – readers already deeply committed to the storyworld and the characters that the story treats. The notion of originality, so central to conceptions of the author since the Romantic period, makes an awkward fit with most fan fiction. When Karen Hellekson and Kristina Busse define the genre as "derivative amateur writing,"[18] their intention is not to belittle fan fiction but to underscore its deliberate rejection of originality as an evaluative criterion. Borrowing characters and settings from popular works of fiction, most fan fiction seeks to rework or extend an existing narrative – filling gaps, imagining sequels, inventing new battles or sexual pairings, but always remaining within the recognized framework of the originating text. Ewan Morrison has described fan fiction writers not as unoriginal but pointedly "anti-original":[19] perfectly content to remain on the less privileged side of Coleridge's imagination/fancy divide and to rearrange preexisting fictional elements rather than create them ex nihilo. Fan fiction authors further unsettle conventional notions of original authorship by working collaboratively. By publishing serially, they are able to solicit feedback on individual installments, rework them, and tailor ensuing episodes to the desires of their readers. Works of fan fiction are "tissues of quotation" stitched together by many hands.

E. L. James's *Fifty Shades of Grey*, one of the best-selling book series of the twenty-first century, presents an illustrative case study in the complexities of authorship in the digital realm. *Fifty Shades* began its life in 2010 as *Masters of the Universe*, one of some 60,000 works of *Twilight* fan fiction then available on FanFiction.net. Working under the pseudonym Snowqueens Icedragon, James transposed the *Twilight* characters Bella Swan and Edward Cullen from remote Forks, Washington, to urban Seattle, jettisoning all vampire elements and focusing entirely on sex. James published episodically, receiving some 35,000 reviews before *Masters of the Universe* was removed from FanFiction.net for violating its seldom enforced rules on sexual explicitness, at which point it was moved to James's own site. There, she continued to publish serially and to respond to readers' feedback; in a November 2010 post, for example, she thanked "Hoot" for "pre-reading and checking my American" and tipped her cap to "the twitterati" for their "continued help with the Amercian [sic]."[20] Eventually, James renamed her characters, renamed the novel, and removed much of the explicit *Twilight* machinery. Though Morrison considers *Fifty Shades* a "collective creation" with "60,000 authors,"[21] it was James alone who collected revenues when the book was sold through Amazon as an e-book, made available through its print-on-demand service, and eventually picked up by Vintage Books, resulting in sales of more than 100 million copies and a lucrative film adaptation. The complexity of authorship in the digital age is neatly embodied by the fact that E. L. James currently holds the immensely valuable copyright to a work of *Twilight* fan fiction – and that, today, FanFiction.net abounds with *Fifty Shades of Grey* fan fiction, shades of a shade.

Though many critics have argued for the artistic and cultural merits of fan fiction,[22] fan fiction authors are less self-consciously literary than members of another contemporary movement, Alternative Literature or Alt Lit. The term "Alt Lit," which came into circulation in the United States around 2010, designates a community, a medium, a style, and a particular subject matter: Alt Lit is a group of young writers tied together by their extremely active use of the internet and social media; it is published and circulated on the internet and social media; it is written in the native styles of the internet and social media; and it is largely concerned with life on the internet and social media. As with fan fiction, Alt Lit is produced and posted for free online, generally on blogs, social media, and personal websites. Like fan fiction, the texts are produced in a collaborative environment, published in progress, and edited based on feedback from readers who are themselves often writers. Many proponents of Alt Lit see the movement as a way of harnessing the power of digital self-publishing to rescue literature from the hierarchical and tightly patrolled world of print and to move it into the mainstream of contemporary online life. In his "doctrine on 'INTERNET POETRY,'" Steve Roggenbuck, a leading figure in Alt Lit, declares "print is dead: publishers are dead: academia is dead: borders [i.e., the bookstore chain] is dead: literary journals are dead: ezra pound is literally dead."[23] Given the enfeebled state of print-based literature, he calls for "the end of gatekeepers in poetry, the end of poetry as an obscured printed product, and the end of poetry as something people intentionally and successfully avoid." The practical advantages of digital publishing, Roggenbuck argues, are essential to carrying out this mission: "long live blogs: long live free literature: long live public domain and creative commons: long live self-publishing: long live torrents: long live free pdf's: long live pay-what-you-want: . . . long live the internet."

Existing in the free-flowing space of digital textuality, works of Alt Lit are dismissive of conventional notions of original authorship. On the website of the digital publisher Muumuu House, run by Alt Lit writer Tao Lin, many featured works are curated Twitter feeds. Lin's 2010 novel *Richard Yates* (which has little to do with the American author) begins with a cut-and-pasted chat log: "'I've only had the opportunity to hold a hamster once,' said Dakota Fanning on Gmail chat. 'Its paws were so tiny. I think I cried a little.'"[24] Marie Calloway's *Adrien Brody* (2011), published by Muumuu House, is an unadorned, detached, and detailed account of a real-life sexual encounter replete with excerpts from text messages, e-mails, and Tumblr blog posts.[25] Roggenbuck's *i love you, before long i die* (2013) is a "walt whitman mixtape," a compilation of his favorite moments from Whitman, delivered as a seventy-five-minute YouTube video.[26] His *DOWNLOAD HELVETICA FOR FREE.COM* – a free PDF download from the eponymous URL – consists of phrases culled from transcripts of MSN Messenger chats with his high-school girlfriend, set in large-type Helvetica. The full text of one poem reads, "I THINK I'M GOING TO EAT THIS BAGEL . . . "[27]

Consisting of recontextualized quotations and repurposed ephemera, the characteristic tone of Alt Lit is flat, monotonous, and brutally undecorated. The experience of reading much Alt Lit, as such, is soporific. As Charles Brock wittily remarks in his *New York Times* review of *Richard Yates*, "In attempting to explore boredom, Lin recreates boredom."[28] For the practitioners and defenders of Alt Lit, however, originality and excitement are beside the point. Kenneth Goldsmith, a supporter of the movement, argues in *Uncreative Writing: Managing Language in the Digital Age* (2011) that such works represent a coherent response to "a new condition in writing": "faced with an unprecedented amount of available text," Goldsmith argues, "the problem is not needing to write more of it; instead, we must learn to negotiate the vast quantity that exists."[29] Drawing on Marjorie Perloff's work on "unoriginal genius," which positions Walter Benjamin's fabulous web of quotation, *The Arcades Project*, as a precursor for digital remix culture,[30] Goldsmith argues that movements like Alt Lit represent a coherent and understandable reaction to life in the Library of Babel. In a digital world where it is so easy to write and publish, and where so much is written and published digitally, it stands to reason that the artist's focus should shift from the pure and perfect expression of her soul to mining vast of quantities of digital text for unexpected or unapprehended beauty.

Yet the celebrity achieved by writers like Tao Lin and Steve Roggenbuck complicates the picture. Though both eschew originality and often renounce copyright, they remain deeply, and somewhat cynically, committed to building up their "author function." If their literary productions are deliberately lazy, flat, and boring, their strategies of self-promotion are tireless and ingenious. Because Alt Lit is transacted on social media – where the line between *talking about* and *writing* Alt Lit is so blurred – its best-known practitioners tend to be those who spend the most time online. As Oscar Schwartz writes,

> [In order] for an Alt Lit writer . . . to "get attention" they have to participate not in punctuated bursts, but constantly, totally, immersively; participation becomes an act of endurance. In a way, the content of the writing becomes less important than the fact it is simply there on the newsfeed, like a type of defensive advertising reminding you of the writer's existence.[31]

Lin, ubiquitous in all variety of social media, has attracted attention by selling shares of future royalties on his then-unpublished *Richard Yates*, by auctioning his MySpace page on eBay, and by paying his followers to spread his reputation on social media.[32] At one point, Lin was so aggressive in soliciting attention from the celebrity website Gawker that it issued a public plea that he stop contacting the site.[33] (Lin, like several other male Alt Lit writers, has attracted further attention in the form of public accusations of sexual assault, sexism, and homophobia.)[34] Roggenbuck, an equally inventive self-promoter and an indomitable presence on social media, is forthright in declaring his allegiance to marketing over literary craftsmanship. In an interview with the Alt Lit site *HTMLGIANT*, Roggenbuck admits, "i don't care about individual poems or writing craft as much as a lot of writers."[35] His interest lies rather in "branding"; not "corporate branding" focused on the selling of products necessarily, but a more "holistic" branding that "captur[es] the essence of some core values." Seeing himself as a purveyor of lifestyle – in his case, one characterized by a commitment to veganism, Buddhism, freedom of expression, and a Whitmanian celebration of nature and the body – Roggenbuck locates the force of his appeal not in individual poems or lines of verse but in the gestalt of his public personality or "brand." This rapprochement of lifestyle marketing with literature has caused no discomfort to Roggenbuck's followers. In a telling comment on the *HTMLGIANT* interview, a user named Morgan writes, "Wow, Steve says some super-smart stuff in this, especially in the answer about style. Really makes it clear/persuasive what 'Steve Roggenbuck' the brand means."[36] What passes for utopia in the Alt Lit community may strike outsiders as a nightmare scenario: in a world of unfettered access to publication, what rises to the top of the literary brew is not the best writing but the cleverest marketing strategy.

Debating the Digital Superorganism: Dash Shaw's *BodyWorld*

Digital production has neither fully liberated the individual author nor totally discredited the notion of original authorship; neither emancipated the individual voice from the gatekeeping, censorship, and compromise of the print model, nor definitively dissolved it into a soup of unrestrained remixing and recombination. Instead, digital production has placed contemporary writers in a delicate position from which they must balance individual self-expression with the need to interest and satisfy the readership's collective mind. Dash Shaw's graphic novel *BodyWorld*, serialized on his website between 2007 and 2009 and revised for book publication in 2010, is a product of this precarious balance. Though first published online, *BodyWorld* stops well short of Alt Lit's full embrace of digital publishing and collaborative authorship. Though it takes as its subject the tension between individuality and the "hive mind" in the digital age, and though it examines the role that digital publishing technology plays in animating this tension, it comes to no definite conclusions, preferring to raise questions rather than to answer them.

BodyWorld explores its themes through a thoroughly bizarre narrative. It is the year 2060, in an America ravaged by the legacy of a Second Civil War. Technologically speaking, Shaw's distant future closely resembles our own recent past, and so the story begins with an alert in an RSS feed: Paulie Panther, a deranged researcher of hallucinogenic drugs, reads a blog post about a new plant that has been discovered in an isolated experimental city called Boney Borough and heads out to investigate. Arriving in town, Paulie finds a rigidly organized communitarian society with little tolerance for outsiders like himself. His first stop is the local high school, where he interrupts a class presentation on "superorganisms": social units like ant colonies in which individuals sacrifice all personal interests to the good of the community. Boney Borough itself functions as a kind of social superorganism, as Shaw implies through the grid-based map of the town on which he meticulously plots the novel's action (Figure 6.2). During the presentation on superorganisms, one student, Billy Borg, sends a note to his girlfriend Pearl Peach, addressing the note not by name but by position: he labels it "4B" (Pearl's desk is second from the front in the fourth row), instructing his classmate, "Pssst: Pass this up two chairs and then across" (Figure 6.3). The community-minded citizens of Boney Borough, Shaw suggests, see themselves not as unique individuals, but as points in the social grid.

Paulie, in contrast, is a strong individual and an artist figure of the Hunter S. Thompson variety: drunken, drug-addled, self-loathing, dubiously visionary, and violently opposed to authority in all its forms. Paulie's rebellious spirit quickly attracts the attention of Jem Jewel, a teacher with a spotty past, and of the aforementioned Pearl Peach, a student possessed of a romantic imagination and a taste for the unconventional. Love affairs with both women play out under the bizarre effects of the new plant Paulie discovers. When smoked, Paulie's plant acts as a powerful drug that induces a state of hyper-sympathy between those who smoke it – a genuine melding of minds in which each smoker inhabits the perspective of the others, thinks their thoughts, and feels the world through their bodies. For Paulie, Jem, and Pearl, smoking the drug is a means of self-expression and an act of antisocial rebellion. Yet, in an ironic reversal, the drug serves in the end to spread further the "superorganism" mentality already so prevalent in Boney Borough. During a tryst in the woods with Pearl, Paulie carelessly flicks a cigarette butt into a grove of the plants. As the ashes stoke a major conflagration, the drug is released into the atmosphere, and as Paulie says, "everyone [takes] a toke." As a result, a vast linked consciousness is formed in which all individuality is merged into a common pool of experience – an "insane hive mind," as Paulie calls it.[37] Because Paulie's own consciousness is drawn into the pool, his many outrageous actions – most pertinently, his seduction of Pearl Peach – become known to the "hive mind." In the graphic novel's conclusion, the merged consciousness of Boney Borough raises a hundred guns against him. It fires, and Paulie falls.

BodyWorld makes no effort to disguise its theme, the fate of the individual artist in a networked society. Late in the narrative, in case we missed it, Shaw goes so far as to depict Jem Jewel seated in her classroom, in front of a chalkboard that bears instructions for a final report on "Superorganism vs. Groupthink" – the same duality that we are asked to ponder as readers (Figure 6.4). *BodyWorld* is only slightly more oblique in identifying the specific

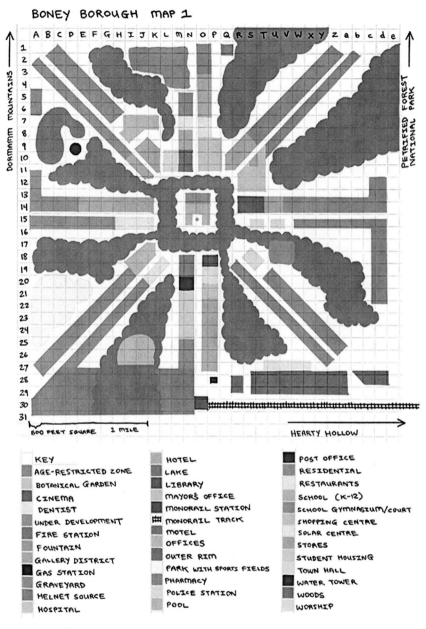

Figure 6.2 *Map of Boney Borough in Dash Shaw's webcomic serial* BodyWorld *(2008–2009).*

Figure 6.3 *"Grid-think" in* BodyWorld: *class note addressed by grid position.*

Figure 6.4 *Jem Jewel lays out the themes of* BodyWorld *in a class assignment.*

networked society in question: though set in the future, it is clearly concerned with the digital present and, more specifically, with the world of digital publishing that allowed for its serialization on Shaw's website. When Paulie arrives in Boney Borough and unpacks his suitcase, we see that it contains an e-reader and a number of "books on crystal."[38] Discussing his twelve-volume *Encyclopedia of the Hallucinogenic Effects of North American Plantlife*, Paulie complains to Jem Jewel about the cost of printed books and magazines in an era when everything has "moved to the net." When Paulie asks Jem if she wrote the blog entry his RSS reader discovered, she replies, "I don't have a blog. I like to keep my secrets."[39]

Perhaps the clearest reference to contemporary debates on the social effects of the internet and digital publishing, however, comes in Paulie's use of the term "hive mind" to describe the murderous linked consciousness of Boney Borough. In *The Gutenberg Elegies*, Sven Birkerts had warned "we are wiring ourselves into a gigantic hive,"[40] naming "telephone, fax, computer-screen networks, e-mail, [and] interactive television" as the "components out of which the hive is being built."[41] More recently, Cathy Davidson has sought to recuperate the term, defining a "hive mind" in *Now You See It* (2011) as the "spontaneous forming of an online community to solve a problem."[42] Citing the example of *World without Oil* – an alternate reality game that applies the collective intelligence of its players to the looming real-world problem of exhausted global oil supplies – Davidson calls the "hive mind" "one of the most inspiring forms of collaboration indigenous to the Internet."[43] Yet in his 2010 "manifesto" *You Are Not a Gadget*, virtual reality pioneer Jaron Lanier sees the "hive mind" as pointedly demonic. Lanier argues that many "Web 2.0" technologies serve to "pull us into life patterns that gradually degrade the ways in which each of us exists as an individual," "deemphasizing personhood and the intrinsic value of an individual's unique experience and creativity."[44] The ease of self-publication and the facility of remixing the work of others have, he argues, replaced "Authorship – the very idea of the individual's point of view" with the "digital flattening of expression into a global mush."[45] In a statement that recalls the fate of Alt Lit stars, Lanier laments the misplaced enthusiasm of young users of social media who "must manage their online reputations constantly" in order to escape "the ever-roaming eye of the hive mind, which can turn on an individual at any moment."[46]

Shaw's treatment of the hive mind theme in *BodyWorld* avoids such stark binaries. Although *BodyWorld* is very much *about* the fate of authorship and individuality in an era of spreading digital interconnectivity, it is not simply a parable of the dangers of the hive. Even though Paulie, the textual figure of the Romantic artist, is murdered by the hive mind, Shaw undercuts any readings

Figure 6.5 *Paulie Panther killed by his own self-loathing: a shadow of Paulie in the mind of Pearl Peach.*

that would position him as a martyr. Paulie is somewhat too convinced of his own status as a heroic outsider to be credible as one. Just before his death, he calls a friend to say, "If you don't see or hear from me in a month, I'm lost. Gone! The Professor Paulie Panther you've known and loved has been absorbed by this emerging colony. The world has lost its great hallucinogenic plant smoker and documentor [*sic*]. Its great lover and leaver."[47] The effect of Paulie's megalomania is to inspire derisive laughter rather than tragic empathy. Paulie is himself too drawn to human interconnection to be a credible symbol of rugged individuality. In the midst of one of his spats with Jem, he tells her, "Yeah, yeah, okay: 'Sympathy.' It's a noun. There's a verb form you should try out."[48] The drug is so attractive to Paulie precisely because it acts as such a verb form: recalling the etymology of "sympathy" in the Greek *sumpatheia*, "feeling with," it allows for a literal sharing of bodily sensations and thus temporarily cures Paulie of his crippling loneliness. Most powerfully, however, Shaw upsets readings of Paulie-as-martyr by suggesting that it is primarily his own self-loathing, rather than the community's conservative rage against an individualistic outsider, that is to blame for his death. In the frame in which Pearl betrays her former lover by yelling "Fire!" Shaw draws a shadow of Paulie's face onto Pearl's own, implying that the word emanates from a vestige of his consciousness inserted into her mind during one of their shared experiences of the mind-merging drug (Figure 6.5).

Shaw's ambivalent treatment of the hive mind theme in *BodyWorld* is reflected in his ambivalent use of the digital medium. Although he first published the work online, his decision to do so was based primarily on practical considerations rather than a desire to exploit the new possibilities of digital presentation. Twenty-four years old at the time that serialization began, with no mainstream reputation, he would have had great difficulty finding a major publisher willing to take on a long, strange, full-color graphic novel with controversial content. By beginning digitally, he was able to avoid the censorship or self-censorship entailed in pitching the work to a major publisher. By serializing, he was able to gauge the reactions of his audience – and also simply to see whether the work was attracting any audience at all and thus worth continuing. As it happened, *BodyWorld* drew a large and devoted audience, attracting the attention of Pantheon Books, an imprint of Knopf Doubleday. Before serialization was complete, he had a deal in place to publish *BodyWorld* as a glossy, full-color, 384-page book, uncensored from the original.[49] When the time came to convert *BodyWorld* into printed form, there was little difficulty in doing so, for the online version made very little use of exclusively digital affordances. Though he has described feeling "weighed down" by the "formal properties of printed books," such as fixed page dimensions and inevitable page breaks,[50] in the digital version of *BodyWorld* Shaw makes almost no use of the "infinite canvas" of the digital screen, aside from a striking vertical journey through the strata of the New York City of 2060 in Chapter 12.[51] Likewise, Shaw made minimal use of "Web 2.0" technology in the digital *BodyWorld*: there was no affordance for user comments, for annotations of particular frames, or even for "liking" certain sequences on social media.

Reflecting his ambivalence to digital authorship both an as idea and as a practical reality, Shaw's artistic process in *BodyWorld* functions as a complex hybrid of digital and analog methods that remain unresolved and in conflict. Shaw has described his art in *BodyWorld* as "a mash-up of pre-Photoshop coloring processes and Photoshop coloring." He generally proceeded by drawing each frame by hand, scanning it into Photoshop and filling in the color with the paint-bucket tool, printing out the Photoshop-colored frame and recoloring it by hand, and then once again scanning this image into Photoshop for final retouching.[52] Individual frames thus combine the smoothness and uniformity of digital coloration with the roughness of analog brushstrokes. *BodyWorld*'s most distinctive visual element – the palimpsestic overlaying of shared experiences that Shaw uses to portray the merging of consciousness effected by the drug – is likewise a peculiar hybrid of digital and analog, employing Photoshop to remix and recombine frames from elsewhere in the narrative (Figure 6.6). In such images, Shaw embodies the message of *BodyWorld* in its form, expressing his forceful but unresolved ambivalence toward the digital world through images that combine and overlay digital and analog design.

Figure 6.6 *Palimpsestic overlaying in* BodyWorld.

Shaw's palimpsest provides a fitting image with which to close this chapter. The palimpsest comes from an earlier period of textuality: the manuscript age, when scribes recycled expensive parchment by rubbing out unneeded texts and writing over top of them, a process that left visible traces of the original beneath the newly written words. This logic of superimposition remains relevant in our own textual moment. As we move from print to the digital, what we should expect to see are not clean and definite breaks, but complex imbrications of the new and the old. Digital production empowers author-ship – freeing the individual from the constraints of competing actors such as editors, publishers, printers, booksellers – while simultaneously challenging the model of individual creation by encouraging collaborative composition, remixing, and "uncreative writing," and by elevating branding over artistic genius. It produces wonderful, monstrous hybrids like *BodyWorld*, a passion-ate but pointedly ambivalent analysis of individuality and group consciousness in the digital age, published both online and in print, drawn in a style that intermingles the conspicuously analog and the unmistakably digital. Digital production is a powerful drug, and we have all taken a toke. But we are all, like Paulie Panther, pioneers in the hallucinogenic: we know the drug is a strong one, but much experimentation is needed before we will be able to discern its specific effects. Precisely where it will take us, we cannot yet know.

Chapter 7

Interactivity: Revolution and Evolution in Narrative

Interactivity is the most recognizably innovative, potentially revolutionary, and intellectually intriguing of the born-digital affordances. Indeed, it is arguably the *only* born-digital affordance to offer something genuinely unprecedented to the literary experience. Digital production, discussed in the previous chapter, may make the publishing process faster, more accessible, and more inclusive – yet however much it improves the print model, it does not reinvent it. Multimodality, the subject of the next chapter, may allow for new combinations of the written word, moving pictures, and sound – yet in doing so, it simply unites into a single medium possibilities that were previously distributed among several. The digital affordance of interactivity, in contrast, offers something entirely new. There is no pre-digital version of a written text that asks *you* to act out the role of its protagonist, to determine the unfolding of the narrative, and to directly affect its outcome. Janet H. Murray thus calls interactivity "the defining activity of the digital medium." In a digital text, she writes, there is "a pleasure of agency," a "sense of participating in a world that responds coherently to our participation." The best that a printed narrative can hope for is to be "immersive"; the experience of interacting with a digital text, in contrast, is "not just immersive, it is *animated.*"[1]

This chapter focuses on two distinct forms of text-based interactive narrative: hypertext and Interactive Fiction (IF). Both present a clear contrast with their print-based predecessors. Whereas a reader moves through a book by turning pages, these interactive digital forms require direct input from their reader in order to move from one chunk of text (called a "lexia") to the next: in a hypertext, the reader must navigate a series of choices, and in IF, the reader must type in textual commands. The first part of the chapter focuses on the reception of hypertext in the 1990s, a decade of bold claims and counterclaims for interactivity in digital fiction. Many critics argued that hypertext fiction would undo the fundamental categories of narrative and usher in a new literary era characterized by a democratic leveling of author and reader. Many others, however, countered that hypertext was neither as revolutionary at the level of narrative as its adherents claimed nor indeed any more "interactive" than print fiction. From the inflated rhetoric of the 1990s, we move to a close investigation of two more recent interactive texts: Stephen Marche's hypertext *Lucy Hardin's Missing Period* and Emily Short's work of IF, *Galatea*. These texts show that, even if interactive literary forms do not fundamentally transform the nature of narrative, they nonetheless allow skilled writers to achieve moving effects unachievable in print.

The Rise and Fall of Hypertext

Given its focus, this book is necessarily oriented toward the future: most of the subjects it investigates are emergent, and one of its refrains is that since we are living the transition to the digital in real time, we cannot stand outside and judge its significance. Hypertext fiction, in this future-oriented context, presents an unusual case: it is one of the few digital literary forms that can be plausibly regarded as dead.[2] Incubated in the 1980s and released into the public imagination in the early 1990s, hypertext was largely forgotten by the dawn of the new millennium. Its spectacular dramatic arc – hypertext's Icarian trajectory – is neatly captured by a pair of essays published in the Books section of the *New York Times* at opposite ends of the 1990s. Robert Coover's "The End of Books," published in June 1992, declared "the print medium . . . a doomed and outdated technology"; "the novel . . . as we know it," Coover said, "has come to its end."[3] Print, he prophesied, would be replaced by the digital medium; the novel, for its part, would be replaced by hypertext fiction. For Coover, the changeover from the printed novel to the electronic hypertext was not just a technological inevitability but a moral imperative as well. Calling the novel a "virulent carrier of the patriarchal, colonial, canonical, proprietary, hierarchical and authoritarian values of a past that is no longer with us," he attacked its distinguishing feature: "the line, that compulsory author-directed movement from the beginning of a sentence to its period, from the top of the page to the bottom, from the first page to the last." Hypertext, by contrast, nonlinear and interactive, heralded a new democratic age. "With its web of linked lexias, its networks of alternate routes (as opposed to print's fixed unidirectional page-turning)," he argued, "hypertext presents a radically divergent technology, interactive and polyvocal, favoring a plurality of discourses over definitive utterance and freeing the reader from domination by the author." Because readers actively choose their path through the web of links in a hypertext and often take on the role of a character in the narrative, Coover argued that in the brave new world of hypertext, the previously isolated figures of reader and author would become "co-learners" and "co-writers." The advent of hypertext marked nothing less than an epochal shift. "Fluidity, contingency, indeterminacy, plurality, discontinuity" were not only "the hypertext buzzwords of the day" but also were "fast becoming principles, in the same way that relativity not so long ago displaced the falling apple."

Just six years later, hypertext's chance had passed. In a March 1998 response to Coover, Laura Miller bookended hypertext's moment in the sun with an article titled, appropriately, "Bookend." Looking back at Coover's prediction that hypertext would displace the printed novel, Miller succinctly noted that, in the intervening years, she had "yet to encounter anyone who reads hypertext fiction," adding, "What's most remarkable about hyperfiction is that no one really wants to read it, not even out of idle curiosity."[4] Hypertext's fundamental premise – that "readers ought to be, and long to be, liberated from two mainstays of the traditional novel: linear narrative and the author" – turned out, Miller argued, to have been doubly flawed. Navigating the linked structure of hypertexts was not liberating or empowering but "profoundly meaningless and dull." Speaking for many nonreaders of hypertext, she asked,

> If any decision is as good as any other, why bother? Hypertext is sometimes said to mimic real life, with its myriad opportunities and surprising outcomes, but I already have a life, thank you very much, and it is hard enough putting that in order without the chore of organizing someone else's novel.

As for Coover's contention that navigating this structure would make her a "co-writer," she retorted, "I could just write my own book if writing is what I really want to do," because no one was stopping her. The "end of books," she concluded, "will come only when readers abandon novels for the deconstructed stories of hypertext, and that is strictly a fiction."

History has taken Miller's side. The works that seemed so revolutionary and world altering to Coover – Michael Joyce's *Afternoon, a story* (1987/1991) and Stuart Moulthrop's *Victory Garden* (1992) – were not only seldom read in their own time, but are today literally unreadable, languishing in antiquated software and hardware formats inaccessible to the contemporary reader. Yet the precipitous rise and fall of hypertext in the 1990s remains a fascinating story, punctuated by bold declarations of a new age for literature and earnest efforts to rethink literary theory in the light of digital innovations. The most enduring legacy of this period is theoretical rather than creative: if works like *Afternoon* have been lost in the shifting sands of technological advancement, the pioneering efforts of hypertext critics such as Jay David Bolter, George Landow, and Espen J. Aarseth remain required reading for anyone looking to understand digital-native narrative forms like videogames. It is fitting, indeed, that theory is the main legacy from the hypertext excitement of the 1990s, because it was theory – particularly poststructuralist theory – that incited this excitement in the first place.

Bolter and Landow: Hypertext and Social Transformation

The two most important early works on the theory of hypertext – Bolter's *Writing Space* (1991) and Landow's *Hypertext* (1992) – explicitly argue its connection with poststructuralism. Landow's *Hypertext* is subtitled *The Convergence of Contemporary Critical Theory and Technology* and opens with the argument that "over the past several decades literary theory and computer hypertext, apparently unconnected areas of inquiry, have increasingly converged."[5] In particular, Landow argues that hypertext "creates an almost embarrassingly literal embodiment" of two crucial poststructuralist ideas: Roland Barthes's conception of the "readerly" text and Jacques Derrida's emphasis on discursive decentering.[6] Landow quotes Barthes's description in *S/Z* (1970) of an "ideal text" in which "the networks are many and interact, without any one of them being able to suppress the rest" – a text that "has no beginning," "is reversible," and to which "we gain access . . . by several entrances, none of which is authoritatively declared to be the main one."[7] For Landow, Barthes's "ideal text" "precisely matches that which has come to be called computer hypertext."[8] Landow argues that Derridean works such as *Glas* (1974) and *Of Grammatology* (1967), emphasizing "openness, intertextuality, and the irrelevance of distinctions between inside and outside," anticipate the logic of digital textuality and offer *avant la lettre* descriptions of "extant hypertext systems."[9] In *Writing Space*, Bolter agrees that "radical theorists" such as Barthes and Derrida "speak a language that is strikingly appropriate to electronic writing."[10] Citing Barthes's distinction between work and text – where the "plural" text links reader and writer "together in a single signifying process"[11] – Bolter finds it remarkable that someone who "did not know about computers" could produce such insightful descriptions of hypertext.[12] Citing Derrida's description of text as "a differential network, a fabric of traces referring endlessly to something other than itself,"[13] Bolter argues that it "sounds very much like text in the electronic writing space."[14]

The appeal of hypertext to critics like Bolter and Landow was closely tied to its amenability to, and embodiment of, poststructuralist theory. Yet they saw hypertext not just as a confirmation of the correctness of Derridean and Barthesian philosophy but also as a vehicle for promoting its political ideals.

Because poststructuralism's political thrust was often buried in abstruse and unreadable works of philosophy, hypertext seemed to them a way to "mainstream" poststructuralist ideology – to make poststructuralism go viral. For Bolter and Landow, hypertext embodied and prefigured a more egalitarian, democratic world. In Bolter's words, "the electronic book reflects a different natural world, in which relationships are multiple and evolving"; if the printed book implies a hierarchical "great chain of being," hypertext promotes a view of the world as a "network of interdependent species and systems."[15] In Landow's view, experiencing hypertext was a consciousness-raising activity that served to explode the notions of authorial property and individual genius embedded in printed books.[16] The "hypertextual dissolution of centrality," Landow argued, "which makes the medium such a potentially democratic one, also makes it a model of a society of conversations in which no one conversation, no one discipline or ideology, dominates or founds the others."[17] Bolter and Landow argued that hypertext would carry out its mission by embedding itself in humanity's most powerful means of self-reckoning: storytelling. By redefining certain basic categories of narrative, it would change our understanding of our world. The two most important changes, Bolter and Landow claimed, were the interactive engagement of the reader and the elimination of linear plot. Whereas the printed text proceeds in a fixed sequence determined by the author, Bolter argued that in hypertext the author merely "lays out a textual space" for the reader, who then "joins in actively constructing the text by selecting a particular order of episodes."[18] Gone is the Romantic mystique of the author-creator; now the reader is on a level plane:

> The author is no longer an intimidating figure, not a prophet or a Mosaic legislator in Shelley's sense. The author's art is not a substitute for religious revelation, and authors do not lay down the law. The electronic author assumes once again the role of a craftsman, working with defined materials and limited goals.... The text is not simply an expression of the author's emotions, for the reader helps to make the text.[19]

For Landow, hypertext "challenges narrative and all literary form based on linearity," in particular notions of "(1) fixed sequence, (2) definite beginning and ending, (3) a story's 'certain definite magnitude,' and (4) the conception of unity or wholeness associated with all these other concepts."[20] The existence of "multiple reading paths" not only "shift[s] the balance between reader and writer"[21] but indeed "blurs the boundaries between reader and writer."[22] By doing so, Landow argues, hypertext "instantiates" one of his most cherished of Barthesian aims: "to make the reader no longer a consumer, but a producer of the text."[23] In ways that a previous generation of writers such as Benjamin and Woolf could only have dreamed of (see Ch. 2), hypertext would quite literally transform the passive reader into an active writer.

The Frustrations and Limitations of Hypertextual Interactivity

Bolter and Landow's ideals – their perception that, in championing hypertext, they were helping promote horizontality, dialogue, and equality in the political as well as the literary sphere – were certainly laudable. But in the years since *Writing Space* and *Hypertext* appeared, many have questioned whether their ideas were firmly grounded in narrative theory. In the *Cambridge Introduction to Narrative*, H. Porter Abbott asks whether hypertext truly effects the "radical" break with print narrative that Bolter and Landow perceived. As Abbott points out, hypertext invented neither nonlinear structure nor readerly choice in determining a narrative path: Julio Cortazar's printed novel *Hopscotch* (1963) allowed readers to choose the order in which they read its chapters, and Marc Saporta's *Composition no. 1* (1962) was presented as a box containing unnumbered pages to be read in the order of the reader's choosing. Indeed, all printed books give their readers the freedom to skip from one section to another, to skim, to flip, to read out of order. Recalling the Russian Formalists' distinction between *fabula* – the raw chronological sequence of events told in a narrative – and *syuzhet* – the manner in which this chronological sequence is narrated in a particular telling – Abbott further points out that even that most ancient of Western literary texts, Homer's *Iliad*, is "nonlinear" in the sense that it begins *in medias res* ("in the middle of things") and then skips forward and backward in time while recounting the Greek victory over the Trojans. Further, although readers of hypertext may have the freedom to create a personalized *syuzhet* as they navigate its pathways, the story that they recover on this path will nonetheless remain linear, because *fabula* is by definition linear and chronological. Homer can construct his telling (*syuzhet*) of the Trojan War in whatever order he likes, beginning in the middle, skipping back to the beginning, flashing forward to the end, and so on. But the actual story on which his narrative is based, the war itself, is inescapably something that happened in a strictly linear chronological order, because that is how time – the medium in which all *fabula* must operate – inescapably moves. "Strictly speaking," Abbot concludes, "hypertext lexia are simply a new twist on an old narrative condition."[24] Readers of hypertexts such as Michael Joyce's *Afternoon, a story* are no different from readers of any novel with a complex and nonlinear *syuzhet*, struggling as they proceed to wrest a firm sense of the underlying story from a sometimes disorienting narration.

Just as pre-digital literature can be conceived as "nonlinear," many critics have argued that literature in print is already deeply "interactive." This is the principal insight of another school of twentieth-century literary criticism, reader-response theory. Critics such as Wolfgang Iser and Stanley Fish argue that written words are only the beginning of the literary experience, insisting that the literary text is "created" as much by the reader as the writer. Though the author puts the words on the page, the reader brings them to life through the process of reading, much as a musician brings an orchestral score to life through performance. In "The Reading Process" (1974), Iser argues that the literary work possesses "two poles": "the text created by the author" and "the realization accomplished by the reader." A work of literature cannot be said to truly exist until it is actualized through the act of reading: "the convergence of text and reader," Iser argues, "brings the literary work into existence."[25] The work of the reader, moreover, consists not in the passive reconstitution of the intentions of the author, but in the active construction – even co-creation – of the text. The literary reader must, for example, fill in "inevitable omissions" that authors leave in narratives: "whenever the flow is interrupted and we are led off in unexpected directions," Iser argues, "the opportunity is given to us to bring into play our own faculty for establishing connections – for filling in the gaps left by the text itself."[26] The filling of such gaps is not an onerous imposition on the reader, but the source of much pleasure, allowing readers to insert themselves imaginatively into the narrative. Hypertext choice cannot possibly *transform* readers into co-authors, reader-response critics argue, because reading already is – and has always been – an intrinsically creative activity.

In *Cybertext: Perspectives on Ergodic Literature* (1997), Espen J. Aarseth offers a reply to such criticisms. The reason that the reader of a hypertext is "a more integrated figure than even reader-response theorists would claim," Aarseth argues, is that while "the performance of [a print] reader takes place all in his head," the user of a hypertext "also performs in an extranoematic [i.e., physical, outside the confines of the mind] sense."[27] Aarseth, notably fond of critical coinages and abstruse terminology, distinguishes "cybertexts" such as hypertexts and Interactive Fictions from traditional narrative on the grounds that cybertexts are "ergodic." "In ergodic literature," he explains, "nontrivial effort is required to allow the reader to traverse the text" – whereas in traditional "nonergodic" literature, "the effort to traverse the text is trivial, with no extranoematic responsibilities placed on the reader except (for example) eye movement and the periodic or arbitrary turning of pages."[28] Contrary to the reader-response model, Aarseth argues that a traditional reader, "however strongly engaged in the unfolding of a narrative, is powerless":

> Like a spectator at a soccer game, he may speculate, conjecture, extrapolate, even shout abuse, but he is not a player. Like a passenger on a train, he can study and interpret the shifting landscape, he may rest his eyes wherever he pleases, even release the emergency brake and step off, but he is not free to move the tracks in a different direction. He cannot have the player's pleasure of influence: "Let's see what happens when I do *this*." The reader's pleasure is the pleasure of the voyeur. Safe, but impotent.[29]

Aarseth's arguments, deliberately controversial, have drawn their own share of rebuttals. In *The Language of New Media* (2002), Lev Manovich warns against overly literal understandings of "interactivity" that equate it with physical interactions such as "pressing a button, choosing a link, moving the body"; Manovich repeats the reader-response theorists' insistence on the active, constructive nature of "the psychological process of filling-in, hypothesis, recall, and identification."[30] In *Reading Machines* (2011), Stephen Ramsay argues that Aarseth underestimates the literal effect that "noematic" or nonphysical interpretation can have on a narrative. For Ramsay, "The minute someone proposes to explain the meaning of a narrative – to speculate, conjecture, extrapolate, or shout abuse at it, whether in the privacy of one's thoughts or in a critical journal – the narrative changes, because we are no longer able to read it without knowledge of the paratextual revolt."[31] One cannot limit oneself to individual texts in considering the question of interactivity, Ramsay argues, because a whole network of communal, collaborative, and constructive discussion surrounds them: discussions that take place in classrooms, in the pages of academic journals, in reading groups, in living rooms, in online forums. These discussions are interactive in themselves, involving many actors in dialogue with one another, and they also interact with the literary texts they bring under discussion, changing how we envision and engage with their narratives.

Another school of thought goes further still in responding to the claims of early hypertext enthusiasts, arguing that hypertext offers its readers *less* choice than traditional printed narratives. In *Planned Obsolescence* (2011), Kathleen Fitzpatrick argues that "hypertext is somewhat deceptive in its claims to activate the reader":

> Upon picking up a book to read, I have the entire text in my hands, all at once, and I can do anything with it that I choose – read the entire thing in a linear fashion, read the end before the beginning, use the index to find the only three pages I really need to read, flip back and forth

> between different sections. With a hypertext, not only do I not have the entire text available to me at the outset – some pathways only becoming activated by prior choices, some choices remaining hidden – but it is also often unclear what options I do have before me, what choices I can make, and what relationship those choices bear to the shape of the text as a whole. All I can do as a reader is follow the choices that the author has allowed. The process of reading a hypertext is thus, in its way, more determined than the process of reading a book, and the experience of reading can at times seem more focused on attempting to divine the author's encoded intent than on creating a reader-centered text.[32]

In *Writing Space*, Bolter wrote enthusiastically of the way that a hypertext reader "can follow paths through the space in any direction, limited only by the constraints established by the author."[33] Yet these constraints are always palpable in a hypertext and very often frustrating. Fitzpatrick reports that many of her students feel "manipulated" by the looming, abstracted, decision-granting power of the author.[34] For Manovich, this feeling comes from the fact that hypertext reifies or objectifies processes of psychological association that, in traditional printed narrative, are left to the reader: "Before, we would read a sentence of a story or a line of a poem and think of other lines, images, memories"; "Now interactive media asks us...to follow pre-programmed, objectively existing associations." "Put differently," Manovich argues, "we are asked to mistake the structure of somebody else's mind for our own."[35]

In her 1998 *New York Times* article, "Bookend," Laura Miller argued that, in the end, it did not matter much whether hypertext granted more or less freedom than its printed alternatives. Reading, she contended, is not a struggle for freedom from the author; it is an act of willing submission to the author's exquisite and dominating consciousness. Responding to Robert Coover's dismissal of readers who "surrender to novels as a way of going on holiday from themselves," Miller argued that this "surrender," "the intimacy to be had in allowing a beloved author's voice into the sanctum of our minds," is exactly what most readers want. "Is it a holiday," she asked, "when we issue this invitation to guests whose appeal lies precisely in their distinctive, unequivocal, undeniably authoritative voices"? Might we rather call this "an expansion of ourselves"?[36] In his contemporaneous *The Gutenberg Elegies* (1997), Sven Birkerts enthusiastically takes Miller's side. Birkerts attempts to give hypertext a fair hearing, yet when he sits down at a computer terminal and actually tries to navigate a real-life hypertext's web of links, he finds the experience an "assault upon what [he] had unreflectingly assumed to be [his] reader's prerogatives." "Domination by the author is the *point* of writing and reading," he writes in the wake of his hypertext experience. "The author masters the resources of language to create a vision that will engage and in some way overpower the reader," and "the reader goes to the work to be subjected to the creative will of another."[37] The debate in the 1990s over the literary politics of hypertext was nothing if not extreme: one the one side, critics foreseeing the liberation of the reader from the enslavement of the author; on the other, critics proclaiming absolute enslavement to be the source of all literary pleasure.

Twenty-First-Century Hypertext: Stephen Marche's *Lucy Hardin's Missing Period*

A quarter-century after the first eruption of enthusiasm for hypertext and long after the dust has settled from the critical controversies that ensued, we find ourselves in an ideal moment for reevaluating the form. With the passing of the poststructuralist moment, hypertext no longer bears the burden of having to confirm or embody the ideas of Barthes and Derrida. Having had time to reflect on the questions of its interactivity and nonlinearity, we no longer ask hypertext to effect a radical break with narrative as it exists in print. Having witnessed its failure to catch on with readers, we no longer expect it to topple social hierarchies nor singlehandedly produce a more egalitarian, democratic world. Approaching the genre with more modest expectations, we are able to see hypertext for what it is: a narrative form that shares much in common with older forms, but whose subtle differences allow skilled writers to achieve poignant artistic effects not possible in print.

Stephen Marche's 2010 *Lucy Hardin's Missing Period*, published on the website of the Canadian general-interest magazine *The Walrus*, presents a compelling example of toned-down twenty-first-century hypertext.[38] Marche, a journalist, print novelist, and, as we have seen, a prominent critic of quantitative approaches to literary analysis (see Ch. 5), approaches the hypertext genre with motivations very different from those that propelled the first wave of hypertext authors. Marche bears no illusions about the marketing appeal of the term "hypertext" in the twenty-first century and pointedly avoids the term in *Lucy Hardin*'s subtitle, which identifies the work as "an interactive novel." The work indeed owes less to Barthes and Bolter than it does to hypertext's contemporaneous print doppelgänger, the Choose Your Own Adventure (CYOA) novel. CYOA succeeded where hypertext failed in the 1980s and 1990s, bringing nonlinear, "interactive," choice-based narrative to the masses, albeit in book form and to an audience of children. (A typical episode in a CYOA novel, for those unfamiliar with the genre, might narrate a walk through the woods on a moonlit night, when suddenly you hear a loud crack. You are given the choice to turn to page 23 to keep walking in the woods – in which case you are eaten by a bear – or to turn to page 36 to turn around, in which case you end up in the arms of your companion and fall in love.) *Lucy Hardin* presents itself not as a return to the hypertext wars of the 1990s but rather as a reworking of CYOA for the generation that grew up reading these novels, but now faces the more difficult decisions of adulthood in the digital age.

Lucy Hardin's Missing Period is a story about a young woman who awakes one morning suspecting she may be pregnant. As the punning title implies, the text unfolds like a sentence without a period, lacking a definitive, authorized ending. Depending on the particular pathway the reader chooses, Lucy might discover she is not pregnant or, if she finds that she is, give birth, have a miscarriage, or decide to end her pregnancy. Other choices for Lucy and for the reader include whether or not to trust her often unreliable boyfriend, Daniel; whether or not to resign herself to the banal security of her job in legal publishing; and what to do about her hoarder mother, who lives entirely through old letters and photographs. As these various scenarios suggest, Marche presents choice not as a blessing – a fun, engaging, empowering diversion in the CYOA style – but as a weighty burden. Indeed, for Marche, hypertext neither offers a fantasy of free choice nor serves as a vehicle for placing author and audience on a level plane. The fact that Marche himself is in charge – that the author retains his hierarchical position in the text – is apparent from the first paragraph, the only passage that every reader must traverse, which contains an unsettling description of Daniel's naked body. As we proceed into the text's tree-like branching structure, the experience of choosing becomes a source of frustration. Often, rather than offering us a choice, the text forces us to click on the sole option presented. Although the words at these no-decision nodes are occasionally written in the voice of the reader, reflecting our curiosity or lack thereof ("Well?"), at other times they are clearly authorial, not only dictating our path through the narrative but also interpreting its meaning ("The ride to her sister's house and to maturity"). When we are given choices, the alternatives are often equally undesirable and difficult to decipher. Some choices are straightforward: when the text presents the alternative of "More College Street" and "Right to the grocery store," it is simply asking us whether we would prefer to read Marche's amusing but inessential descriptions of a busy Toronto shopping street or to skip over them and advance directly to the next important moment in the plot. But when we are asked to choose between "Her own fury, in the figure of a fly" and "A glimpse of how others must see her," we must do so blindly, because the meaning of the choice becomes clear only after we have taken it.

Clear choices are particularly crucial in *Lucy Hardin* not only because of the high narrative stakes – Lucy's happiness or misery – but also because they cannot be undone. Whereas in a printed CYOA novel, one can return to an especially important decision by marking the spot with one's fingers, in *Lucy Hardin* our options disappear as soon as we have made a choice: there is no back button. The experience of choosing in *Lucy Hardin* thus tracks with that of Kathleen Fitzpatrick and her students: we routinely feel "manipulated" by a lack or clear or desirable choices and acutely aware of the hierarchical presence of the option-granting author. The difference between *Lucy Hardin* and most earlier hypertexts, however, is that in Marche's text this frustration is cultivated deliberately. Real life, Marche suggests, is itself a series of unsatisfying, constricted, and obscure choices, none of which can be undone. Though Laura Miller dismisses the notion that hypertext's "myriad opportunities and surprising outcomes" mimic real life, she would perhaps have been more sympathetic to the realism of Marche's limited choices and dreary outcomes.

Lucy Hardin's recasting of choice as a burden rather than a boon is under-scored by a powerful detail of its narrative technique: its abandonment of the distinctive CYOA second person in favor of the third person. CYOA, as does much hypertext, stresses the interactive dimension of the reading experience by collapsing the reader/character distinction into the second-person pronoun "you": *you* are the camper being chased by a bear in the woods; *you* are the pilot of the space ship on whose fate the universe depends; *you* are the detective seeking to crack the case. The second person functions not only to draw the reader in but also to simplify the process of choosing: in deciding to turn and fight the marauding bear, for instance, one chooses simultaneously for oneself as a reader and for one's avatar in the story. In *Lucy Hardin*, the third person keeps the author/character/reader triad in play, forbidding such simplifica-tions. Our position is paradoxical and indeterminate: we are not Lucy, yet we control her fate, albeit through an awkward and unclear choice mechanism controlled by the author. As such, each decision node binds us in an ethical dilemma: will we choose what is more interesting to ourselves as readers, or will we choose what we consider best for Lucy, the character, based on the information passed on to us by the author? When Lucy is offered a job as a dealer in an illegal card game – work that would take her away from her secure position at the legal publisher – we are offered a stark choice between "Risk" and "Security." As a reader, the narrative pull of an illegal card game is clearly stronger than that of a stable nine-to-five job; yet for Lucy, who may need to support a child, safety is clearly the more responsible option. The interests of reader and character are at odds in such instances; deciding which path to pursue requires a conscious decision whether to put Lucy's interests first or our own.

The ethical dimension is compounded by the fact that once we make a decision for Lucy, she immediately misrecognizes it as her own. In one scenario, Lucy's pregnancy test comes back positive, and we are asked whether she should call her mother or sister. If we choose her sister, the text reads "Stumbling to the phone beside the bed, Lucy knew that her sister was the woman to talk to" – but we know better: Lucy could not possibly have *known* she would call her sister, because we had just made this choice for her. Lucy indeed repeatedly misconstrues the pathways we have selected – however blindly or selfishly – as the inevitable workings of fate. In one lexia, the narrator reports, "She had known she was pregnant from the moment she woke up"; in another, Lucy holds her newborn son in her arms "at last, as it had always had to be." The disjuncture between what we know about Lucy's narrative trajectory and what Lucy thinks she knows about it – a form of dramatic irony possible only through choice-based storytelling – reveals something fundamental about the way narrative functions in everyday life. Because the choices we are presented with in life are so often limited and unsatisfying, and because decisions themselves are often out of our hands, we use narrative as a form of compensation: like Lucy, we tell ourselves stories of "it was meant to be" as a way of imposing a retrospective order and coherence onto what is largely the result of chance. As the critic Erich Auerbach writes,

> There is always going on within us a process of formulation and interpretation whose subject matter is our own self. We are constantly endeavoring to give meaning and order to our lives in the past, the present, and the future, to our surroundings, the world in which we live; with the result that our lives appear in our own conception as total entities – which to be sure are always changing, more or less radically, more or less rapidly, depending on the extent to which we are obliged, inclined, and able to assimilate the onrush of new experience.[39]

By stepping into Lucy's life at a moment of particularly intense change and watching as she weaves a narrative thread to encompass the twists and turns that we know are completely out of her hands – because they are mostly in ours – we not only receive a poignant demonstration of this function of narrative but also participate in acting it out.

This is not to say that *Lucy Hardin* could not have achieved similar effects in print; one can certainly imagine a printed CYOA version of the novel with identical lexia and options. Yet Marche makes subtle uses of digital-specific affordances to emphasize his theme. In a printed edition, we might still notice Lucy's mistaken perception that she had "known" she would call her mother; but we notice this far more readily when it appears instantly, as soon as we have made our choice, rather than after we have gone searching for the proper page. Further, we take our choices more seriously when we know we cannot go back; we pause longer over the ethically loaded question of whose interests are served by a particular choice. The most effective digital affordance in *Lucy Hardin* comes in the form of its disappearing choices. In Marche's text, choices appear in green text at the end of paragraphs (Figure 7.1a). Once we have made our selection, however, the green choices dissolve, giving the illusion of an unbroken narrative and erasing all evidence of the points where Lucy's story might have branched out differently (Figure 7.1b). This digital feature, unachievable in print, captures beautifully the process of retrospective reformulation at work in Lucy's own mind. Through the use of such a simple and restrained device, Marche shows the promise of second-wave hypertext: not to revolutionize storytelling, but to use digital affordances to tell good stories better.

How to Talk to Machines: Interactive Fiction and Emily Short's *Galatea*

Twenty-first-century hypertexts such as *Lucy Hardin* are refreshingly honest: they turn down the volume on hypertext hype, they acknowledge the occasionally "manipulative" nature of hypertextual interactivity, and they use the genre's limitations productively in telling their stories. Yet, in their very humility, they can sometimes leave us wanting more. The unrealized vision of born-digital literature theorized in the 1990s continues to resonate; in theory, if not in practice, we are still drawn to the idea of a narrative able to develop in direct response to the desires and inputs of its reader. Indeed, the frustrations of hypertext help us imagine what such an ideal text might look like. Whereas hypertext offers us predetermined choices and often asks us to take them blindly, a genuinely interactive born-digital text would unfold with all the reciprocity of a good conversation, allowing us to say and do anything we choose, while still shaping our responses into a gripping story.

The genre of Interactive Fiction (IF) was the first textual form to approach this ideal. IF was invented in the mid-1970s by Will Crowther, a programmer at MIT whose working life was devoted to ARPANET, the foundation of the modern internet, and whose spare time was devoted to exploring caves. Uniting his vocation and avocation, Crowther developed a text-based computer game called *Adventure*, the aim of which was to gather treasures while navigating a labyrinthine network of caves. A few years after Crowther's first version, Don Woods, a programmer at Stanford, sought permission to tidy up the code and

A BLUE +. Lucy sat down on the toilet seat, reached for the back of the box. A blue + meant pregnancy. Stunned numbness and angry panic circled each other with bouts of clenching, and she sat on the toilet fingering the test strip like a ticket. To where?

Never having dealt with a pregnancy before, she was already screwing it up, ordinary thoughts intruding on what was obviously a crisis. The craftsmanship of the turquoise tiles in the bathroom was impeccable, no breaks on the edging or shaved pieces. Lucy craved a cigarette, raisiny and relieving, and then deeply craved red wine, osso bucco with roasted garlic spread on unsalted bread. The test could be wrong. She would do more tests. The test wouldn't be wrong.

Dampered knowledge blazed forth: Daniel, four, five weeks ago, fiddling with the condom, running the tap in the bathroom, returning nervously, but he had said, he had specifically said, that everything was all right.

CALL HER SISTER ● ● ● CALL HER MOTHER

(a)

A BLUE +. Lucy sat down on the toilet seat, reached for the back of the box. A blue + meant pregnancy. Stunned numbness and angry panic circled each other with bouts of clenching, and she sat on the toilet fingering the test strip like a ticket. To where?

Never having dealt with a pregnancy before, she was already screwing it up, ordinary thoughts intruding on what was obviously a crisis. The craftsmanship of the turquoise tiles in the bathroom was impeccable, no breaks on the edging or shaved pieces. Lucy craved a cigarette, raisiny and relieving, and then deeply craved red wine, osso bucco with roasted garlic spread on unsalted bread. The test could be wrong. She would do more tests. The test wouldn't be wrong.

Dampered knowledge blazed forth: Daniel, four, five weeks ago, fiddling with the condom, running the tap in the bathroom, returning nervously, but he had said, he had specifically said, that everything was all right.

STUMBLING TO THE PHONE beside the bed, Lucy knew that her sister was the woman to talk to. With five kids and at least one abortion, fertility had always been Judith's illness.

The line picked up halfway through the third ring — a squeal, the high whine of Lucy's nine-year old niece Julianna, and the barked authority of the twelve-year-old Margaret. A muted thud meant the receiver dropped on the carpet, a rustling like wrapping paper meant its retrieval.

(b)

Figures 7.1a–b *Disappearing choices in Stephen Marche's* Lucy Hardin's Missing Period.

expand the network of caves. The 1977 Woods-Crowther release of *Adventure* proved immensely popular in the small computing community of the time – so popular that it is said to have effectively stalled all computing work in the United States in the two weeks after it was released. *Adventure* also established ground rules for a new narrative form that, in the 1980s, became the most commercially successful genre of computer games, with titles such as *Zork* and the IF adaptation of *The Hitchhiker's Guide to the Galaxy* selling millions of copies. In IF, the player controls the actions of the "player character," an avatar for the player who exists within the fictional world, by entering textual commands ("go north," "pick up gold," "ask about the artist") that are in turn interpreted by a computer "parser." If the parser understands the command, the player is moved through the world and rewarded with lexia that further describe the world and suggest subsequent actions. The parser is the feature that most clearly distinguishes IF from hypertext: at a hypertextual decision node, the computer is merely asked to produce the lexia corresponding to the reader's choice; yet in IF the computer has a more active role, because the parser must *interpret* the player's command before it can produce any output.

Though the commercial apogee of IF has long passed, a small but dedicated community of writers continues to pursue the form. Emily Short's *Galatea* (2000–2004)[40] is among the most remarkable of its products. Through its title, *Galatea* announces a complex chain of associations that connects it both to literary history and to the history of computing. The primary reference of the title is to Greek myth, Galatea being the name most often associated with Pygmalion's statue, so perfectly sculpted that it came to life. In *Pygmalion* (1909), George Bernard Shaw's dramatic adaptation of the myth, the Galatea figure is renamed Eliza Doolittle, a young Cockney girl whose uncouth speech is so thoroughly transformed by the phoneticist Henry Higgins that he falls in love, Pygmalion-style, with his own creation. Shaw's renaming of Galatea provides the link to Emily Short's other major reference: Joseph Weizenbaum's pioneering work of artificial intelligence (AI), ELIZA. Working at MIT in the mid-1960s, Weizenbaum developed a computer program that could convincingly replicate the naïve conversational style of a Rogerian psychotherapist. If one typed in a simple sentence such as "I'm depressed," ELIZA would respond in a manner implying both understanding and empathy: "I am sorry to hear you are depressed." When Weizenbaum released versions of the program in 1966, ELIZA came to resemble the Galatea of the Pygmalion myth in ways he had not anticipated. Though the program was quite crude, mostly regurgitating inputted text in the form of a question, those who used ELIZA routinely mistook it for a living thing – a sculpture come to life. Weizenbaum's own secretary asked him to leave the room when she was interacting with ELIZA, given the intimacy of their conversations, and professional psychiatrists began recommending its use as an inexpensive means of bringing therapy to the masses. Though this reaction stunned Weizenbaum, ELIZA seemed for many of its users to pass the famous test that Alan Turing proposed for artificial intelligence: engaging with ELIZA in a typed conversation, many were unable to tell whether they were interacting with a human or a machine – proof enough, as Turing hypothesized in 1950, that the machine should be considered intelligent.[41]

Short's *Galatea* presents itself as an extension of the Galatea myth as filtered through Shaw and Weizenbaum. Its action unfolds in a single room in an art gallery, where our player character, a near-future art critic, has been dispatched to analyze Galatea, the latest in "animate" robotic statuary. In his capacity as a critic of AI art, the player character's goal is to perform an extended Turing Test – to draw Galatea out in conversation in such a way that she shows her robotic seams. If the critic takes too long to address Galatea at the beginning of the game, Galatea protests, "You might try speaking to me. . . . It's not polite merely to stare. And I've gotten very bored, standing here." The critic's detached response to Galatea's words (he silently classes them as "An attempt to engage the audience") shows that he approaches her not as an equal in conversation, but as an AI specimen to be probed, critiqued, and evaluated. In some instances, the critic is impressed by Galatea's performances. After he removes his hand from her shoulder following a tactile inspection, she shivers in response. "Animates don't do that," he thinks. "There's a conventional limit to their interactivity. They're meant to be touched – but not to react." In other instances, however, the critic is disappointed. When he presses Galatea for details on the process of her carving, she has very little to offer. When she tells the critic, "You've heard what I know," he responds, "No piece is going to get a serious critical reception with such a pathetic database"; as he tells her elsewhere, "I wouldn't say you exactly pass the Turing Test."

The narrative situation of *Galatea* closely mirrors our own situation. On the one hand, we approach the text as readers, eager to uncover Galatea's story. On the other hand, because we must navigate *Galatea*'s clunky parser to access this story, we also find ourselves in the position of the critic, standing back to observe the all-too-apparent limits of the text's interactivity. Indeed, if the character Galatea appears at times to be passing the critic's Turing Test, *Galatea* the work of IF never comes close to passing our own version of that test. Certain aspects of *Galatea*'s interactivity are impressively realistic. For instance, Galatea reacts differently to identical inputs depending on her mood: she will only agree to look into your eyes if you have first listened to her story, and she will only kiss you if you have shown her sufficient sympathy. Yet the immensely awkward interface through which we must interact with *Galatea* precludes any genuine immersion in the story. Because the parser understands so few commands, we spend much of our time struggling to find the magic words that will unlock the narrative. The following exchange, recorded in one of my own logs, is frustratingly typical:

```
>ask about her
(Galatea)
"Read the placard," she says. "That's what it's
there for, after all."
>read placard
Large cream letters on a black ground.
47. Galatea White Thasos mar-
ble. Non-commissioned work by the
late Pygmalion of Cyprus. (The artist has since
committed suicide.) Originally not an
animate. The waking of this piece from
its natural state remains unexplained.
>ask about waking
Which do you mean, which god woke her or the
experience of waking?
>ask about experience of waking
You can't form your question into words.
>experience
That's not a verb I recognize.
>ask about waking experience
"What was it like, waking up?"  you ask.
```

By this point in the game, I was sufficiently familiar with the interface to know that I would need to ask about something in the previous lexia to produce an interesting response. Yet just as I became interested in the dawn of Galatea's consciousness – her "awakening" – I was woken from the spell of narrative by a frustrating sequence of simple commands that the parser failed to understand.

As in *Lucy Hardin*, the feeling of playing *Galatea* is more often one of constraint than of freedom. One cannot type anything one wishes in an interactive fiction like *Galatea*. If one were to type, "Hey, Galatea, let's get out of here and grab a pizza" or "Look! Aliens! Run!" the parser would blandly respond, "You can't form your questions into words" or "That's not a verb I recognize." When the reader inevitably becomes frustrated in *Galatea* and types "help," the brief set of commands that *Galatea*'s parser is able to understand is revealed, and the player is directed to a URL with a series of walkthrough "cheats" – step-by-step recipes for producing interesting narratives. On the cheats page, Short writes,

> I've said it over and over: I don't want people playing to particular endings. I want them to play the game and get whatever result comes naturally, because that is what the game is built for. It's a dispenser of stories, customized to the individual who is playing at the moment.
>
> That's my vision as the author.
>
> Players, however, seem to have a different idea: a lot of them want to see *all* the text, or at least all the endings. And I have to admit that, while I hate to provide helps to that end (as the author), I can also see their point (as a player of other games). *Galatea* is horribly Protean; her moods change and you don't always know exactly why; she responds differently to the same question at different times, and this makes it difficult to recover endings that one has already reached once. From my point of view as an author, these features were all desiderata, and I worked hard to produce them, in the name of realism and complexity and richness. From the point of view of the (re)player, they can get confusing after a while.[42]

It is Short's authorial goal to grant readers the freedom to create their own customized story. In my experience, however, very few players have the patience to exercise this freedom. The vast majority almost immediately end up on the cheats page and then derive whatever pleasure they take from *Galatea* by following the prompts of one of Short's walkthroughs. In practice, Short remains very much the master of *Galatea*, pulling the levers that control not only what Galatea says but also what we type into the command line. Indeed, Short acknowledges this in one of her proffered walkthroughs, "Wizard of Oz." This particular sequence ends with the critic pulling down the velvet curtain that lies behind Galatea, revealing a "rather short" woman – "a little on the dumpy side, and dressed in a ripped pair of blue jeans" – who has been controlling Galatea's performance all along. "Sorry to disappoint," this woman tells the critic: "It was an experiment that – well, it seemed like a good idea at the time." The critic, taken aback, tells the woman, "You could start by telling me your *real* name." We, of course, already know her name – because, if we have made it to the end of her walkthrough script, she has been controlling our performance as well.

Short's frustration with her indolent readership is both understandable and justified, because the text's most powerful effects emerge only when we accept the limitations of its maladroit parser and struggle against them. Only by rejecting the easy refuge of the "help" command – only by repeatedly reformulating our textual commands until the parser finally understands them – do we gain access to the final and most fascinating symmetry between form and content in *Galatea*. To succeed in his task of analyzing and interacting with Galatea, the critic must accept the rapidly shifting landscape of her moods and learn to navigate it. Likewise, to succeed as players in *Galatea*, we must accept the limitations of another impetuous machine, *Galatea*'s parser, and then learn how to express our individual human wishes – the things we want to say to Galatea and to learn from her – in a machine language that this parser can understand. In this symmetry lies *Galatea*'s signature effect: its most ingenious use of the digital medium, and its most compelling comment on life in the digital age. As critics such as Sherry Turkle and Katherine Hayles have argued, human language and human interaction are today becoming increasingly reliant on machine language and human-machine interaction. In *Alone Together* (2011), Turkle describes a dangerous tendency to seek shelter from the risks and disappointments of human relationships in the clumsy but comparatively safe company of artificial intelligence. Turkle, a colleague of Joseph Weizenbaum at MIT in the 1970s, draws one of her most pertinent examples from ELIZA. She recalls that when graduate students interacted with ELIZA, a few would "[learn] enough about the program to trip it up," yet many more would "[use] this same inside knowledge to feed ELIZA responses that would make it seem more lifelike."[43] These students "knew all about ELIZA's limitations, but they were eager to 'fill in the blanks'"; they knew that ELIZA failed the Turing Test, but for some reason, they wanted it to *seem* as if ELIZA could pass it. Turkle calls this phenomenon "the ELIZA effect" and argues that this "human complicity in a digital fantasy" is becoming increasingly widespread in the digital age, because we are increasingly emotionally dependent on interactions with machines.[44] Katherine Hayles, however, argues that Turkle's "ELIZA effect" is inevitable in a period when nearly all human communication, from e-mail and text messages to phone calls and snail mail, is mediated through some form of digital code.[45] As Hayles suggests, we have simply reached a point at which we can no longer express our humanity without the help of machine language. It is this paradoxical situation, finally, that *Galatea* dramatizes. Emily Short's work does not merely *describe* this increasing intermingling of human and machine language, but asks its readers to *act it out*. The words of Hayles and Turkle will resonate most strongly with a player who has persevered through *Galatea*'s many frustrations and learned its central lesson: that to please a machine, you must learn to think like a machine, and to learn a computer's story, you must learn to speak its language.

Interactive digital texts such as *Lucy Hardin* and *Galatea* succeed artistically in a manner that defies the expectations of early enthusiasts of the genre. These texts achieve their effects not by granting their readers perfect freedom but by deliberately frustrating their ability to choose. Interactivity for Marche and Short is not a vehicle for empowerment, but a way of asking readers to act out intractable problems: to have them navigate the ethical terrain of a particularly difficult day in someone else's life or to throw them into the communicative difficulties of a world where human and machine intelligence have become increasingly interwoven. The most fascinating interactive fiction being written today does not do what Bolter or Landow predicted it would. Instead, it does what literature has always done: it finds new ways to bring readers more directly in contact with what it means to be alive in their place and time.

Chapter 8

Literature in the Digital Master Medium

It took many decades for the computer to develop into an expressive medium. The first computers were entirely unfit to serve as carriers of artistic expression: the only inputs they could understand were numerical, and the only operations they could perform were mathematical. With the development of standards like ASCII, text was the first expressive modality to go digital. In short order, textual artistic forms such as Interactive Fiction and hypertext emerged and took advantage of the unique expressive properties of the digital medium. It took much longer to devise means of representing the expressive modalities of music, images, and moving pictures. When such methods were finally perfected and popularized, from the 1990s onward, the computer became something more than merely another expressive medium. It became a master medium.

In 1985, Friedrich Kittler prophesied a time when "for the first time in history or for the end of history," "people will be connected to a communication channel which can be used for any kind of media."[1] "When films, music, phone calls, and texts are able to reach the individual household via fiber optic cables," he wrote, "the previously separate media of television, radio, telephone, and mail will become a single medium."[2] Kittler did not have to wait long for such a medium to come into being: the World Wide Web, developed in the early 1990s and still rapidly expanding, was exactly the communication channel he imagined. Capitalizing on developments in audio, image, and video compression, the development of graphical web browsers, and the increasing bandwidth of high-speed and dial-up connections, the Web was the first widely accessible carrier of the digital master medium. In *The Language of New Media* (2001), Lev Manovich wrote, "Today we are witnessing the emergence of a new medium – the meta-medium of the digital computer": "graphics, moving images, sounds, shapes, spaces, and texts have become computable; that is, they comprise simply another set of computer data."[3]

As the computer has transitioned from a device capable of transmitting only numbers and text to one able to carry multiple modalities, it has increasingly brought into question the notion of "literariness." In *Electronic Literature:*

New Horizons for the Literary (2008), Katherine Hayles divides the history of born-digital fiction into two "generations." First-generation works, beginning with Interactive Fiction in the 1970s, tended to be composed of blocks of text, with limited graphics, animations, colors, and sound. In contrast, the second-generation works that began to appear around 1995 took full advantage of the multimodal possibilities of the Web. If the hypertext link was the defining feature of first-generation born-digital texts, Hayles argues, then second-generation works, with their "wide variety of navigation schemes and interface metaphors," are defined only by their lack of a defining feature.[4] As co-editor of the first volume of the *Electronic Literature Collection* (2006)[5] – the first major anthology of born-digital fiction – Hayles was confronted with the greatest definitional dilemma posed by second-generation born-digital works: their often tenuous relationship to that most fundamental of literary modalities, text. "Created and performed within a context of networked and programmable media," Hayles writes, such second-generation texts were informed not only by literature but also by "computer games, films, animations, digital arts, graphic design, and electronic visual culture."[6] Although Hayles included a number of text-based works, such as Short's *Galatea*, in the collection, nearly all works incorporated some visual effects, most included sound, and a third of them had no words at all.[7] By calling such works "electronic *literature*," Hayles and her fellow editors sought to challenge that word's text-centric definition. Rather than limiting ourselves to "literature" – works made up primarily of text – Hayles proposes a shift in focus to the concept of "the literary," a broad category that includes "creative artworks that interrogate the histories, contexts, and productions of literature," and not only those that practice "the verbal art of literature proper."[8]

This chapter takes up Hayles's challenge. How are multimodal forms forcing us to reevaluate literature and the literary? What happens to the traditional literary modality, text, when it is incorporated into one of Hayles's second-generation born-digital texts? Is it really possible to integrate a form like literature – a form that usually requires slow, careful, close reading – into a noisy, colorful, flickering space combining music and moving images, or do such environments overwhelm the literary experience? If we accept McLuhan's basic premise that the medium affects the user more profoundly than the message it carries, how might multimodal literary forms reshape the consciousnesses of their readers? We begin by looking at two born-digital texts that insert themselves determinedly into the literary tradition: *Inanimate Alice* by Kate Pullinger and Chris Joseph, and *Dakota* by Young-Hae Chang Heavy Industries. Although clearly "literary" in Hayles's terms, both texts use the resources of electronic literature to question the very possibility of electronic literature. These works' manifest discomfort with their own forms opens the way for the second part of the chapter, which asks whether we should look elsewhere for the survival of the literary impulse in the digital age – to videogames, a form that bears little conscious relation to literature and thus falls outside Hayles's definition of the "literary." Are *videogames* literature? Simply to pose the question is to feel how fundamentally the digital age is forcing us to reconsider our notions of literature and the literary.

Harmony among the Art Forms: the Prehistory of Digital Multimodality

As with so many topics encountered in this book, the multimodality of artistic expression is not so novel as it may at first appear. Hayles's second-generation electronic texts were by no means the first to pursue the status of a "meta-medium" – to seek to combine in a single form "graphics, moving images, sounds, shapes, spaces, and texts." Indeed, that honor belongs to the opera, a 500-year-old medium that envisioned itself as the re-creation of an artistic form much older still. Opera's multimodal ambitions are reflected in its name, *opera* being the plural of *opus*, a work of art. The *OED*'s earliest recorded usage of the word to designate an artistic form, in 1639, describes it as "a composition in which poetry, dance, and music are combined." In practice, the combinations were greater still; as the form spread throughout Europe in the seventeenth and eighteenth centuries, it came to encompass not only literature, drama, music, and dance but also, through set design, painting and sculpture. Yet the Renaissance opera strived not to *unify* so much as to *reunify* the arts, because its deliberate aim was to re-create the integrated form of the Greek tragedy from the scattered fragments of modern Western art.

Although the opera initially cast its gaze backward toward ancient Greece, its most ambitious practitioners sought to use the opera's multimodal form to craft a new form of art that would in turn remake the world. The most determined to do so was Richard Wagner, the German composer who, along with Giuseppe Verdi, dominated opera's nineteenth-century golden age. In his pamphlet *Art and Revolution* (1849), Wagner follows his operatic predecessors in seeing the form as a means of revitalizing Western art through a return to ancient precedents. After the fall of Greek tragedy, he argues, "the Drama separated into its component parts; rhetoric, sculpture, painting, music, &c. forsook the ranks in which they had moved in unison before; each one to take its own way, and in lonely self-sufficiency to pursue its own development."[9] Though endorsing the aims of the first operatic composers, Wagner dismisses their actual achievements: the first two hundred years of opera, he says, produced only "a foolish restoration of a sham Greek mode of art."[10] Rather than a genuine unification of the arts, it was "an inane patchwork,"[11] a "chaos of sensuous impressions jostling one another without rhyme or reason."[12] For Wagner, the Renaissance opera failed to grasp that Greek tragedy was more than a mechanical unification of the arts; it was also, in its place and time, a vehicle for unifying the public consciousness. In another pamphlet of 1849, *The Art-Work of the Future,* Wagner sees the potential for a perfected form of opera that would, through its balanced integration of the separate arts, serve as a model for a perfected polis. In such a form, he argues, "the separate artist, like each several art, must quell each selfish, arbitrary bent";[13] by presenting a work in which "each separate branch of the arts" participates in "reciprocal agreement and co-operation" to deliver a "common message," Wagnerian opera would serve as a formal symbol of the subordination of individual wills toward a common purpose.[14] In *Art and Revolution,* Wagner says that such a "united utterance of a free and lovely public" would stand as a "perfect Art-work."[15]

Friedrich Nietzsche's first book, *The Birth of Tragedy* (1872), is propelled by a manic enthusiasm for Wagner and Wagnerian opera. For Nietzsche, there was no question that Wagner had finally fused the arts. The consequences, he believed, would be world-historical. *The Birth of Tragedy* begins with a reinterpretation of Greek tragedy. For Nietzsche, the genius of the form rested on its perfect balance of two basic psychological impulses: the Apollinian and the Dionysian. Apollinian artworks, Nietzsche argues, are beautiful, ordered, and well proportioned: appealing to the audience's desire for clarity and intelligibility, they impart a keen sense of individuality by drawing sharp lines between represented people and objects. Dionysian art, by contrast, inspires feelings of drunken rapture, transport, and awe; under its sway, Nietzsche writes, the spectator "feels himself not only reconciled, and fused with his neighbor, but as one with him."[16] The singular achievement of Greek tragedy was to balance these warring psychological impulses – and this feat was possible only because of its multimodal form, in which music provided the Dionysian rapture and poetry the counterbalancing Apollinian clarity. According to Nietzsche, the downfall of the Greek tragedy came about through the triumph of what he calls "aesthetic Socratism": the notion that "to be beautiful, everything must be intelligible."[17] After Socrates, Apollo predominates over Dionysus in Western cultural history, which becomes increasingly preoccupied with "the desire for knowledge and the optimism of science."[18] Like Wagner, Nietzsche dismisses the Renaissance opera's attempts to re-create Greek tragedy: rather than balancing the two forces, he argues, its "rapidly changing endeavor to affect now the concepts and imagination of the hearer, now his musical sense" was "intrinsically contradictory both to the Apollinian and Dionysian artistic impulses."[19] In the Wagnerian opera, in contrast, Nietzsche perceives a genuine *"rebirth of tragedy"*[20] – a true reversal of the long dominance of "aesthetic Socratism" and a genuine *"awakening of the Dionysian spirit* in our modern world!"[21] Wagner's achievement is not merely aesthetic but also political for Nietzsche: by uniting the two great streams of Western art and the two great human psychic impulses, Wagner promised the dawn of a new political era. More specifically, Nietzsche says – or rather, desperately *hopes*– that Wagnerian opera heralds the triumph of the German nation. In works such as *Tristan und Isolde*, "Dionysus speaks the language of Apollo; and Apollo, finally the language of Dionysus; and so the highest goal of tragedy and of all art is attained."[22] Through such works, Nietzsche argues, lies the "renovation and purification of the German spirit."[23]

Beneath Nietzsche's dangerously overblown rhetoric lies an account of the social significance of multimodal art that remains relevant today. Nietzsche's theory of the interaction of the Apollinian and the Dionysian remains relevant because it maps so neatly onto the McLuhanian analysis of print and electronic media. In McLuhan's account, the psychic effects of print are recognizably Apollinian, fostering and privileging linearity, rationality, and individuality. The electronic media, by contrast, are decidedly Dionysian, encouraging participation and breaking down the barriers separating individuals. Few digital multimodal artists have been drawn to the grand historical arguments of Nietzsche and Wagner – the notion that new combinations of artistic media might usher in a new era of world history. Yet many more have been attracted to the notion that multimedia art holds the promise of balancing the Apollinian effects of print – its linearity and its focus on the concentrated individual reader – with the Dionysian character of modalities such as music and moving pictures. Though they may not expect empires to fall or be founded, the social change that such artists seek through cognitive reorientation is nonetheless real.

Self-Reflexive Leitmotifs in *Inanimate Alice*

Among the most self-conscious recent attempts to employ the multimodality of the digital medium as a vehicle for literary expression is the *Inanimate Alice* series by Kate Pullinger and Chris Joseph. Launched in 2005, when it was envisioned as a ten-episode story arc, *Inanimate Alice* unfolds as a born-digital *Bildungsroman*, recounting the maturation of Alice through her itinerant childhood. At the heart of the project is the collaboration between Pullinger – who, as a print novelist, received Canada's 2009 Governor General's Award for fiction – and Chris Joseph, an animator and multimedia artist. Pullinger has argued that storytelling comes first in their collaborative process; as she put it in a 2006 interview, "It's all about good stories, well-told, whatever the medium."[24] Yet a central goal of her collaboration with Joseph is to use the unique capacities of the digital medium to craft new kinds of narratives – to "us[e] the computer to tell stories in new ways."[25] Their work is motivated by their frustration with the popular e-book formats that function merely as "electronic replicas of books" – "paper under glass."[26] "If you are going to put a work of fiction on a computer," Pullinger asks, "why would you not use the multimedia components a computer has to offer you – image and sound and interactive games?"[27] *Inanimate Alice* responds by using them all. Asked which art forms *Inanimate Alice* employs, Chris Joseph lists "linear and non-linear fiction; generative and static art; electronic music; games; and some mashups of these that are still in search of suitable descriptions."[28] Yet embracing so many forms while still envisioning themselves primarily as storytellers has placed Pullinger and Joseph in an uncomfortable generic space. On the *Inanimate Alice* "About" page, labels proliferate: the authors call their work "born-digital," "interactive," "multimedia," and a "digital novel."[29] When *The Guardian* published "Episode 3: Russia" on its website in 2006, Pullinger wrote a post for its Books Blog titled "Fact is we need a better name for 'digital fiction.'" "It's tricky working in a genre that has no name," she wrote: "What would you call it?" she asks the *Guardian*'s readers. "Is it a kind of all-singing, all-dancing book? Is it a game? Is it a movie with text?"[30]

Reading (or "playing" or "viewing") *Inanimate Alice*, the reader (or "player" or "viewer" or "user") experiences for herself the discomfort of existing in the undefined spaces between art forms. "Episode 1: China"[31] is unsettling on several levels. The story is dark: Alice, eight years old and living in a remote oil station in northern China, discovers that her father is missing; she and her mother head out in a Jeep to search for him. The episode's multimodal form adds to the discomfort for a reader accustomed to print. Though the narrative is driven by first-person text in Alice's voice, it requires action from the reader to advance it: clicking on arrows, completing a simple game, and navigating the smartphone-like "Zeron" device on which Alice plays a game called ba-xi, records her diary, and has created a skateboarding cartoon figure she calls Brad. Although these user actions can have the effect of disrupting the flow of the narrative – one becomes, at times, more interested in clicking through and completing tasks than in reading Alice's thoughts – the more serious challenge comes in the form of the digital animations and electronic music that accompany the text. Experiencing *Inanimate Alice* for the first time, I was reminded of Wagner's assessment of the early opera as a "chaos of sensuous impressions jostling one another without rhyme or reason."[32] The combined effect of the individual modalities was grating, as each distracted from the other rather than complementing it. The interactive games and the clicking interface kept me from lingering on the words, whereas the busy animations and cacophonous electronic music removed all possibility of entering a state of aesthetic contemplation. The total work was less than the sum of its parts.

Although the multimodal experience of "Episode 1" is occasionally unpleasant, this unpleasantness is nevertheless brilliantly acknowledged in *Inanimate Alice* through its "electrosmog" leitmotif. The backstory of *Inanimate Alice*'s engagement with "electrosmog" is peculiar. As Edward Picot has uncovered, *Inanimate Alice* was originally commissioned as a promotional vehicle for a device called the Electrosmog Detector, marketed by a company named Sensory Perspective.[33] In the artistic statement accompanying "Episode 1" in the first volume of the *Electronic Literature Collection*, Pullinger and Joseph state that the work was "created to help draw attention to the issue of electro-sensitivity and the potentially harmful pollution resulting from wireless communications."[34] "Episode 1" incorporates "electrosmog" as an aural motif that echoes throughout the work: the grating, buzzing, popping, static-filled sound many of us have heard after placing our mobile phones too close to an older, unshielded audio device, such as a radio or stereo system. The sound serves a double purpose in *Inanimate Alice*. On the one hand, perhaps in fulfillment of the authors' arrangement with Sensory Perspective, it brings attention to health concerns, though always obliquely, as when the sound fills the reader's ears as Alice writes, "The sky hums up here, I don't know why, as though it's electronic." More significantly, however, the electrosmog sound provides a self-reflexive symbol of the clash between old and new media. As one of the most grating and distracting multimodal effects in the work, the sound of electrosmog calls attention to its own obnoxiousness in order to turn the question back on the reader. Is the multimodal form of *Inanimate Alice* distracting or disorienting because of the work's inherent artistic failures, the motif implicitly asks – or is the problem rather that we come to the text with a set of anachronistic expectations derived from reading fiction in print? If electrosmog is the sound of a new medium clashing with an antiquated device, perhaps it is *us* – we readers who are not yet attuned to an emerging form – who are the antiquated device in question.

The inclusion of interactive game play in *Inanimate Alice* presents a similar challenge to readers accustomed to print. The type of interactivity in *Inanimate*

Alice is markedly different from that in either hypertext or Interactive Fiction (see Ch. 7). Rather than offering choices in a branching narrative or requiring user input to advance the narrative, each episode in *Inanimate Alice* tells an entirely linear narrative bereft of any choices: users simply click an arrow to advance to the next "lexia," an action akin to turning the page in a printed book. Occasionally, however, we are required to complete a game to reach the next segment of text – as, for example, when we must photograph flowers with Alice's Zeron player in "Episode 1." Kate Pullinger has defended such games as a means of immersing her readers in the narrative. "As a reader, I'm not interested in choice," Pullinger said in a 2006 interview: "I'm not interested in having to make decisions as I'm being told a story." "The kind of gameplay in *Inanimate Alice*," she explained, "is the kind of interactivity I'm interested in as it's part of the story, not a diversion from the story."[35] These ambitions are largely fulfilled in "Episode 1": although the photography game is quite primitive, it succeeds in placing us in Alice's perspective by having us capture the natural world with the Zeron device that mediates so much of her experience.

The gameplay in "Episode 3: Russia,"[36] by contrast, goes entirely against Pullinger's characterization: it feels gratuitously tacked on to the story rather than meaningfully integrated into it. The narrative of "Russia" is even more menacing than that of "China." Alice, now living in Moscow, hides in a closet as her father is berated by thugs and then joins her parents' hasty flight from the country. As this narrative progresses, the reader plays a clumsy game called Matryoshka: in every chapter of the story, we are asked to locate a hidden matryoshka (a Russian nesting doll) that, once discovered and clicked on, falls from the top of the screen at increasing speed, to be captured by moving a small iconic representation of Brad, the skateboarding character from "Episode 1." The image of the matryoshka dolls is again self-reflexive: here, one hopes, is gameplay perfectly nested inside an already deeply nested array of text, images, animations, and music. The actual gameplay falls well short of the promise of this harmonious image, however. To play the game well, we must devote most of our resources to looking for the obscured dolls, which makes it very difficult to pay attention to the story or the text. In direct contradiction to one of Pullinger's stated ambitions, gameplay detracts – "diverts" – from the supposedly preeminent story. The self-reflexivity of "Russia" goes further, however. In the narrative context of the story, the Matryoshka game is the creation not of Pullinger and Joseph – but of Alice herself. Looking at a screen on Alice's Zeron player, we are told early on, "I'm playing a game I made up – Matryoshka. I need to collect all the dolls in order to finish the game." The same logic is repeated for the reader in "Russia": to pass through a security checkpoint at the airport and escape the country, Alice must show a guard that she has collected all the dolls, and if she fails to do so, we must return to earlier points in the story and collect the missing dolls. Recognizing that Alice is the author of Matryoshka unlocks the governing conceit of the *Inanimate Alice* series, in which each episode is presented as an autobiography – a multimodal narrative in which Alice is the author of both form and content. Borrowing a stylistic device from James Joyce's *A Portrait of the Artist of a Young Man*, the increasing complexity of each episode is intended to reflect Alice's increasing skills as a game designer. *Inanimate Alice* is not just a digital-age *Bildungsroman*, then, but also a born-digital *Künstlerroman*: not merely a novel of development, but the story of Alice's maturation as an artist, the stages of which are immediately visible to the reader as the episodes progress.

As a self-reflexive device, the authors' Joyce-derived conceit has the effect of justifying the artistic shortcomings of *Inanimate Alice*, reminding readers that the form in which it is being produced is still in its infancy. If the Matryoshka game is primitive and distracting, that is only because Alice is still young and has not had the chance to develop fully as an artist. It is telling, however, that although ten episodes were originally envisioned for the series, only five have been released; Pullinger and Joseph released four episodes in the project's first three years, and then paused for seven years before releasing the fifth. Pullinger and Joseph's skills perhaps have simply not been able to keep up with those projected for their character Alice. If they envisaged the tenth episode as a decisive demonstration of the power of multimodal digital storytelling, it seems unlikely they will be able to deliver it. To date, their skills have only hinted at the medium's potential. Still, we must recall that some two hundred years passed between the dawn of the opera and Wagner's *Tristan und Isolde*. By this logic, we may have to wait until the twenty-third century for the perfection of the form.

A Dictatorial Stranglehold: Young-Hae Chang Heavy Industries' *Dakota*

Inanimate Alive strives to create a new literary form by surrounding a text-centered narrative with all the modalities of which the digital medium is capable. It goes out of its way, however, to present itself as a form in its awkward adolescence and to suggest that an audience of literary readers may not yet possess the interpretive machinery to engage fully with or even enjoy it. Balancing a commitment to formal innovation against the concern that treading new ground will alienate readers, Pullinger and Joseph are reminiscent of modernists such as Virginia Woolf who, in a 1924 essay on Joyce and Eliot, argued, "We must reconcile ourselves to a season of failures and fragments. We must reflect that where so much strength is spent on finding a way of telling the truth, the truth itself is bound to reach us in rather an exhausted and chaotic condition."[37] By contrast, Young-Hae Chang Heavy Industries *Dakota* – another prominent and much-discussed example of multimodal born-digital literature – invokes modernist literature to express an almost opposite intention. Their aim is not to excuse the "exhausted" or "chaotic" condition of the form, but to explode the very notion of multimodal born-digital literature.

Young-Hae Chang Heavy Industries (YHCHI) – a Seoul-based collaboration between Young-Hae Chang and Marc Voge founded in 1999 – works in the genre generally called "Flash poetry": text heavy, music driven, temporally sequenced, and designed in Adobe (formerly Macromedia) Flash for viewing in a web browser. YHCHI's work has been widely published and exhibited in a range of venues that collectively attest to its permeation of the boundaries separating artistic forms: the Tate Modern, the Pompidou Center, the Whitney, *The Iowa Review Web*, and *Poemsthatgo.com*. YHCHI's *Dakota* (2002)[38] is formally representative of their multimodal oeuvre. It begins with a blank screen and the opening notes of "Tobi Ilu," a rhythmic instrumental track from jazz drummer Art Blakey's album *The African Beat* (1962). As the screen fades through shades of gray from black to white, Blakey's beat begins to kick in as we see a countdown sequence reminiscent of the early cinema. After this sequence is complete, text begins to flash by at a fixed and steady pace, in a huge, black, all-caps Monaco typeface. The first word of the poem proper, gyrating alone on the screen in all its manifest boldness, is "FUCKING." The narrative that unfolds is in two parts: first, we follow a group of friends on a drunken road trip through the Dakota Badlands; then, halfway through *Dakota*'s runtime, this storyline breaks down and we find ourselves in Seoul where *Dakota*'s authors present a series of local vignettes and metacritical reflections.

I must confess that when I first encountered it, I failed to recognize *Dakota*'s literary heritage and ambitions. I had begun a unit on born-digital fiction by asking students to bring to class any text fitting that description. One student suggested *Dakota*, and it proved extremely popular with the rest of the class, which was immediately drawn in by the music, the stylish and arresting presentation of text, and the energetically worded account of the trip in the Badlands. Though we all enjoyed it, neither the audience, the presenter, nor I recognized *Dakota*'s complex negotiation of literary history. As Jessica Pressman has shown,[39] *Dakota* is an intricately structured retelling of Ezra Pound's first and second *Cantos* – which in turn present an intricately structured retelling of Homer's *Odyssey*, a foundational text of the Western literary tradition. The parallels between the works are overwhelming once you begin to look for them. Book 11 of the *Odyssey* describes Odysseus's journey into the underworld; this katabasis, retold in Pound's first *Canto*, is reproduced in *Dakota* when the drunken narrator converses with one of his dead friends. The name of the dead friend in question, Elie, echoes the Elpenor of Homer and Pound, one of the fallen comrades Odysseus meets in Hades. Tiresias, addressed with the apostrophe "O King" in Pound's *Canto* I,[40] reappears in *Dakota* as Elvis Presley, the king of rock 'n' roll. Just as Pound begins *Canto* II, "Hang it all, Robert Browning, / there can be but one 'Sordello,'"[41] YHCHI begin the second section of their narrative, "GØDDAMMITT,/ ART BLAKEY, – NØ MIND/ HEARD – 'Ø' TINDE'/ ØR – 'DINGA/ DINGA' – BEFØRE/ YØURS DID." Just as Pound acknowledges that he is reading Homer not in the original Greek but in a Latin translation ("Lie quiet Divus. I mean, that is Andreas Divus, / In officina Wecheli, 1538, out of Homer"[42]) YHCHI more crudely point out that they are reading *The Cantos* in an anthology ("FUCK – YØU, – ELLMANN, – THAT'S RIGHT – RICHARD – ELLMANN – NØRTØN – NEW YØRK, – 1973, – ØN – PØUND").

In an interview, Young-Hae Chang has stated that *Dakota* "is based on a close reading of Ezra Pound's cantos part I and part II"[43] – and as Jessica Pressman has confirmed, *Dakota* is a text that "invit[es] and reward[s] close reading."[44] Yet there is something strange and contradictory about *Dakota*'s relationship to close reading, a hermeneutic approach that the text both demands and forbids. Paradoxically, *Dakota* requires a form of attention – careful, alert, deep, concentrated – that its fast-moving, hyperactive, rhythmic form precludes. The text in *Dakota* passes by so fast that, as Pressman notes, "it is often impossible to read, let alone close read."[45] Further, the text to which *Dakota* refers – Pound's *Cantos* – is one of the most famously difficult in the English tradition. As the name-checked Richard Ellmann remarks in his prefatory notes to *The Cantos* in the 1973 *Norton Anthology of Modern Poetry*, part of what makes Pound's poem so difficult is that it is not at all clear what sources he is subjecting to close reading: "The famous obscurity of the *Cantos*," he writes, "results partly from Pound's disjunctive arrangement of his materials, but partly from the obscurity of the materials themselves."[46] The concatenation of difficulty that lies beneath *Dakota*'s stylish and flamboyant exterior is truly dizzying.

Reading *Dakota*, one feels a bit like Alex undergoing the Ludovico Technique in *A Clockwork Orange*: head strapped in place, eyelids held open, images flashing by so quickly that they bypass the conscious mind completely. In *Dakota*, we are light years from the hypertext fantasy of a reader liberated by the interactivity of the digital medium. Asked in an interview with *Dichtung-Digital* why their work incorporates no interactive features, YHCHI provided two reasons: "Because we don't know how" (they claimed to have mastered only the most basic functionality of Flash) and, more intriguingly, because "we would like our work to exert a dictatorial stranglehold on the reader."[47] *Dakota* recognizes the passive, dominated position of its reader within its last frames. With text flashing by faster than ever before, the authors depict a scene of eating jajangmyeon, a fast-food noodle dish that is best "WØLFED – DØWN – WITH – YØUR – HEAD – TILTED – LEFT – IF – YØU'RE – A – RIGHTY." The connection between literary and alimentary consumption is clear: as Pressman writes, just as "the reader struggles to absorb the text being hurled at her," she is "figured as literally eating a foreign substance speedily without identifying the food she ingests."[48] In their *Dichtung-Digital* interview, YHCHI argue that "digital media invite less thoughtfulness than analog media"; in the midst of the "tsunami of digital information on the Web," they suggest, it is increasingly difficult to find a still place for concentrated artistic contemplation.[49] *Dakota* criticizes this unsettling situation by reproducing it in amplified form: by constructing a richly meaningful, deeply literary narrative, yet delivering it in a tsunami-like digital medium that makes its meaning almost impossible to access. *Dakota*, as such, is a perplexingly divided work: a demonstration not only of the immense literary potential of multimodal digital art but of how out of place the slow, complex, historically interconnected literary text is in the fast, high-intensity, ahistorical universe of ones and zeros – how vulnerable Apollinian clarity becomes when it is placed within the pulsing, flashing stream of the digital Dionysian.

Both *Inanimate Alice* and *Dakota* come to us from the literary community: they are the products of serious writers and poets working in collaboration with serious visual and musical artists to develop new forms of art that incorporate the literary into a multimodal mixture. Yet both provide us with reasons to look beyond the literary community for alternate models of multimodal fiction. If *Inanimate Alice* succeeds artistically, it is not as a demonstration of the power of born-digital storytelling, but as a brilliant apologia: a subtle evocation of all the reasons why audiences are not ready to engage with such work and writers are not equipped to produce them. The primary artistic message of *Dakota*, likewise, is the impossibility of its digital form: a brilliant demonstration of how a loud and fast-moving multimodal presentation serves effectively to bury a complex literary argument that requires stillness and concentration for its comprehension. These two prominent examples of born-digital literature present us with deliberate dead ends: self-conscious and sophisticated "Check back later" signs. While we bide our time, then, we would do well to look beyond the literary community to a multibillion-dollar industry that has been producing compelling, and wildly popular, multimodal born-digital narratives for several decades. It is time for us to ask an uncomfortable question: might videogames be the vessel in which the literary impulse will survive in the digital age?

Are Videogames Literature?

Can a Computer Make You Cry? Videogames as Art and Narrative

The June 1983 issue of *Creative Computing* magazine is in most ways an entirely typical document of the rabidly optimistic but relatively primitive computer scene of the early 1980s. The cover promises in-depth reviews of leading applications in the then-new field of word processing, and the accompanying illustration shows a small human figure tossing books, pencils, and bits of paper into a robotic brain. Among such bits of techno-nostalgia lies the most confident early assertion of the videogame's status as art form: an advertisement titled "Can a Computer Make You Cry?" It features a moody black-and-white photograph of seven men and one woman dressed in leather jackets and turtlenecks, posed like an arty post-punk band or a group of neo-beat poets. "Why do we cry," the advertisement asks:

> Why do we laugh, or love, or smile? What are the touchstones of our emotions?
>   Until now, the people who asked such questions tended not to be the same people who ran software companies. Instead, they were writers, filmmakers, painters, musicians. They were, in the traditional sense, artists.
>   We're about to change that tradition. The name of our company is Electronic Arts.[50]

The message of the advertisement was implicit in the new company's name: videogames were about to become a fully fledged art form. "The computer is more than just a processor of data," the ad read. "It is a communications medium: an interactive tool that can bring people's thoughts and feelings closer together." The advent of videogames had the potential to become more important than the arrival of cinema or television; videogames had the power, Electronic Arts claimed, to be "something along the lines of a universal language."

More than thirty years later, the videogames industry is more successful today than most would have predicted in 1983. At the time of this writing, videogames generate in excess of $80 billion worldwide yearly; in the

United States alone, the industry grosses $20 billion annually, more than double the domestic market for fiction. Yet videogames have failed to achieve the artistic recognition prophesied in the *Creative Computing* advertisement. James Newman attributes this lack of cultural recognition to a pair of widespread assumptions: first, that videogames are a children's medium, "easily and readily denigrated as trivial – something that will be 'grown out of' – and demanding no investigation"; and second, the sense that they are "mere trifles – low art – carrying none of the weight, gravitas, or credibility of more traditional media."[51] Since 1983, Electronic Arts has itself supplied some evidence to support these perceptions. Though it is today the third largest game company in the world, with annual revenues of nearly $5 billion, its best-selling titles – sports franchises such as *Madden NFL* and *NBA Live*; first-person shooters like *Battlefield* and *Medal of Honor* – bear little relation to the high-brow masterpieces prophesied in its founding advertisement. Rather than striving to create anything as grand as a universal language, Electronic Arts – which tellingly now calls itself "EA," as if to mask its arty roots – exists today to entertain and to make money.

If the question "Are videogames art?" remains very much unresolved, the question "Are videogames literature?" is more vexed still. It was easier to perceive the literary inheritance of early videogames like *Adventure*, which were at least entirely text based; the connection is much less apparent in the multimodal blockbusters produced by today's videogame industry, in which text takes a back seat to visual design, animation, music, recorded dialogue, and sound effects. The most frequently asserted connection between videogames and literature is their shared status as narrative forms – yet this, too, has proven controversial. Citing storyless games such as *Tetris*, critic Jane McGonigal leaves narrative out of her definition of videogames in *Reality is Broken* (2011): "A compelling story makes a game more enticing," she argues, but is not necessary.[52] Setting aside games like *Tetris*, how do we deal with the large number of games that involve narrative elements such as characters, events, and plots? Most scholars in the burgeoning field of game studies have resisted the effort to view even such games through the lens of traditional narrative. In the inaugural 2001 issue of *Game Studies* – the first peer-reviewed academic journal in the field – Jesper Juul presents a pair of arguments against the narrative approach. First, echoing an argument raised in the debate over hypertext (see Ch. 7), Juul argues that the reader of literary narrative bears little similarity to the player of a game: whereas a reader exists wholly outside the narrative – peering in from the outside, as it were – a game player "inhabits a twilight zone where he/she is both an empirical subject outside the game *and* undertakes a role inside the game."[53] Second, Juul argues that time works differently in games than in narratives. Whereas a narrative presents itself as a retelling of some already completed action, in a game, "the events are *happening* now" and "what comes next is not yet determined." For Juul, the interactivity of videogames means that they will never fit within the traditional confines of narrative: because "it is impossible to influence something that has already happened," he argues, "you cannot have interactivity and narration at the same time." In his own contribution to the inaugural issue of *Game Studies*, Espen Aarseth argues that we should approach videogames not as narratives but as "simulations": not as representations of some existing story, but as an alternate reality in which players are able to craft their own narratives free from the constraints and consequences of the real world.[54] Reframing this same idea through the *syuzhet/fabula* distinction of the Russian Formalists (see Ch. 7), H. Porter Abbott agrees that many videogames are more akin to an alternative life than to a narrative: "As in life," he says, "we are aware of something happening that has not been planned or written or scripted in advance – something making itself up as it goes along."[55] One is not told a story in such games; rather, one is presented with an arena in which to enact a story of one's own.

As with the hypertexts and Interactive Fictions encountered in the last chapter, however, the "second life" ideal presented by videogames is much easier to formulate in theory than to realize in practice. A truly open "simulated" word of the kind theorized by Juul and Aarseth is, alas, extremely difficult to design. The example of Emily Short's *Galatea* (see Ch. 7) is again instructive, for although we can ask Galatea many things and her answers depend on a number of on-the-fly considerations, our interactions are nevertheless extremely limited. We can only ask Galatea about the subjects she has been programmed to answer, and we can only ask them in language she understands. In every videogame, as in *Galatea*, we soon come to a point where our freedom to craft the narrative brushes up against the programmed limitations of the "simulation." At such points, we are thrown back into the world of traditional narrative. This situation is captured elegantly by Austin Grossman in *You: A Novel*, whose protagonist muses repeatedly on what he calls "The Ultimate Game":

> There was still and always would be the problem of storytelling. You –
> you in the game – *should* wake up in a world with total choice. Go
> searching for a legendary jewel, stay home and make paper dolls, or run
> out into the street and punch a stranger in the nose. Somehow the
> computer copes. In a normal game, a real game, you couldn't do it. The
> world is a narrative channel, a single story that you can follow but never
> escape. Or maybe there's an open world, but only a specific range of

actions you can perform – you can punch a stranger in the nose but you can't talk to them; you can't make a friend or fall in love. Or you can talk to strangers but they can only say a few things – they're not really people, just shallow repositories of canned speech. At some point, sooner or later but usually very, very soon, the world just runs out of stories it can tell. And every time you run into that point, there's a jarring, illusion-breaking bump that tells you it's just a game.[56]

Although videogames possess the theoretical capacity to take us beyond the traditional boundaries of narrative, in practice they seldom do. However much theorists like Juul and Aarseth may wish to banish the concept of narrative from game studies, it remains a crucial, if occasionally unwelcome, element of the form. As inconvenient as it for game theorists, however, the persistence of narrative serves our own purposes better, because it provides a firm link connecting the world of literature to that of videogames and thus provides a basis for evaluating their suitability as a carrier of the literary impulse into the digital future.

Indie Games and/as the Future of Narrative

There has never been a better time for readers of literature to think seriously about the videogame as an artistic form and a new vehicle for narrative. Although the field of game studies has produced excellent, perceptive studies of games such as *World of Warcraft*, *Doom*, and *Call of Duty*, such blockbuster games – often loud and violent, usually presenting predictable genre narratives – have failed to resonate with audiences accustomed to the quieter pleasures of *War and Peace*, the *Odyssey*, or *Mansfield Park*. However, the advent of "indie games" – an "arty" subgenre of games given to bold experiments in narrative – heralds a new rapprochement of videogames with the sphere of the literary. Indie games are plausibly the ultimate born-digital form. Not only are they, in the words of indie game designer Phil Fish, "the sum total of every expressive medium of all times, made interactive"[57] but they also take full advantage of all the liberating practical possibilities of digital production and distribution. The "indie" in indie games refers primarily to their independent production, a relatively novel option in gaming made possible by the development of online channels of distribution. Before the internet, most videogames were designed for consoles, such as the Atari 2600 or the Nintendo Entertainment System. To write for a console platform, developers had to pay an expensive licensing fee, arrange for the production of expensive game cartridges, and have these physical commodities distributed and sold in stores. The realities of console production, combined with the immense technical difficulty of making a good game, meant that most games were produced by large teams in large studios. Because games were so expensive to produce and disseminate, the financial risks were considerable. Big studios developing for consoles thus tended to conservatism, sticking to the genres and narratives they knew would sell. Beginning in the early 2000s, however, two major developments spurred the emergence of indie games. Though games had been distributed on floppy disks and on the internet as "shareware" since the 1990s, services such as Apple's App Store and Valve's Steam made their distribution to mobile and computer platforms significantly easier. At the same time, the release of several sophisticated and easy-to-use new game creation tools – "game engines" such as Unity and Unreal – reduced the need for large, studio-based development teams. The result has been the creation of an alternative model of videogame production – one that resembles literary production much more closely. Rather than being developed in large teams that are commercially motivated to develop broadly palatable products, games can now be developed by individuals or small teams in pursuit of creative expression.

Though indie games have been produced in all the canonical videogame genres – first-person shooters, role-playing games, racers, real-time strategy, and so on – the most conspicuous indie games are those of a type that hardly existed in the console era: self-consciously "arty" or literary titles. As Jamin Warren notes, the label "indie game" has even come to designate not a method of production but a particular genre and style: in his words, "8-bit chiptune platformers with terrible gameplay that reflect on the existential reality of life."[58] Whatever their stylistic consistency, the effect of indie games in the videogame world as a whole has been to add much-needed diversity. In *The Rise of the Videogame Zinesters*, Anna Anthropy argues that because mainstream games are so difficult and expensive to make, they have tended to reflect the values of the restricted community that produces and consumes them – a community that is disproportionately young, white, and male. (Anthropy's assessment was lent considerable force by the Gamergate controversy of the mid-2010s, which underscored the entrenched sexism, homophobia, and xenophobia of the games community.) Although she finds many novels, films, and comics that speak to her experience as a queer transgender woman, Anthropy is unable to point to a single mainstream videogame that addresses her. She argues, however, that independent and amateur production – made possible by digital distribution and accessible game-creation tools – presents a possible way forward. Not only are "smaller games with smaller budgets and smaller audiences" more likely to be "more experimental or bizarre or interesting"[59] than big-budget games but they are also far more likely to "come from a wider set of experiences and present a wider range of perspectives."[60]

Gone Home, released in 2013 by the Fullbright Company, serves as a succinct demonstration of the artistic merits of indie games.[61] Presenting itself as "a story exploration videogame," it offers an adventurous and recognizably "literary" narrative that pushes against conventional boundaries of videogame subject matter by centering on a coming-out story. The game's production was typically "indie": its three-person team, composed of two men and one woman, met while working on the acclaimed blockbuster *BioShock 2* and committed to develop a similarly sophisticated game entirely without violence. Living together in a rented house in Portland, they developed the game in the Unity engine. In *Gone Home*, we inhabit the first-person perspective of Kaitlin Greenbriar, who has returned home from a year abroad and whose family, in the meantime, has moved into a dilapidated mansion. Kaitlin enters the home on a dark and stormy night to find it entirely empty. Her task, and ours, is to find out what has happened – to piece together the narrative threads that will explain the unexpected emptiness of the Greenbriar home. The story we recover is of a sort familiar to readers of literature yet still extremely atypical of mainstream videogames: Kaitlin's parents, trapped in an unhappy marriage, are at a marriage counselling session; her younger sister Samantha, having fallen in love with a female classmate and encountered the disapproval of her parents and peers, has run away from home. The precise manner in which we recover this story in *Gone Home* is markedly different both from literary fiction and mainstream games: we wander around the house, picking up letters and bits of paper, snooping through bookshelves, and listening to audio diaries recorded by Samantha. *Gone Home*'s method of storytelling is often extremely effective. We recover the entire backstory of Kaitlin's father simply by poking around in his study: the boxes of unsold JFK conspiracy novels tell us that he is a writer fallen on hard times; a rejection letter from a publisher sits next to an empty bottle of whiskey, suggesting the consequences of his literary failures; an angry letter from his current employer, the reviews editor at a stereo equipment magazine, shows us how far he has fallen. "A whole life in boxes, in a single room," as *PC Gamer* wrote in the article naming *Gone Home* their 2013 Narrative Game of the Year.[62]

At the same time, *Gone Home* ably illustrates the real difficulties that videogames present as vehicles for narrative. On the one hand, *Gone Home* seems to many literary readers too game-like. Although there are no monsters to kill and few puzzles to solve, the mansion's locked doors, hidden keys, and secret passageways detract from any sense of genuine realism. On the other hand, even to inexperienced gamers, it may feel too limited in its interactive possibilities to be satisfyingly game-like. Although there is some degree of freedom in the way we unfurl the story by moving around the house, there is clearly an "intended" route, which the authors prioritize through devices such as locked doors and hidden passageways. In this sense, the game is *too much* like print fiction: the story, the *fabula*, is already fixed, and we can have no impact on it; although we are responsible, to some extent, for the order in which this story is uncovered (the *syuzhet*), we are still left with only the rather limited options the developers grant us. When we open a work of print fiction, we do so with the tacit acceptance that both *fabula* and *syuzhet* are unavoidably fixed in advance by the author and that our role will be limited to that of "reader response." In videogames, we know that affordances exist for allowing us to affect the narrative. When these affordances are not employed, the experience can feel disappointingly passive.

Another unlikely 2013 indie game sensation, *The Stanley Parable*, takes this narrative conundrum as its theme.[63] The basic scenario of *The Stanley Parable* is similar to that of *Gone Home*: Stanley, a downtrodden office employee, looks up from his desk one day to find that all his co-workers have disappeared, and he sets out to discover what has happened. The main formal innovation of *The Stanley Parable* is the inclusion of an intrusive narrator. At every step of the journey, the narrator's affable voice interprets the action and provides clear suggestions for what course the player should pursue. As we approach a set of doors, the narrator says, "When Stanley came to a set of two open doors, he entered the door on his left." Entering the left door and following all of the narrator's subsequent suggestions leads to the game's so-called freedom ending: we discover the company's Mind Control Facility, we disable it heroically, and we are rewarded with an escape into a pastoral scene. If we disobey the narrator, on the other hand, he acknowledges our dissension and tries to steer us back onto the intended track. Entering the right door, we are told, "This was not the way to the meeting room, and Stanley knew it perfectly well." If we linger in the patently uninteresting employee lounge, the narrator expresses his indignation with our refusal to follow the suggested course of his linear narrative. Eventually he says, "Stanley waited around for more dialogue, but when none came, he decided the game was trying to send him a message."

Many endings are possible in *The Stanley Parable* if we disobey the narrator. In general, disobedience produces the most interesting stories. A particularly entertaining and self-reflexive outcome is the "confusion ending," in which our repeated refusal to follow the narrator's directions causes him to lose the narrative thread entirely. He repeatedly restarts the game in an effort to get his bearings, but simply cannot get back on track. After one restart, the narrator resorts to drawing a yellow line through the game – he calls it

"The Stanley Parable Adventure Line" – but even following this line leads nowhere. Restarting yet again, the narrator becomes briefly enthusiastic about the freedom that might come from being lost in the narrative: "Now, this is exciting! Just Stanley and me, forging a new path, a new story!" Again, however, we encounter no one and learn nothing. Finally, we are led into a room that reveals that all this confusion has, alas, been scripted in advance; laid out on a series of large screens is the developer's outline for "The Confusion Ending." As the narrator says elsewhere in the game, "every path you can walk has been created for you long in advance" – even the path of confusion. *The Stanley Parable* is, in effect, a game-long demonstration of the tension in videogames between granting players enough freedom to forge their own narratives while also keeping them on a meaningful narrative track. Although it provides an amusingly self-conscious demonstration of this tension, it stops well short of offering a solution. Rather than providing a way forward for videogames as a narrative form, it makes delightful fun of how far they still have to go.

Instilling Mental Balance: *Superbrothers: Sword and Sworcery EP*

More constructive than *The Stanley Parable* is *Superbrothers: Sword & Sworcery EP*, a 2011 indie game originally released for the iPhone and co-developed by lead designer Craig D. Adams, musician Jim Guthrie, and independent studio Capybara Games.[64] *Sworcery*'s narrative is simple and relatively threadbare: we are the Scythian, a warrior sent to the remote Caucasus region to save a village from an evil spell, and by solving a series of oblique puzzles and fighting several "boss battles" against triangular adversaries known as Trigons, we eventually achieve our quest, though we perish in the process. Whereas *Gone Home* and *The Stanley Parable* seek to prioritize, redefine, theorize, or criticize the place of narrative in videogames, *Sworcery*'s main interest lies in achieving a careful *balance* between narrative and non-narrative elements. While the game was in development, Adams published a polemical essay on the webzine *Boing Boing* in which he outlines his vision of "the native language of videogames." Titled "Less Talk More Rock," the essay is, in one sense, literally a call for less "talk" in videogames – particularly in big-budget studio games, which Adams dismisses as "bloated cross media confections loaded with various kinds of talk and nonsense."[65] The problem with such confections, he argues, is their overemphasis on "disruptive, dissonant" narrative elements such as "overlong and condescending tutorials" and "over-explained idiotic stories." For Adams, the "magic" of videogames exists in underexplained, intuitive moments in which "you are seeing things, hearing things, spotting patterns, flowing through spaces, experiencing moods and locations." When ham-handed narrative intrudes into such spaces, Adams argues, it has the damaging effect of "stirring our intellect, forcing us to switch gears and pay attention."

Adams's use of the word "intellect" suggests an affinity with Nietzsche's reading of Wagnerian opera – and indeed, the connection between Adams and Nietzsche is explicit. Just as Nietzsche celebrated Wagner's careful counterbalancing of Apollinian logic and Dionysian rapture, Adams argues for renewed balance in videogames between end-directed, intellect-driven narrative and directionless, exploratory gameplay. One of Adams's acknowledged sources for *Sworcery* is Leonard Shlain's *The Alphabet versus the Goddess: The Conflict between Word and Image* (1998), a bizarre scientific popularization of Nietzsche's Apollinian/Dionysian duality. Shlain, a neurosurgeon, equates the Apollinian with the left hemisphere of the brain (the verbal, time-keeping site of sequential processes like logic and narrative) and the Dionysian with the right hemisphere (the nonverbal, visual site of spatial processes such as pattern recognition). Drawing on McLuhan, Shlain presents a historical argument in which the spread of the alphabet – abstract, linear, sequential – prioritizes the left over the right brain. For Shlain, who genders the left brain male and the right brain female, the spread of alphabetic literacy goes hand in hand with the subjugation of women. With the dawn of multimodal entertainment in the form of television and computer games, Shlain sees the possibility for "a renewed respect for iconic information, which, *in conjunction with* the ability to read, can bring our two hemispheres into greater equilibrium and allow both individuals and cultures to become more balanced."[66]

Shlain's influence is palpable in many aspects of the game. The creators have cited him as the inspiration for their decision to give *Sworcery* a female protagonist[67] – a choice that feminist videogame critic Anita Sarkeesian has greeted as an "assert[ion] that women can fill the role of the mythic hero as effectively as men can."[68] Shlain also inspired *Sworcery*'s effort to balance Apollinian "left-brain" linear narrative with Dionysian "right-brain" exploration and pattern recognition. The game is carefully egalitarian in its deployment of available modalities. Not only does it use text, images, animation, and music but its gameplay also makes each reactive to the other. Guthrie's adaptive score, for example, responds to the narrative, offering a happy tune for a moment of achievement or a grave one before battle. *Sworcery* balances narrative advancement against nonlinear exploration by developing innovative ways of slowing down its gameplay. Between each of the game's four "sessions," the player is warned by the Archetype – *Sworcery*'s narrator figure – not to move too quickly through the game's story: after Session One, he cautions, "Our research shows that prolonged exposure to the mythopoetic psychocosmology of S:S&S EP can have adverse side effects." The game's signature device is another delaying technique. To advance from one level to another, we must wait for particular moon phases: only when there is a full moon in the real world can we enter the game's Bright Moon Phase and recover the Bright Moon Trigon; we must then wait a few weeks, for a new moon, to make our attempt on the Dark Moon Trigon.

Such devices ask players to set aside their usual compulsion to make their way as quickly as possible through the game's narrative – to "beat" the game – inviting them instead calmly to explore its sounds and spaces. Likewise, *Sworcery*'s gameplay encourages "right-brain" pattern recognition and Dionysian transport even while advancing the game's "left-brain" sequential plot. Moving through the game's later sessions requires us to release a number of Sylvan Sprites, a task accomplished not through combat but by solving oblique audiovisual puzzles that reward intuitive exploration. In one sequence, we must learn to play waterfalls like strings on a guitar; in a forest scene, we are asked to notice subtle visual discrepancies between the woods and the image they reflect in a nearby pool. Any attempt to blast quickly past such obstacles results only in frustration; to solve the puzzles successfully, we must achieve a mental state of almost meditative serenity. Although each session culminates in a conventional "boss battle," these battle sequences also work to instill sensory equilibrium. Experienced gamers would no doubt have little trouble defeating the Trigons – dodging lightning blasts, avoiding triangular projectiles, engaging in extended ping-pong battles with rays of energy. Yet for novices, the only way to succeed is by relaxing and listening to the music, which contains implicit cues for when to dodge and when to strike. We graduate to the next level only when we have learned to achieve the requisite mental balance.

In *Persuasive Games* (2007), videogame critic Ian Bogost argues that the most powerful native form of expression in videogames is what he calls "procedural rhetoric." Although Bogost has no doubt that videogames are an art form and "an expressive medium,"[69] he argues that they achieve their effects in a manner distinct from all the other arts. Rather than simply presenting their audience with words, images, or moving pictures, Bogost argues, videogames achieve their rhetorical force through "rule-based representations and interactions." To convince its audience of a particular social ill, a film or a novel would describe it in a persuasive fashion; a videogame, by contrast, would not merely *describe* the problem but would also have its player *act it out*. For Bogost, "the very way videogames mount their claims through procedural rhetorics" has the power to "disrupt and change fundamental attitudes and beliefs about the world."[70] We can see this power in a game like *Sword & Sworcery*. Whereas writers such as Nietzsche, McLuhan, and Shlain describe and argue for the importance of achieving a balance among linear, logical, and individualistic modes of thought and intuitive and communal ones, *Sword & Sworcery* presents itself as a framework in which that mental balance can be actuated in the player. For Craig D. Adams, *Sworcery* is a very deliberate exercise in procedural rhetoric: to play it successfully is to act out the psychic recalibration it seeks to achieve.

Sworcery's ambitions are clearly hyperbolic and likely unrealistic: though several million people have downloaded and played the game, we have no way of measuring its disruption of "fundamental attitudes and beliefs about the world."[71] Yet this very over-ambitiousness provides the strongest link we possess between indie videogames and the literary tradition. If there is a trait held in common between the literary writers and thinkers we have encountered in this volume – Woolf, Benjamin, Blake, Dickinson – it is an earnest faith, sometimes to the point of absurdity, that new forms of expression have the power to change the world. "I must Create a System, or be enslav'd by another Mans,"[72] wrote Blake in *Jerusalem*, an illuminated prophetic text that Blake intended, like all his prophetic works, to usher in a new phase of human perception. In *A Room of One's Own*, Virginia Woolf noted that, by the time women were granted the freedom to write, "all the older forms of literature were hardened and set in place." "The novel alone was young enough to be soft in her hands,"[73] and so it was to the novel that she devoted herself. Today, it is the form of the videogame that is most malleable and most amenable to the shaping touch of a new generation of ambitious artists. With few rules in place, with growing access to independent creation and distribution, and with the expressive language of "procedural rhetoric" on their side, videogame artists possess a powerful toolkit. Let's pay close attention to what they do with it.

Coda: Print in the Digital Age

The BlackBerry-Borne Invasive: Jonathan Franzen's *Freedom*

Nicholas Carr would have found an enthusiastic reader in Jonathan Franzen. In 2010, the year that Carr published *The Shallows*, Franzen published *Freedom* – precisely the sort of long, weighty, unabashedly literary novel that Carr argued was increasingly endangered in the digital age. In a cover story in *Time*, Lev Grossman said *Freedom* "look[ed] more like a 19th century novel than a 21st century one"[1]; on *Salon*, Laura Miller agreed that this "long, realistic novel" was oddly out of step with its time.[2] In the interviews Franzen gave during the book tour for *Freedom*, he went out of his way both to reaffirm his commitment to novels of Victorian scope and proportions and to argue that such novels could only be composed through a studied and disciplined avoidance of the digital. In the "10 Rules for Writing Fiction" he submitted to *The Guardian*, number eight read, "It's doubtful that anyone with an internet connection at his workplace is writing good fiction."[3] In *Time*, Grossman reported that Franzen composed his novel on a "heavy, obsolete Dell laptop" from which he had not only removed the wireless card but also physically blocked the Ethernet port ("What you have to do," Franzen said, "is you plug in an Ethernet cable with superglue, and then you saw off the little head of it").[4] In defending his malicious aversion to the internet, Franzen described a fundamental opposition between digital life and literary activity. "We are so distracted by and engulfed by the technologies we've created, and by the constant barrage of so-called information that comes our way, that more than ever to immerse yourself in an involving book seems socially useful," Franzen said: "The place of stillness that you have to go to to write, but also to read seriously, is the point where you can actually make responsible decisions, where you can actually engage productively with an otherwise scary and unmanageable world."[5] As in Carr, the sphere of the digital is for Franzen one of distraction, superficiality, and passivity. The quiet world of printed literary fiction, by contrast, provides a counter-environment for active, sustained, and concentrated reflection.

Opposition to the internet was a prominent theme not only in Franzen's *Freedom*-era interviews but also in *Freedom* itself. One of the novel's four protagonists, Walter Berglund, an environmental and population-control activist, describes the internet as a symptom and a motivator of the general processes of social fragmentation ravaging America's culture and environment. "We might have enough land for other species to survive if it wasn't all so fragmented," Walter tells Richard Katz, an estranged musician friend he is trying to recruit for a campaign:

> It's like the internet, or cable TV – there's never any center, there's no communal agreement, there's just a trillion little bits of distracting noise. We can never sit down and have any kind of sustained conversation, it's all just cheap trash and shitty development. All the real things, the authentic things, the honest things are dying off. Intellectually and culturally, we just bounce around like random billiard balls, reacting to the latest random stimuli.[6]

Rather than rebutting Walter's characterization of the digital world as an echo chamber in which individuals are cordoned off from one another, each to pursue their selfish consumerist desires, Richard obliquely affirms it with a joking retort: "There's some pretty good porn on the internet."[7] Richard, who toils in obscurity for decades before achieving musical celebrity in middle age, has his own reasons for disdaining internet culture. After a teenage fan posts a ranting interview on his blog, Richard is exposed to the instantaneous feedback loop of digital stardom. Even Richard, the book's figure of imperturbable rock 'n' roll authenticity, listens intently as his interviewer summarizes the response: "there's a tiny minority now that's saying you sounded like an asshole and a whiner," he tells Richard, "but that's just the player-hating fringe. I wouldn't worry about it."[8] For the critic Gerard Moorey, such episodes are at the heart of Franzen's attack on the "internet-facilitated degeneration of the culture of popular music into a culture of banal gossip – a welter of trivial comments and asides that render meaningful communication between an artist and his or her audience increasingly difficult."[9] Yet at least pop music still possesses an audience in *Freedom*'s version of the internet age. No such consolation exists for literature, which Franzen tersely eulogizes through his description of a character's chosen career in "literary publishing," "a declining and endangered and unprofitable enterprise."[10]

Franzen is a self-consciously anti-digital literary author, and *Freedom* is an explicitly anti-digital literary text. For all this determined posturing, however, irony abounds. Walter Berglund's tirade against internet-borne fragmentation is undercut by the fact that it is delivered in an attempt to convince Richard to participate in an internet-borne "viral" marketing campaign. "We need to make it cool, and we need to make it viral," Walter tells Richard, trying to sell him on his series of concerts and local musical festivals designed to spread awareness of overpopulation.[11] Though the musical festival fails, it is indeed a digital video ("CancerOnThePlanet.wmv") that finally "[goes] viral" and spreads his message.[12] Further, *Freedom* itself is, whether Franzen likes it or not, a hybrid of digital and analog processes. The novel was composed digitally, even if on an old laptop whose internet terminals were removed or physically blockaded. It was reviewed online, in the digital editions of newspapers, on book blogs, on sites like Goodreads, and in online book clubs such as that led by Laura Miller on *Salon*. And the novel was sold not only as a printed book but also as an e-book. The novel was delivered wirelessly on August 31, 2010, to the digital devices of Amazon customers who had preordered the Kindle edition, which offered bonus features such as plot summaries, lists of major characters, errata, and suggestions for further reading. Once downloaded, readers of the digital edition quickly proceeded to highlight their favorite passages, to post reviews of the novel, and to discuss it among themselves. As Matthew Kirschenbaum and Sarah Warner argue, scholarship of this avowedly anti-digital book will nonetheless have to proceed digitally, through the examination of digital drafts of Franzen's manuscripts, electronic correspondence between the author and his editor, digital editions of the completed novel, and digital traces of its reception by readers.[13]

The inescapability of the internet, even for the most resolutely print-focused novelists, is the underlying theme of Franzen's essay "Farther Away," published in *The New Yorker* a year after the release of *Freedom*. The essay describes Franzen's desire to flee the "modern distractions" of internet-connected life after going on a book tour in which he found himself "checking [his] e-mail every ten minutes."[14] His quest takes him, somewhat hyperbolically, to one of the most isolated places on the planet: a remote island 100 miles off the coast of Chile known to locals as Más Afuera, Spanish for "Farther Away." Though he goes to the island to escape the grip of the digital, his thoughts – and even his metaphors – return obsessively to the internet. At one point, while describing the disastrous effects of a non-native species, the blackberry bush, on local plant life, he finds himself unable to resist the lure of an easy pun, launching into a Walter Berglund-style attack on "the Internet, that BlackBerry-borne invasive" – the "virulent" and "radically individualistic invader that is now displacing the novel."[15] Franzen's ruminations on the history of the novel – instigated by the fact that Daniel Defoe's *Robinson Crusoe*, one of the earliest realistic novels in English, was inspired by accounts of Más Afuera – lead him back around to the internet. Citing Ian Watt and

Catherine Gallagher, Franzen ties the eighteenth-century rise of the novel to its glorification of the "enterprising individual" during a period of rapidly increasing social mobility. Propelled from its inception by the growing cult of the individual, Franzen contends, the novel is now being displaced by an even more radically individualistic force. "Instead of mapping the self onto a narrative," he writes, the internet "maps the self onto the world." "With 'Robinson Crusoe,'" he writes, "the self had become an island; and now, it seemed, the island was becoming the world."[16] Even in far-flung Más Afuera, there is no escape from the digital. Not only is his entire journey negatively motivated by the internet, and not only does the internet haunt his language and imagination, but the climax of his solitary speculations is a theory of the novel that positions the internet as its ultimate realization.

The Death of the Book and the Birth of Bookishness

So far, we have discussed digitization – the process of turning print-era books into digital forms – and we have discussed born-digital fiction: works created digitally for digital consumption. What we skipped over, in moving from one to the other, are the printed books that continue to be produced in the period of their threatened obsolescence, when the printed codex is no longer the dominant textual medium but only one choice among many. Despite the gloomy predictions of writers like Carr and Birkerts, printed books continue to be produced and read. Indeed, some evidence points to their resurgence. Recent studies have shown that the exponential growth of e-book sales in the early years of the twenty-first century has slowed dramatically. Whereas the Association of American Publishers reported 252% annual growth in e-book sales in 2010, for example, that figure had dwindled to 5% by 2013.[17] Though e-books now make up nearly a quarter of book sales in the United States, their share of the market appears to have reached a plateau. In a blog post on these surprising figures, Nicholas Carr speculates that readers have discovered that, although e-books formats are suited to certain titles and situations, such as genre fiction and romance, or reading on an airplane, printed books are better adapted to literary fiction and to reading on a couch at home.[18] My own experience, and that of my students over the years, suggests that digital forms like the e-book have allowed us to better "see" the physical book. Not until we are forced to click or swipe our way through the screens of an e-book do we realize how satisfying it is to flip through the physical leaves of a book, scanning forward to the start of the next chapter, marking the spot with a finger. Not until we are given the choice between a few pixelated fonts do we truly appreciate the importance of typography to the reading experience. Of the many achievements of e-books, one of the greatest is to have reminded us what a wonderful technology the book is – how perfectly adapted it has become, through centuries of incremental advancement, to the presentation of text.

Electronic texts have not only changed the way that readers perceive printed texts but also powerfully affected how authors conceive of the printed book as an artistic medium. Jessica Pressman has argued for the emergence of an "aesthetic of bookishness" in twenty-first century literature, in which "the threat posed to books by digital technologies becomes a source of artistic inspiration and formal experimentation."[19] To make her case, Pressman turns to Mark Z. Danielewski's *House of Leaves* (2000), a novel that leverages an abundance of print-specific elements of book design – spiraling and upside-down text that forces the reader to rotate the book in her hands, footnotes that send her flipping in all directions, endless variations in typography – to convey the comparatively impoverished experience of digital textuality. In the words of Danielewski, who composed the novel in pencil, *House of Leaves* serves to remind readers of "the analogue powers of these wonderful bundles of paper [that] have been forgotten"; reflecting on his aims, he adds, "I'd like to see the book reintroduced for all it really is."[20] Katherine Hayles presents Jonathan Safran Foer's *Tree of Codes* (2010) as another example of Pressman's aesthetic of bookishness. In a forcefully un-digitizable tour de force of book design, Foer constructs his narrative literally by cutting away words from another book, Bruno Schulz's *The Street of Crocodiles*. The text left over from this process of excision makes up *Tree of Codes*, which Foer calls "a die-cut book by erasure, a book whose meaning was exhumed from another book."[21] Hayles argues that Foer's unusual method, which produces pages so lace-like and delicate that they must be handled with care in order not to tear them, is part of a broader desire to "entice readers to become intimate with . . . novels' bodies through physical manipulations of their printed forms."[22]

As both Pressman and Hayles themselves acknowledge, however, it would be a mistake to consider texts like *House of Leaves* or *Tree of Codes* strictly anti-digital. Instead, like Franzen's *Freedom*, they emerge from the complex interplay at work today between print and digital forms. Describing a video released by Foer's publisher that shows *Tree of Codes* being manufactured by a computer-controlled laser die-cutter, Kirschenbaum and Werner argue that Foer's text "turns out to be a book which, despite its flagrant *bookishness*, could not have been practically fabricated as a trade object . . . without the employment of sophisticated digital technologies."[23] Likewise, *House of Leaves*, composed in pencil, could not have been laid out in its final form without the assistance of digital desktop publishing software. Indeed, Danielewski's text might not have been released as a printed book at all if not for the viral buzz created when he posted a draft as a free PDF download from his website two years before its eventual publication. If print is undergoing a renaissance in the early twenty-first century, this phenomenon must be understood as a reaction against the digital that is paradoxically abetted by the digital. Texts like *House of Leaves* and *Tree of Codes* show us that, far from standing as isometric opposites, print and the digital have become so forcefully intertwined as to be meaningful only in relation to one another.

The Pressures and Opportunities of the Digital Age: Jennifer Egan's *A Visit from the Goon Squad*

Citing texts like *House of Leaves* and *Tree of Codes*, Jessica Pressman argues that the aesthetic of bookishness is predominantly found in "*experimental* writing."[24] Yet Jonathan Franzen's *Freedom* shows us that the logic of "bookishness" is also at work in more conventional and popular literary works. Jennifer Egan's *A Visit from the Goon Squad* (2010) presents an equally compelling example of a best-selling literary text bound up in the complexities of bookishness. Published the same year as *Freedom* – when it rivaled Franzen's novel for several major American book awards, claiming both the Pulitzer Prize and the National Book Critics Circle Award for Fiction – *Goon Squad* is distinguished from Franzen's novel by its relative comfort in the paradoxes of print in the digital age. Like *Freedom*, *Goon Squad* is clearly a print novel *about* the digital world; its Pulitzer citation called it "an inventive investigation of growing up and growing old in the digital age."[25] Yet rather than arguing for or against the digital world, Egan is content to leave its complexities unresolved. The most vocally anti-digital of *Goon Squad*'s protagonists is Bennie, an erstwhile punk rocker who has gone on to found a successful music label. Listening to an old Dead Kennedys track, a favorite of his youth, he delights in the recording's "muddiness" – its "sense of actual musicians playing actual instruments in an actual room."[26] He recognizes, by contrast, that "what he was bringing into the world was shit. Too clear, too clean." "The problem," he reflects, "[is] precision, perfection"; the problem, more precisely still, is "*digitization*" – an "*aesthetic holocaust*" that "suck[s] the life out of everything that [gets] smeared through its microscopic mesh."[27] Scotty, a former bandmate of Bennie's who has gone on to a less distinguished career in janitorial work, is, much like *Freedom*'s Richard Katz, a figure of un-digitizable authenticity. The climax of the novel's final chapter – set in a near-future New York where smartphone-like "handsets" mediate all social experience – occurs when a large crowd responds exultantly to Scotty's stripped-down slide guitar blues at an outdoor concert. Scotty's fans recognize him in this moment as "a man you knew had never had a page or a profile or a handle or a handset, who was part of no one's data, a guy who had lived in the cracks all these years, forgotten and full of rage, in a way that registered as pure. Untouched."[28] Yet Egan forcefully undercuts this apparent climax of un-digitizable authenticity. The exultant crowd has assembled not spontaneously, but rather because of a sophisticated digital marketing campaign funded by Bennie – one so sophisticated that the vast numbers of so-called parrots who promote Scotty's concert to their friends via social media have done so without realizing their involvement in a coordinated plot. The social media campaign owes its success, moreover, to the widespread thirst for unmediated authenticity that has sprung out of a hypermediated lifestyle. In one scene, the two young people Bennie has hired to direct the campaign, in the midst of an oral discussion of its particulars, take up their handsets when the discussion gets especially complex, continuing it in the exaggerated text-speak that has become for them the more natural form of communication.[29] It is the hypermediation of everyday life that makes Scotty's unrefined, direct, live performance so appealing to the assembled crowd. Though Scotty's performance starts well, the active participation and obvious elation of this large crowd are what push the experience to its crescendo. As Egan's narrator relates,

> It may be that a crowd at a particular moment of history creates the object to justify its gathering. . . . Or it may be that two generations of war and surveillance had left people craving the embodiment of their own unease in the form of a lone, unsteady man on a slide guitar. Whatever the reason, a swell of approval as palpable as rain lifted from the center of the crowd and rolled out toward its edges, where it crashed against buildings . . . and rolled back at Scotty with redoubled force.[30]

The scene's irony is deep and ultimately irreducible. Propelled by a crowd that has assembled only through the manipulation of prevailing digital media, Scotty rises to his feet and becomes the symbol of the crowd's own lost authenticity.

Such intertwining of the digital and the analog, with each shown to depend on the other in an infinite recursion, is characteristic not only of Egan's themes but also of her form. Although very much at home in the pages of a printed book, *Goon Squad* deploys an unusual narrative structure that some critics have read as an adaptation of contemporary social media. The novel is composed of thirteen chapters, each of which exists in the same storyworld, but is told from a different perspective and deals with a different set of characters. These chapters are told out of chronological sequence, ranging backward to late-1970s San

Francisco and forward to the near future of 2020s New York. Each is connected in a loose linking structure: a minor character or incident from one chapter becomes the focus of the next, and the "full story" – if such a thing exists in *Goon Squad* – emerges slowly from the gradual exploration of this networked structure. In a perceptive review for *Newsweek*, Jennie Yabroff argues that *Goon Squad* is "the first novel to be structured like a Facebook page": beginning from a particular character's "wall," we radiate outward from friend to friend, understanding each individual character only through his or her position in a social network. Yabroff reads this structure as a critique of the "narcissism and fragmentation" of networked social life, yet she also praises the way that Egan's structure hybridizes print-based and digital narrative strategies, seeking not to "explode traditional storytelling" but rather to "explore how it responds to the pressures and opportunities of the digital age."[31] The novel's most conspicuous digital nod comes in its twelfth chapter, which is delivered in the form of a young girl's PowerPoint presentation on her brother's obsession with "Great Rock and Roll Pauses." In the pages of the printed book, individual slides are printed in landscape-oriented monochrome, forcing the reader to turn the book on its side to take in the presentation. As physically awkward and narratologically unprepossessing as the PowerPoint chapter may seem at first, it is among the most affecting and engrossing in the book. Yet the version Egan posted on her personal website, jenniferegan.com, is more engrossing still, presented in full color and – more importantly – with a soundtrack allowing us to *listen* to the "Great Rock and Roll Pauses" in question.

The existence of this digital surrogate makes *Goon Squad* an example of what Katherine Hayles calls a "Work as Assemblage": a narrative that exists not within the enclosed space of a physical volume but rather as "a cluster of related texts" – print and digital – "that quote, comment upon, amplify, and remediate one another."[32] Egan's particular cluster was enlarged further still in 2012, with the publication of "Black Box," a short story that extends the narrative of *Goon Squad* by imagining the future spy career of one of its protagonists (Lulu, co-coordinator of the PR campaign for Scotty's concert). As a textual object, "Black Box" sets forth the fabulously complex intertwining of print and the digital in contemporary fiction. Though printed in its full 8,500-word form in the pages of *The New Yorker* and published on the magazine's website and mobile app, the story was first serialized on Twitter, where it was delivered as a series of several hundred tweets in one-hour bursts over a period of ten days. The formal limitations of Twitter clearly influence Egan's story, which unfolds in short paragraphs of 140 characters or less. Yet, as Egan explains in a post on the *New Yorker's* blog, she composed the entire story in longhand, in a Japanese notebook ruled with rectangular black boxes approximately the correct size for handwritten passages the length of a tweet.[33]

Kirschenbaum and Werner argue that "Black Box" – a hybrid print/digital extension of a hybrid print/digital novel, and a text shaped both by the formal constraints of a digital form and those of a paper notebook – should be viewed as "an artifact of multi-faceted interchange, a generative friction, between print and digital writing platforms."[34] It lends force to the status of *A Visit from the Good Squad* as an exemplary print novel of the digital age – one that is exemplary precisely because it refuses to be contained by any theory of contemporary textuality that envisions print and the digital as irreconcilable, rival categories.

In the Preface, I said that this book exists to facilitate a conversation: that digital and print perspectives each have something to offer the other; that they must be placed in dialogue; and that, in accordance with Mikhail Bakhtin's notion of the "excess of seeing," each stands to benefit when it shares its vision with the other. The examples we have encountered in this final chapter show that this conversation is not only potentially beneficial but also necessary. Franzen and Egan remind us that, whatever our attitude to the networked present, there is no escaping it. To rework a much-abused phrase of Derrida's, *il n'y a pas de hors-numérique*: there is no outside the digital.[35] This is not to say that we are inmates in a digital prison or that the print-based literary tradition is doomed, but simply that no account of literature going forward will be complete unless it attends to the digital. Writers and artists like Dash Shaw, Emily Short, Young-Hae Chang, and Craig D. Adams show us that working in digital forms does not entail an abandonment of print traditions, for the born-digital works they produce are hybrids of print and digital traditions, deployed to better understand and grapple with the world we are living in today. As students and scholars of literature, we must follow their lead. Following the example of modernist critics like Walter Benjamin and Virginia Woolf, we need to understand that a deepened knowledge of literature and its future will come not from retreating into the comfort of existing forms, but through active engagement with emerging ones. As critics like Jerome McGann, Stephen Ramsay, Katherine Hayles, and Tanya Clement show us, the critical power of digital approaches comes largely from their ability to defamiliarize – to re-present the seemingly familiar in such a way that it begins to look strange, teeming with new possibilities, abounding in new questions. The advent of the digital heralds not the death of literature, but an opportunity to look at it with fresh eyes. This is not the end of the book, but the beginning of an exploration.

Notes

Preface: The Excess of Seeing

1 For an extended introduction to Digital Humanities and its place in literary studies, see Matthew G. Kirschenbaum, "What Is Digital Humanities and What's It Doing in English Departments?", *ADE Bulletin*, no. 150 (2010), http://perma.cc/UX7Q-8PLG.

2 William Pannapacker, "The MLA and the Digital Humanities," *The Chronicle of Higher Education, Brainstorm*, December 28, 2009, http://perma.cc/A2GE-ALGU.

3 See Kirschenbaum, "What Is Digital Humanities and What's It Doing in English Departments?"

4 In an astounding turnaround, I was asked precisely these questions at the poster session of the 2014 MSA conference in Pittsburgh. I believe this reflects both the rapid expansion of digital methods in literary studies and the geographic unevenness of this expansion.

5 N. Katherine Hayles, *How We Think: Digital Media and Contemporary Technogenesis* (Chicago: University of Chicago Press, 2012), 6.

6 Matthew G. Kirschenbaum and Sarah Werner, "Digital Scholarship and Digital Studies: The State of the Discipline," *Book History* 17 (2014): 408–9.

7 Maryanne Wolf, *Proust and the Squid: The Story and Science of the Reading Brain* (New York: Harper Perennial, 2008), 226.

8 Virginia Woolf, *A Room of One's Own* (Peterborough, ON: Broadview Press, 2001), 116.

9 Mikhail Bakhtin, "Author and Hero in Aesthetic Activity," in *Art and Answerability: Early Philosophical Essays*, ed. Michael Holquist and Vadim Liapunov, trans. Vadim Liapunov (Austin: University of Texas Press, 1990), 23.

10 Although many excellent books exist that aim at comprehensive introductions to DH and digital literary studies, the best starting points remain, respectively, Susan Schreibman, Ray Siemens, and John Unsworth, eds., *A Companion to Digital Humanities* (Oxford: Blackwell, 2004), http://www.digitalhumanities.org/companion/, and Ray Siemens and Susan Schreibman, eds., *A Companion to Digital Literary Studies* (Oxford: Blackwell, 2008), http://www.digitalhumanities.org/companionDLS/.

Chapter 1. The Digital Medium and Its Message

1 *Marshall McLuhan,* Heritage Minutes (Historica Canada), accessed April 7, 2015, https://www.youtube.com/watch?v=GHzAerGKYnc.
2 "At the Feet of the Master," *Ideas* (CBC Radio, July 21, 2011), http://www.cbc.ca/ player/Radio/Ideas/ID/2064712136/.
3 Ibid.
4 Ibid.
5 Nicholas Carr, "Is Google Making Us Stupid?" *The Atlantic,* July 1, 2008, http:// perma.cc/E6V4-2BFL.
6 Clay Shirky, "Why Abundance Is Good: A Reply to Nick Carr," *Encyclopedia Britannica Blog,* July 17, 2008, http://perma.cc/2V9D-9NLY.
7 Clay Shirky, "Why Abundance Should Breed Optimism: A Second Reply to Nick Carr," *Encyclopedia Britannica Blog,* July 21, 2008, http://perma.cc/2TMY-96R9.
8 Larry Sanger, "A Defense of Tolstoy & the Individual Thinker: A Reply to Clay Shirky," *Encyclopedia Britannica Blog,* July 18, 2008, http://perma.cc/3YJ6-2Z2B.
9 Nicholas Carr, "Why Skepticism Is Good: My Reply to Clay Shirky," *Encyclopedia Britannica Blog,* July 17, 2008, http://perma.cc/P2JY-M27V.
10 Sven Birkerts, *The Gutenberg Elegies* (London: Faber and Faber, 2006), 191.
11 Ibid., 193.
12 Ibid., 208.
13 Ibid., 219.
14 Ibid., 224.
15 Ibid., 5.
16 Ibid., 217.
17 Ibid., 76.
18 Ibid., 197.
19 James Joyce, *A Portrait of the Artist as a Young Man* (New York: B. W. Huebsch, 1921), 134.
20 Birkerts, *The Gutenberg Elegies,* 229.
21 Sven Birkerts, "A Know-Nothing's Defense of Serious Reading & Culture: A Reply to Clay Shirky," *Encyclopedia Britannica Blog,* July 28, 2008, http://perma .cc/TD9M-UEMP.
22 Sven Birkerts, "Reading in the Open-Ended Information Zone Called Cyberspace: My Reply to Kevin Kelly," *Encyclopedia Britannica Blog,* July 25, 2008, http://perma .cc/DM8S-JE55.
23 This list of "salient features" is condensed and simplified from the more detailed investigation in Adriaan van der Weel, *Changing Our Textual Minds: Towards a Digital Order of Knowledge* (Manchester: Manchester University Press, 2011), 142–192.
24 Ibid., 149.
25 Ibid., 193.
26 Ibid., 193–194.

27 Disqus Comments on "Is Google Making Us Stupid" by Nicholas Carr (*The Atlantic*), accessed March 8, 2015, https://perma.cc/Y54E-LG75?type=pdf.

28 Nicholas Carr, *The Shallows: What the Internet Is Doing to Our Brains*, paperback (New York: Norton, 2011), 198.

29 Ibid., 131.

30 Ibid., 127.

31 Ibid., 112.

32 Clay Shirky, *Cognitive Surplus: How Technology Makes Consumers into Collaborators* (New York: Penguin, 2010), 55.

33 Ibid., 52.

34 Cathy Davidson, *Now You See It: How the Brain Science of Attention Will Transform the Way We Live, Work, and Learn* (New York: Viking, 2011), 152.

35 Ibid., 17.

36 Ibid., 284.

37 Ibid., 285.

38 Hayles, *How We Think*, 62–67.

39 Ibid., 11–12.

40 Ibid., 69.

41 Ibid., 99.

42 Ibid., 247.

Chapter 2. Medium Shifts: Literary Thought in Media History

1 Nicholas Carr, "Minds like Sieves," *Rough Type*, July 14, 2011, http://perma.cc/GA5Z-AWUL.

2 Betsy Sparrow, Jenny Liu, and Daniel M. Wegner, "Google Effects on Memory: Cognitive Consequences of Having Information at Our Fingertips," *Science* 333, no. 5 (August 2011): 778.

3 Carr, "Minds like Sieves."

4 Plato, *Phaedrus*, ed. and trans. Alexander Nehamas and Paul Woodruff (Indianapolis: Hackett, 1995), 79–80.

5 Ibid., 80.

6 Walter Ong, *Orality and Literacy: The Technologizing of the Word* (New York: Routledge, 2002), 78.

7 Alexander Nehamas and Paul Woodruff, "Introduction," in *Phaedrus* (Indianapolis: Hackett, 1995), xxv–xxvii.

8 Ong, *Orality and Literacy*, 24.

9 Quoted in Harold Love, *The Culture and Commerce of Texts: Scribal Publication in Seventeenth Century England* (Amherst, MA: University of Massachusetts Press, 1998), 153.

10 See van der Weel, *Changing Our Textual Minds*, 88.

11 Ann M. Blair, *Too Much to Know: Managing Scholarly Information before the Modern Age* (New Haven: Yale University Press, 2010), 11.

12 Ibid., 55.

13 Ibid., 57.

14 Martin J. C. Lowry, *The World of Aldus Manutius: Business and Scholarship in Renaissance Venice* (Ithaca, NY: Cornell University Press, 1979), 29–31.

15 Blair, *Too Much to Know*, 55.

16 Ibid., 56.

17 Martin Luther, *The Table Talk of Martin Luther*, ed. and trans. William Hazlitt (London: Bell & Daldy, 1872), 369, https://archive.org/details/cu31924029255184.

18 Blair, *Too Much to Know*, 58.

19 Edgar Allan Poe, *The Works of Edgar Allan Poe*, ed. John H. Ingram, vol. 3 (Edinburgh: Adam and Charles Black, 1875), 412.

20 Blair, *Too Much to Know*, 60.

21 Andrew Piper, *Book Was There: Reading in Electronic Times* (Chicago: University of Chicago Press, 2012), xi.

22 Carr, "Is Google Making Us Stupid?"

23 Piper, *Book Was There*, x.

24 Alan Liu, *Local Transcendence: Essays on Postmodern Historicism and the Database* (Chicago: University of Chicago Press, 2008), 324.

25 Lev Manovich, "Avant-Garde as Software," *Artnodes*, no. 2 (2002): 2, http://perma.cc/PU8B-GZYB.

26 Ibid., 1.

27 Ibid., 8.

28 Friedrich Kittler, "Gramophone, Film, Typewriter," in *Literature, Media, Information Systems: Essays*, ed. John Johnston, trans. Philippe L. Similon and Dorothea von Mücke (Amsterdam: G+B Arts, 1985), 39.

29 Ibid.

30 Philip G. Hubert Jr., "The New Talking Machines," *The Atlantic Monthly*, February 1889, 259.

31 Octave Uzanne, "The End of Books," *Scribner's Magazine*, August 1894, http://perma.cc/CC4T-32P8.

32 Walter Benjamin, "The Work of Art in the Age of Its Technological Reproducibility," in *Selected Writings*, ed. Howard Eiland and Michael W. Jennings, trans. Edmund Jephcott and Harry Zohn, vol. 3 (Cambridge, MA: Belknap, 2002), 104. All emphases in original.

33 Ibid., 123n8.

34 Ibid., 114.

35 Ibid.

36 Walter Benjamin, "The Author as Producer," in *Selected Writings*, ed. Michael W. Jennings, Howard Eiland, and Gary Smith, trans. Edmund Jephcott, vol. 2 (Cambridge, MA: Belknap, 2005), 771.

37 Ibid., 777.

38 Ibid., 779.

39 Ibid., 778.

40 Virginia Woolf, "Poetry, Fiction, and the Future," in *The Essays of Virginia Woolf*, ed. Andrew McNellie, vol. 4 (New York: Harcourt Brace Jovanovich, 1988), 433–434.

41 Ibid., 423–433.

42 Ibid., 434.

43 Ibid., 429.

44 Ibid., 435–436.

45 T. S. Eliot, "Marie Lloyd," in *Selected Prose of T. S. Eliot*, ed. Frank Kermode (New York: Farrar, Straus and Giroux, 1975), 174.

46 Ibid.

47 T. S. Eliot, "The Possibility of a Poetic Drama," in *The Sacred Wood* (London: Methuen, 1950), 70.

48 T. S. Eliot, *The Use of Poetry and the Use of Criticism* (London: Faber and Faber, 1933), 154.

49 I. A. Richards, *Principles of Literary Criticism* (London: Routledge & Kegan Paul, 1926), 21.

50 Ibid., 2.

51 Ibid., 231. Emphasis in original.

52 Ibid.

53 F. R. Leavis and Denys Thompson, *Culture and Environment: The Training of Critical Awareness* (London: Chatto & Windus, 1933), 1.

54 Ibid.

55 Ibid., 4–5.

56 Friedrich Kittler, "Preface to *Gramophone, Film, Typewriter*," in *Literature, Media, Information Systems: Essays*, ed. John Johnston, trans. Stefanie Harris (Amsterdam: G+B Arts, 1985), 28.

57 Marshall McLuhan, Jerome Agel, and Quentin Fiore, *The Medium Is the Massage* (New York: Bantam, 1967), 26.

58 Geoffrey Wintrop-Young and Michael Wutz, "Translators' Introduction," in *Gramophone, Film, Typewriter* by Friedrich Kittler (Stanford: Stanford University Press, 1999), xvi.

59 Jessica Pressman, *Digital Modernism: Making It New in Modernism* (Oxford: Oxford University Press, 2014), 5.

60 Philip Marchand, *Marshall McLuhan: The Medium and the Messenger* (Toronto: Random House, 1989), 37.

61 Matthew G. Kirschenbaum, *Mechanisms: New Media and the Forensic Imagination* (Cambridge, MA: MIT Press, 2008).

62 Ibid., 16.

Chapter 3. The Universal Library

1 Woolf, *A Room of One's Own*, 11.

2 Gary Hall, *Digitize This Book! The Politics of New Media, or Why We Need Open Access Now* (Minneapolis: University of Minneapolis Press, 2008), 7.

3 Cf. Andrew Erskine, "Culture and Power in Ptolemaic Egypt: The Museum and Library of Alexandria," *Greece & Rome* 42, no. 1 (April 1995): 38–48.

4 Ibid., 45.

5 H. G. Wells, "World Brain: The Idea of a Permanent World Encyclopaedia," *Encyclopédie Française*, August 1937, http://perma.cc/462H-BLLK.

6 Ibid.

7 Matthew Steggle, "'Knowledge Will Be Multiplied': Digital Literary Studies and Early Modern Literature," in *A Companion to Digital Literary Studies*, ed. Susan Schreibman and Ray Siemens (Oxford: Blackwell, 2008), http://perma.cc/99U6-3364.

8 Michael Hart, "The History and Philosophy of Project Gutenberg," *Project Gutenberg*, August 1992, http://perma.cc/T28A-VKRN.

9 Ibid.

10 Ibid.

11 Ibid.

12 Sam Vaknin, "The Ubiquitous Project Gutenberg: Interview with Michael Hart, Its Founder," November 15, 2005, http://perma.cc/KZZ3-3J4N.

13 U.S. Constitution, art. 1, sec. 8, cl. 8.

14 U.S. Copyright Act, 1790, sec. 1.

15 Robert Darnton, "A World Digital Library Is Coming True!," *New York Review of Books*, May 22, 2014, http://perma.cc/R34Z-ZU9U.

16 Aaron Swartz, *Guerilla Open Access Manifesto* (Eremo, Italy: self-published, 2008), http://perma.cc/EDR9-FAYM.

17 "Annual Summary: JSTOR in 2012" (JSTOR, March 19, 2013), http://perma.cc/M2F6-KV82.

18 Jennifer Howard, "JSTOR Tests Free, Read-Only Access to Some Articles," *Chronicle of Higher Education*, January 13, 2012, http://perma.cc/AHD8-5ELB.

19 *Lessig on "Aaron's Laws – Law and Justice in a Digital Age"* (Harvard Law School, 2013), https://www.youtube.com/watch?v=9HAw1i4gOU4.

20 Hall, *Digitize This Book!*, 7.

21 "Company – Google," *Google*, accessed March 9, 2015, http://perma.cc/243Q-Y232.

22 Sergey Brin, "A Library to Last Forever," *New York Times*, October 8, 2009, http://perma.cc/484Q-DRQJ.

23 Jean Noël Jeanneney, *Quand Google défie l'Europe: plaidoyer pour un sursaut* (Paris: Mille et une nuits, 2005).

24 Leigh Phillips, "Merkel Speaks out on Google Books," *Bloomberg Businessweek*, October 12, 2009, http://perma.cc/SSY9-LVQ4.

25 Darnton, "A World Digital Library Is Coming True!"

26 Robert Darnton, "Google & the Future of Books," *New York Review of Books*, February 12, 2009, http://perma.cc/TNE4-2ZCA.

27 Ibid.

28 Ibid.

29 Robert Darnton, "Can We Create a National Digital Library?," *New York Review of Books*, October 28, 2010, http://perma.cc/G47C-R5U8.

30 Robert Darnton, "Google's Loss: The Public's Gain," *New York Review of Books*, April 28, 2011, http://perma.cc/WY7H-SUYG.

31 "About DPLA," DPLA, accessed March 9, 2015, http://perma.cc/6Y7D-3DX3.

32 Nicholas Carr, "The Library of Utopia," *MIT Technology Review*, April 25, 2012, http://perma.cc/T4ZN-WM2L.

33 Ibid.

34 Darnton, "A World Digital Library Is Coming True!"

35 Digital accessibility – the imperative to make digitized texts accessible to persons with disabilities such as those who are deaf, hard of hearing, blind, or have low vision or difficulty distinguishing particular colors – is a growing concern in the Digital Humanities. For more on this question, see Jen Giuliano and George H. Williams, "Accessibility and the Digital Humanities," *Chronicle of Higher Education*, March 30, 2012, http://perma.cc/EG79-5YE9.

36 Jorge Luis Borges, "The Library of Babel," in *Ficciones*, ed. and trans. Anthony Kerrigan (New York: Grove Press, 1962), 83.

37 Ibid., 86–87.

38 Robert Darnton, *The Case for Books: Past, Present, and Future* (New York: Public-Affairs, 2009), 44.

39 Borges, "The Library of Babel," 87.

40 Ibid., 84.

41 Ibid., 85.

42 Ibid., 86.

43 Carr, *The Shallows*, 156.

Chapter 4. Digital Editions and the Complexity of Remediation

1 Jerome McGann, *Radiant Textuality: Literature after the World Wide Web* (New York: Palgrave, 2001), 168.

2 Vannevar Bush, "As We May Think," *Atlantic Monthly*, July 1945, http://perma.cc/KSY8-8RRS.

3 William Blake, *The Marriage of Heaven and Hell*, in *The Complete Poetry & Prose of William Blake*, ed. David V. Erdman (New York: Anchor, 1988), 34.

4 Ibid., 39.

5 Alexander Gilchrist and Anne Gilchrist, *Life of William Blake, "Pictor Ignotus"* (London: Macmillan and Co., 1863), 80, https://archive.org/details/lifewilliamblak06gilcgoog.

6 Joseph Viscomi, "Digital Facsimiles: Reading the William Blake Archive," *Computers and the Humanities*, no. 36 (2002): 27, 29.

7 Virginia Jackson, *Dickinson's Misery* (Princeton, NJ: Princeton University Press, 2005), 53.

8 Ibid., 1.

9 Mark van Doren, "Foreword," in *Bolts of Melody: New Poems of Emily Dickinson*, ed. Mabel Loomis Todd and Millicent Todd Bingham (New York: Harper & Brothers, 1945), v.

10 Emily Dickinson, "Alone and in a Circumstance" (Amherst, MA), Amherst College, accessed March 9, 2015, http://www.edickinson.org/editions/1/image_sets/240377.

11 Emily Dickinson, "Alone and in a Circumstance," in *Bolts of Melody: New Poems of Emily Dickinson*, ed. Mabel Loomis Todd and Millicent Todd Bingham (New York: Harper & Brothers, 1945), 102–103.

12 McGann, *Radiant Textuality*, 63.

13 David Porter, *Dickinson: The Modern Idiom* (Cambridge, MA: Harvard University Press, 1981), 17.

14 Quoted in Jeanne Holland, "Scraps, Stamps and Cutouts: Emily Dickinson's Domestic Technologies of Publication," in *Cultural Artifacts and the Production of Meaning: The Page, the Image, and the Body*, ed. Margaret J. M. Ezell and Katherine O'Brien O'Keefe (Ann Arbor, MI: University of Michigan Press, 1994), 158.

15 Ibid., 159.

16 Ibid., 165.

17 Jackson, *Dickinson's Misery*, 167.

18 McGann, *Radiant Textuality*, 63.

19 R. W. Franklin, "Introduction," in *The Manuscript Books of Emily Dickinson* (Cambridge, MA: Belknap, 1981), ix.

20 Martha Nell Smith, "Because the Plunge from the Front Overturned Us: The Dickinson Electronic Archives Project," *Studies in the Literary Imagination* 32, no. 1 (Spring 1999), http://perma.cc/D42P-3QN2.

21 Jackson, *Dickinson's Misery*, 45.

22 "About," *Emily Dickinson Archive*, accessed March 10, 2015, http://perma.cc/U26J-MG5E. Controversy nonetheless surrounded the launch of the Harvard-hosted Emily Dickinson Archive. Though Amherst College, holders of many Dickinson manuscripts (including that for "Alone and in a Circumstance – "), agreed to allow the site to display its images, it was unhappy with various aspects of the site. See Meg P. Bernhard and Jennifer Leung, "Launch of Digital Dickinson Archive Clouded by Controversy," *Harvard Crimson*, October 23, 2013, http://perma.cc/57MF-ULDT.

23 Lawrence Rainey, *Revisiting "The Waste Land"* (New Haven: Yale University Press, 2005), 100. The discussion of the publication history of *The Waste Land* in this chapter is deeply indebted to Rainey.

24 Quoted in ibid., 37.

25 Quoted in ibid., 97.

26 T. S. Eliot, "The Frontiers of Criticism," *Sewanee Review* 64, no. 4 (December 1956): 533.

27 Ibid., 534.

28 Although the footnotes common in anthology editions of *The Waste Land* are more intrusive than the endnotes found in the Boni and Liveright edition (and in most present-day Faber and Faber editions of Eliot's work), the endnotes present serious reading difficulties of their own. Most serious is that, as one flips from the endnotes section to the main text and back, one very quickly loses the narrative thread – a situation parodied brilliantly in Vladimir Nabokov's novel *Pale Fire*, where the editor Arthur Kimbote's endnotes act as a parasite on the text of John Shade's poem "Pale Fire," distracting the reader from it almost completely.

29 N. Katherine Hayles, *My Mother Was a Computer: Digital Subjects and Literary Texts* (Chicago: University of Chicago Press, 2005), 89.

30 Ibid., 90.

31 Ibid.

32 Ibid., 91.

33 Jay David Bolter and Richard Grusin, *Remediation: Understanding New Media* (Cambridge, MA: MIT Press, 1999), 45.

34 Ibid., 46.

35 Jackson, *Dickinson's Misery*, 45.

36 Ong, *Orality and Literacy*, 34.

37 Samuel Johnson, *The Works of Samuel Johnson, LL. D.*, vol. 2 (New York: Alexander Blake, 1842), 46.

38 John Milton, "Paradise Lost," in *The Complete Poems*, ed. John Leonard (London: Penguin, 1998), 172, book III, lines 35–44.

39 Johnson, *The Works of Samuel Johnson, LL. D.*, 2:46.

40 R. C. Trevelyan, *Thamyris; or, Is There a Future for Poetry?* (London: Kegan Paul, 1925), 5.

41 Ibid., 72.

42 T. S. Eliot, *The Letters of T. S. Eliot*, ed. Valerie Eliot, vol. 1 (London: Faber and Faber, 1988), 596.

43 T. S. Eliot, "The Waste Land," in *Collected Poems, 1909–1962* (London: Faber and Faber, 1963), 70, lines 173–176.

44 Ibid., lines 185–186.

45 Ibid., 71, lines 203–204.

46 "A Note on This Edition," WikiBooks, *The Devonshire Manuscript*, (2014), http://perma.cc/QP5F-TFW9.

47 Constance Crompton, Ray Siemens, and Alyssa Arbuckle, "Understanding the Social Edition through Iterative Implementation: The Case of the Devonshire MS," *Scholarly and Research Communication* 4, no. 3 (2013): 2.

48 Johanna Drucker, *SpecLab: Digital Aesthetics and Projects in Speculative Computing* (Chicago: University of Chicago Press, 2009), 166.

49 Ibid.

50 Jerome McGann, "Texts in N-Dimensions and Interpretation in a New Key," *TEXT Technology* 12, no. 2 (2003): 4.

51 Ibid., 12.

52 Drucker, *SpecLab*, 173.
53 Johanna Drucker and Geoffrey Rockwell, "Introduction: Reflections on the Ivanhoe Game," *TEXT Technology* 12, no. 2 (2003): vii.
54 McGann, "Texts in N-Dimensions and Interpretation in a New Key," 10.
55 Ibid.
56 Drucker, *SpecLab*, 69.
57 Ibid., 68.
58 Ibid., 88–89.
59 Ibid., 66.
60 Drew Nelles, "Solitary Reading in an Age of Compulsory Sharing," in *The Edge of the Precipice: Why Read Literature in the Digital Age?*, ed. Paul Socken (Montreal: McGill-Queens University Press, 2013), 43.
61 Ibid., 47.
62 Piper, *Book Was There*, 100.

Chapter 5. Quantitative Approaches to the Literary

1 Roberto Busa, "The Annals of Humanities Computing: The Index Thomisticus," *Computers and the Humanities* 14 (1980): 83.
2 Ibid.
3 See Susan Hockey, "The History of Humanities Computing," in *A Companion to Digital Humanities*, ed. Susan Schreibman, Ray Siemens, and John Unsworth (Oxford: Blackwell, 2001), http://perma.cc/L3A8-EJHV.
4 Quoted in Julia Flanders, "Data and Wisdom: Electronic Editing and the Quantification of Knowledge," *Literary and Linguistic Computing* 24, no. 1 (2009): 58. The analysis of the debate surrounding the New Shakspere Society and its relationship to quantitative analysis of literature in this chapter is deeply indebted to Flanders's essay.
5 Ibid.
6 Ibid.
7 Algernon Charles Swinburne, "The Three Stages of Shakespeare," *Fortnightly Review* 17, no. 101 (May 1, 1875): 615.
8 James M. Hughes et al., "Quantitative Patterns of Stylistic Influence in the Evolution of Literature," *Proceedings of the National Academy of Sciences* 109, no. 20 (May 15, 2012): 7682, doi:10.1073/pnas.1115407109.
9 Laura Miller, "Are Literary Classics Obsolete?" *Salon*, May 31, 2012, http://perma.cc/2KV3-T78N.
10 Stephen Marche, "Literature Is Not Data: Against Digital Humanities," *Los Angeles Review of Books*, October 28, 2012, http://perma.cc/D2AQ-P3SB.
11 Hockey, "The History of Humanities Computing."
12 Rosanne G. Potter, *Literary Computing and Literary Criticism: Theoretical and Practical Essays on Theme and Rhetoric* (Philadelphia: University of Pennsylvania Press, 1989), xvi.

13 Ibid., xvii.

14 Stephen Ramsay, *Reading Machines: Toward an Algorithmic Criticism* (Urbana, IL: University of Illinois Press, 2011), 85.

15 Tanya Clement, "Text Analysis, Data Mining, and Visualizations in Literary Scholarship," in *Literary Studies in the Digital Age: An Evolving Anthology*, ed. Kenneth M. Price and Ray Siemens (MLA Commons, 2013), http://perma.cc/2CED-BNEK.

16 Geoffrey Rockwell et al., *TAPoR List Words*, 2011, http://taporware.ualberta.ca/~taporware/textTools/listword.shtml. Many readers will prefer to use the more modern outgrowth of TAPoR, *Voyant* (http://voyant-tools.org/), which offers similar functionality in a more attractive integrated environment. The older version, however, allows for clearer illustration of my points.

17 J. F. Burrows, *Computation into Criticism: A Study of Jane Austen's Novels and an Experiment in Method* (New York: Oxford University Press, 1987).

18 Julia Flanders, "Detailism, Digital Texts, and the Problem of Pedantry," *TEXT Technology* 14, no. 2 (2005): 57.

19 Words clouds can also be generated in Voyant (see note 16).

20 See Adam Hammond and Julian Brooke, *He Do the Police in Different Voices: Exploring Voices in T. S. Eliot's* The Waste Land, 2012, http://hedothepolice.org/.

21 Clement, "Text Analysis, Data Mining, and Visualizations in Literary Scholarship."

22 Gertrude Stein, *The Making of Americans: Being a History of a Family's Progress* (Normal, IL: Dalkey Archive Press, 1995), 290.

23 Franco Moretti, "Conjectures on World Literature," in *Distant Reading* (London: Verso, 2013), 48.

24 Melba Cuddy-Keane, Adam Hammond, and Alexandra Peat, *Modernism: Keywords* (Chichester: Wiley-Blackwell, 2014).

25 Raymond Williams, *Keywords: A Vocabulary of Culture and Society* (London: Fontana, 1976), 18–19.

26 "A Practical Present [Advertisement for Rubdry Towels]," *Cosmopolitan*, June 1911, *The Modernist Journals Project*, http://modjourn.org/render.php?view=mjp_object&id=1236613507359375.

27 Matthew L. Jockers, *Macroanalysis: Digital Methods and Literary History* (Urbana, IL: University of Illinois Press, 2013), 9–10.

28 Jean-Baptiste Michel et al., "Quantitative Analysis of Culture Using Millions of Digitized Books," *Science* 331, no. 6014 (January 14, 2011): 176–182, doi:10.1126/science.1199644.

29 Ryan Heuser and Long Le-Khac, *A Quantitative Literary History of 2,958 Nineteenth-Century British Novels: The Semantic Cohort Method*, Stanford Literary Lab Pamphlets 4 (Stanford, 2012), http://litlab.stanford.edu/LiteraryLabPamphlet4.pdf.

30 Ibid., 19.

31 Ibid., 44. Ted Underwood and Jordan Sellers offer an important alternate explanation of the phenomenon noticed by Heuser and Le-Khac. They argue that the quantitative patterns are indicative not of a shift in the perception of "social spaces," but rather of a broader shift in literary language from Latinate to Anglo-Saxon diction ("abstract value" words being predominantly Latinate and "hard seed" words

being predominantly Anglo-Saxon). See Ted Underwood and Jordan Sellers, "The Emergence of Literary Diction," *Journal of Digital Humanities* 1, no. 2 (Spring 2012), http://perma.cc/K655-GMLG.

32 Heuser and Le-Khac, *A Quantitative Literary History of 2,958 Nineteenth-Century British Novels,* 19.

33 Ibid., 49.

34 Jockers, *Macroanalysis,* 122.

35 Ibid., 128.

36 Ibid., 127.

37 These topics can be browsed on Jockers's website, http://www.matthewjockers.net/macroanalysisbook/macro-themes/.

38 Jockers, *Macroanalysis,* 151–153.

39 Mark Algee-Hewitt and Grace Muzny at Stanford University are currently undertaking a reconsideration of Jockers's findings on "female" versus "male" themes. Their preliminary results reveal a fundamental shortcoming in Jockers's approach. Rather than working at the level of the text, as Jockers does, Algee-Hewitt and Muzny break individual novels into narration and character speech and identify the gender of speaking characters. They find that male and female authors distinguish male and female characters in broadly similar ways (i.e., that regardless of whether the novel is written by a male or a female author, female characters tend to speak disproportionately about emotion). The more telling difference, Algee-Hewitt and Muzny find, is that female authors have more female characters and more female character speech in their novels than male authors do. Their work suggests that the more revealing difference between female and male authors is not that the former are more interested in themes such as "female fashion," but simply that they are more likely to have female characters speak in their novels.

40 Matthew L. Jockers, *Text Analysis with R for Students of Literature* (New York: Springer, 2014), viii.

41 Julian Brooke and I are presently working on developing an automatic method of performing basic structural tagging on plain text literary files. Even though our method works well for basic structural divisions (paragraphs, stage directions, passages of dialogue, and so on), working on this project has only reinforced to me the extreme difficulty of making machines understand distinctions that are, to humans, extremely simple. See Julian Brooke, Adam Hammond, and Graeme Hirst. "GutenTag: An NLP-Driven Tool for Digital Humanities Research in the Project Gutenberg Corpus," *Proceedings of the NAACL '15 Workshop on Computational Linguistics for Literature,* (Denver, CO: June 2015), 42–47.

42 Hayles, *My Mother Was a Computer,* 96.

43 McGann, *Radiant Textuality,* 185–186.

44 Virginia Woolf, *To the Lighthouse* (London: Penguin, 1992), 33.

45 Erich Auerbach, *Mimesis: The Representation of Reality in Western Literature,* trans. Willard Trask (Garden City, NJ: Doubleday, 1957), 531.

46 Julian Brooke, Adam Hammond, and Graeme Hirst, "Using Models of Lexical Style to Quantify Free Indirect Discourse in Modernist Fiction," *Digital Scholarship in the Humanities* (forthcoming, 2015). See also Adam Hammond and Julian Brooke, *The Brown Stocking: Exploring Voices in Virginia Woolf's* To the Lighthouse, 2013, http://brownstocking.org/.

47 McGann, *Radiant Textuality*, 175.

48 Ibid., 207.

Chapter 6. Short-Circuiting the Publication Process

1 Leonard Woolf, *Beginning Again* (London: Hogarth, 1964), 234.

2 J. H. Willis, *Leonard and Virginia Woolf as Publishers: The Hogarth Press, 1917–41* (Charlottesville, VA: University of Virginia Press, 1992), 44.

3 Jack London, *Martin Eden* (New York: Macmillan, 1913), 201.

4 Ibid., 118.

5 Quoted in Richard Findlater, ed., *Author! Author!* (London: Faber and Faber, 1984), 104.

6 Virginia Woolf, *The Letters of Virginia Woolf*, ed. Nigel Nicolson and Joanne Trautmann, vol. 2 (London: Hogarth, 1976), 231.

7 See Robert Darnton, "What Is the History of Books?" *Daedalus* 111, no. 3 (1982): 65–83.

8 Adriaan van der Weel, "The Communications Circuit Revisited" (SHARP, Mainz, 2000), http://perma.cc/7HPY-WKHV.

9 Borges, "The Library of Babel," 87.

10 Ong, *Orality and Literacy*, 131.

11 Roland Barthes, "The Death of the Author," in *Image-Music-Text*, trans. Stephen Heath (New York: Hill and Wang, 1977), 146.

12 Michel Foucault, "What Is an Author?" in *The Essential Foucault*, ed. Paul Rabinow and Nikolas Rose, trans. Josué V. Harari (New York: New Press, 2003), 390.

13 Mark Poster, *What's the Matter with the Internet?* (Minneapolis: University of Minneapolis Press, 2001), 68.

14 Ibid., 91.

15 Ibid., 68.

16 Ibid.

17 Karen Hellekson and Kristina Busse, "Fan Identity and Feminism," in *The Fan Fiction Studies Reader*, ed. Karen Hellekson and Kristina Busse (Iowa City: University of Iowa Press, 2014), 75–81.

18 Karen Hellekson and Kristina Busse, "Introduction: Why a Fan Fiction Studies Reader Now?" in *The Fan Fiction Studies Reader*, ed. Karen Hellekson and Kristina Busse (Iowa City: University of Iowa Press, 2014), 5.

19 Ewan Morrison, "In the Beginning, There Was Fan Fiction: From the Four Gospels to Fifty Shades," *The Guardian*, August 13, 2012, http://perma.cc/S4TU-XVHQ.

20 Quoted in Jason Boog, "The Lost History of *Fifty Shades of Grey*," *GalleyCat*, November 21, 2012, http://perma.cc/GR6G-GFDT.

21 Morrison, "In the Beginning, There Was Fan Fiction."

22 See, for example, Henry Jenkins, *Textual Poachers: Television Fans and Participatory Culture* (New York: Routledge, 2013); Maria Lindgren Leavenworth, "The Paratext of Fan Fiction," *Narrative* 23, no. 1 (January 2015): 43; and Karen Hellekson and Kristina Busse, eds., *The Fan Fiction Studies Reader* (Iowa City: University of Iowa Press, 2014).

23 Steve Roggenbuck, "Doctrine on 'INTERNET POETRY,'" February 2011, http://perma.cc/JH9E-W32X.

24 Tao Lin, *Richard Yates* (Brooklyn, NY: Melville House, 2010), 1.

25 Marie Calloway, *Adrien Brody* (New York: Muumuu House, 2011), http://perma.cc/PGF6-P8C4.

26 Steve Roggenbuck, *1 Hour and 15 Minutes of Walt Whitman's Poetry*, 2014, https://www.youtube.com/watch?v=hxeEc7hp04M.

27 Steve Roggenbuck, *DOWNLOAD HELVETICA FOR FREE.COM* (Chicago: self-published, 2011), 82, http://perma.cc/Y3QD-YHGZ.

28 Charles Brock, "Young Love," *New York Times*, September 24, 2010, http://perma.cc/2FQ8-FDEH.

29 Kenneth Goldsmith, *Uncreative Writing* (New York: Columbia University Press, 2011), 1.

30 Marjorie Perloff, "Unoriginal Genius: Walter Benjamin's Arcades as Paradigm for the New Poetics," *Études Anglaises* 61, no. 2 (June 2008): 229–252.

31 Oscar Schwartz, *Can I Have Your Attention Please?* (Self-published, 2013), 16, http://perma.cc/4QKC-B55N.

32 Ibid., 11.

33 Emily Gould, "Now We Also Hate Miranda July," *Gawker*, June 27, 2007, http://perma.cc/WT6L-35WJ.

34 Miles Klee, "Stephen Tully Dierks, Tao Lin, and the Alt Lit Scene's Rape Problem," *The Daily Dot*, October 2, 2014, http://perma.cc/U68F-XFK2.

35 Noah Cicero, "'ultimately Beautiful': An Interview with Steve Roggenbuck," *HTMLGIANT*, June 1, 2012, http://perma.cc/Q93W-XPWP.

36 Ibid.

37 Dash Shaw, *BodyWorld* (self-published, 2009), Chapter 11, Part 1, http://perma.cc/PJX9-Y83F.

38 Ibid., Prelude, http://perma.cc/CE6S-NV5G.

39 Ibid., Chapter 1, Part 1, http://perma.cc/Y68C-BA8D.

40 Birkerts, *The Gutenberg Elegies*, 219.

41 Ibid., 224.

42 Davidson, *Now You See It*, 143.

43 Ibid.

44 Jaron Lanier, *You Are Not a Gadget: A Manifesto* (New York: Vintage, 2011), x.

45 Ibid., 47.

46 Ibid., 70.
47 Shaw, *BodyWorld*, 2009, Chapter 11, Part 1, http://perma.cc/PJX9-Y83F.
48 Ibid., Chapter 3, Part 2, http://perma.cc/X5KT-CKUX.
49 Dash Shaw, *BodyWorld* (New York: Pantheon Books, 2010).
50 Dash Shaw, "Dash Shaw," in *Creating Comics! 47 Master Artists Reveal the Techniques and Inspiration behind Their Comic Genius*, ed. Judith Salavetz and Spencer Drate (Beverly, MA: Rockport, 2010), 128.
51 Shaw, *BodyWorld*, 2009, Chapter 12, http://perma.cc/D6CU-SGEA.
52 Shaw, "Dash Shaw," 130.

Chapter 7. Interactivity: Revolution and Evolution in Narrative

1 Janet H. Murray, "Inventing the Medium," in *The New Media Reader*, ed. Noah Wardrip-Fruin and Nick Montford (Cambridge, MA: MIT Press, 2003), 6–7.
2 Though the label "hypertext fiction" is indeed plausibly dead, hypertextual fiction continues to thrive under other genre labels. The immensely popular hypertexts produced in the Twine software platform, for example, are usually called (and call themselves) "videogames."
3 Robert Coover, "The End of Books," *New York Times*, June 21, 1992, http://perma.cc/M7EV-GX3Z.
4 Laura Miller, "Bookend: www.claptrap.com," *New York Times*, March 15, 1998, http://perma.cc/J5YE-C5J7.
5 George P. Landow, *Hypertext: The Convergence of Contemporary Critical Theory and Technology* (Baltimore: Johns Hopkins University Press, 1992), 2.
6 Ibid., 33.
7 Roland Barthes, *S/Z*, trans. Richard Miller (New York: Hill and Wang, 1974), 5–6.
8 Landow, *Hypertext*, 3.
9 Ibid., 8.
10 Jay David Bolter, *Writing Space: The Computer, Hypertext, and the History of Writing* (Hillsdale, NJ: Lawrence Erlbaum, 1991), 161.
11 Roland Barthes, "From Work to Text," in *Textual Strategies: Perspectives in Post-Structuralist Criticism*, ed. and trans. Josué V. Harari (Ithaca, NY: Cornell University Press, 1979), 74–76.
12 Bolter, *Writing Space*, 161.
13 Jacques Derrida, "Living On," in *Deconstruction and Criticism*, ed. and trans. James Hulbert (New York: Seabury, 1979), 84.
14 Bolter, *Writing Space*, 162.
15 Ibid., 105.
16 Landow, *Hypertext*, 33.
17 Ibid., 70.
18 Bolter, *Writing Space*, 122.
19 Ibid., 153.
20 Landow, *Hypertext*, 101–102.

21 Ibid., 23.
22 Ibid., 5.
23 Barthes, *S/Z*, 4.
24 Porter H. Abbott, *The Cambridge Introduction to Narrative*, 2nd ed. (Cambridge: Cambridge University Press, 2008), 34.
25 Wolfgang Iser, "The Reading Process: A Phenomenological Approach," in *Reader Response Criticism: From Formalism to Post-Structuralism*, ed. Jane P. Tompkins (Baltimore: Johns Hopkins University Press, 1980), 50.
26 Ibid., 55.
27 Espen J. Aarseth, *Cybertext: Perspectives on Ergodic Literature* (Baltimore: Johns Hopkins University Press, 1997), 1.
28 Ibid., 1–2.
29 Ibid., 4.
30 Lev Manovich, *The Language of New Media* (Cambridge, MA: MIT Press, 2001), 75.
31 Ramsay, *Reading Machines: Toward an Algorithmic Criticism*, 41.
32 Kathleen Fitzpatrick, *Planned Obsolescence: Publishing, Technology, and the Future of the Academy* (New York: NYU Press, 2011), 63.
33 Bolter, *Writing Space*, 163.
34 Fitzpatrick, *Planned Obsolescence*, 98.
35 Manovich, *The Language of New Media*, 61.
36 Miller, "Bookend."
37 Birkerts, *The Gutenberg Elegies*, 163.
38 Stephen Marche, *Lucy Hardin's Missing Period* (Toronto: The Walrus, 2010), http://walrusmagazine.com/lucyhardin/.
39 Auerbach, *Mimesis*, 549.
40 Emily Short, *Galatea*, 2004, https://emshort.wordpress.com/my-work/.
41 A. M. Turing, "Computing Machinery and Intelligence," *Mind* 59, no. 236 (October 1950): 433–460, doi:10.1093/mind/LIX.236.433.
42 Emily Short, "Game Cheats and Walkthroughs," 2000, http://perma.cc/8V9Y-B8U5.
43 Sherry Turkle, *Alone Together* (New York: Basic Books, 2011), 24.
44 Ibid.
45 N. Katherine Hayles, *Electronic Literature: New Horizons for the Literary* (Notre Dame, IN: University of Notre Dame Press, 2008), 37, 130–131.

Chapter 8. Literature in the Digital Master Medium

1 Kittler, "Gramophone, Film, Typewriter," 31.
2 Ibid.
3 Manovich, *The Language of New Media*, 19–20.
4 Hayles, *Electronic Literature*, 6–7.
5 N. Katherine Hayles et al., eds., *Electronic Literature Collection* (College Park, MD: Electronic Literature Organization, 2006), http://collection.eliterature.org/1/.

6 Hayles, *Electronic Literature*, 4.
7 Ibid.
8 Ibid.
9 Richard Wagner, "Art and Revolution," in *Richard Wagner's Prose Works*, trans. William Ashton Ellis, 2nd ed., vol. 1 (London: Kegan Paul, Trench, Trübner & Co, 1895), 43. https://archive.org/details/richardwagnerspr011341mbp.
10 Ibid., 54.
11 Ibid.
12 Ibid., 43.
13 Richard Wagner, "The Art-Work of the Future," in *Richard Wagner's Prose Works*, trans. William Ashton Ellis, 2nd ed., vol. 1 (London: Kegan Paul, Trench, Trübner & Co, 1895), 193. https://archive.org/details/richardwagnerspr011341mbp.
14 Ibid., 184.
15 Wagner, "Art and Revolution," 53.
16 Friedrich Nietzsche, "The Birth of Tragedy," in *The Birth of Tragedy and The Case of Wagner*, trans. Walter Kaufmann (New York: Random House, 1967), 36.
17 Ibid., 83–84.
18 Ibid., 106.
19 Ibid., 115.
20 Ibid., 121.
21 Ibid., 119.
22 Ibid., 130.
23 Ibid., 123.
24 Michelle Pauli, "Down with Alice," *The Guardian*, December 7, 2006, http://perma.cc/YYP2-RL3R.
25 Ibid.
26 Kate Taylor, "Digital Lit: How New Ways to Read Mean New Ways to Write," *The Globe and Mail*, July 9, 2011, http://perma.cc/6JHP-R5PZ.
27 Ibid.
28 "Q&A with Artist Chris Joseph," *Alice's School Report*, 2011.
29 "About Alice," *Inanimate Alice*, n.d., http://perma.cc/6HW7-UTEU.
30 Kate Pullinger, "Fact Is We Need a Better Name for 'Digital Fiction,'" *The Guardian*, December 11, 2006, http://perma.cc/U55H-6XQU.
31 Kate Pullinger and Chris Joseph, "Episode 1: China," in *Inanimate Alice* (London: Bradfield Company, 2005), http://inanimatealice.com/episode1/.
32 Wagner, "Art and Revolution," 43.
33 Edward Picot, "Unanswered Questions," *The Hyperliterature Exchange*, November 2005, http://perma.cc/55DM-M7RL.
34 Kate Pullinger and babel, "Author Description: Inanimate Alice, Episode 1," in *Electronic Literature Collection*, ed. N. Katherine Hayles et al. (College Park, MD: Electronic Literature Organization, 2006), http://perma.cc/3576-2CPJ.
35 Pauli, "Down with Alice."
36 Kate Pullinger and Chris Joseph, "Episode 3: Russia," in *Inanimate Alice* (London: Bradfield Company, 2006), 3, http://inanimatealice.com/episode3/.

37 Virginia Woolf, "Mr. Bennett and Mrs. Brown," in *The Hogarth Essays* (Garden City, NY: Doubleday, 1928), 27.

38 Young-Hae Chang and Marc Voge, "Dakota," in *Young-Hae Chang Heavy Industries*, 2002, http://yhchang.com/DAKOTA.html.

39 Pressman, *Digital Modernism*.

40 Ezra Pound, "Canto I," in *The Norton Anthology of Modern Poetry*, ed. Richard Ellmann and Robert O'Clair (New York: W. W. Norton & Company, 1973), 358, line 53.

41 Ibid., 357, lines 1–2.

42 Ibid., 359, lines 68–69.

43 Pressman, *Digital Modernism*, 91.

44 Ibid., 96.

45 Ibid., 81.

46 Richard Ellmann and Robert O'Clair, eds., *The Norton Anthology of Modern Poetry* (New York: W. W. Norton & Company, 1973), 356.

47 Hyun-Joo Yoo, "Intercultural Medium Literature Digital: Interview with YOUNG-HAE CHANG HEAVY INDUSTRIES," *Dichtung-Digital*, February 2005, http://perma.cc/FAJ9-UHCA.

48 Pressman, *Digital Modernism*, 93.

49 Yoo, "Intercultural Medium Literature Digital."

50 "Can a Computer Make You Cry?" *Creative Computing*, June 1983, http://perma.cc/7UD9-6JZ8.

51 James Newman, *Videogames* (London: New York: Routledge, 2004), 5.

52 Jane McGonigal, *Reality Is Broken: Why Games Make Us Better and How They Can Change the World* (New York: Penguin, 2011), 21.

53 Jesper Juul, "Games Telling Stories? A Brief Note on Games and Narrative," *Game Studies* 1, no. 1 (2001), http://perma.cc/T4MA-UA79.

54 Espen Aarseth, "Computer Game Studies, Year One," *Game Studies* 1, no. 1 (2001), http://perma.cc/5MEJ-S2UJ.

55 Abbott, *The Cambridge Introduction to Narrative*, 36.

56 Austin Grossman, *You: A Novel* (New York: Mulholland Books, 2013), 20–21.

57 James Swirsky and Lisanne Pajot, *Indie Game: The Movie* (BlinkWorks Media, 2012).

58 Jamin Warren, *Does "Indie Game" Mean Anything Anymore?* Game/Show (PBS Digital Studios, 2014), https://www.youtube.com/watch?v=E8iwDkE8mw4.

59 Anna Anthropy, *Rise of the Videogame Zinesters: How Freaks, Normals, Amateurs, Artists, Dreamers, Dropouts, Queers, Housewives, and People Like You Are Taking Back an Art Form* (New York: Seven Stories Press, 2012), 19.

60 Ibid., 8.

61 Steve Gaynor, Karla Zimonja, and Johnnemann Nordhagen, *Gone Home* (Portland, OR: Fullbright Company, 2013).

62 "Best Narrative Game of the Year: Gone Home," *PC Gamer*, December 27, 2013, http://perma.cc/FKK4-JX5L.

63 Davey Wreden and William Pugh, *The Stanley Parable* (Galactic Cafe, 2013).

64 Superbrothers, Jim Guthrie, and Capybara Games, *Superbrothers: Sword & Sworcery EP* (Toronto: Capybara Games, 2011).

65 Superbrothers, "Less Talk, More Rock: The Native Language of Video Games Is Neither Spoken nor Written," *Boing Boing*, March 24, 2010, http://perma.cc/ZTQ9-87M6.

66 Leonard Shlain, *The Alphabet versus the Goddess: The Conflict between Word and Image* (New York: Viking, 1998). Emphasis in original.

67 The creators write, "The Scythian's gender may have something to do with Leonard Schlain's [*sic*] The Goddess & The Alphabet: The Conflict Between Text & Image [*sic*], a book that offers an alternate perspective on the received wisdom of thousands of years of male-dominated written literature & history." Superbrothers, Jim Guthrie, and Capybara Games, "About," *Swordandsworcery.com*, 2011, http://perma.cc/SPW6-MFBM.

68 Anita Sarkeesian, "The Scythian – Sword & Sworcery," *Feminist Frequency: Conversations with Pop Culture*, March 31, 2015, http://perma.cc/J8F9-C8Z6.

69 Ian Bogost, *Persuasive Games: The Expressive Power of Videogames* (Cambridge, MA: MIT Press, 2007), vii.

70 Ibid., ix.

71 Ibid.

72 William Blake, *Jerusalem*, in *The Complete Poetry & Prose of William Blake*, ed. David V. Erdman (New York: Anchor, 1988), 153.

73 Woolf, *A Room of One's Own*, 92.

Coda: Print in the Digital Age

1 Lev Grossman, "Jonathan Franzen: Great American Novelist," *Time*, August 12, 2010, http://perma.cc/9ZHN-TLDY.

2 Laura Miller, "Let's Talk about Jonathan Franzen's 'Freedom,'" *Salon*, September 4, 2010, http://perma.cc/B8V3-WWUY.

3 Jonathan Franzen, "Ten Rules for Writing Fiction," *The Guardian*, February 20, 2010, http://perma.cc/S8FU-TD2G.

4 Grossman, "Jonathan Franzen: Great American Novelist."

5 Ibid.

6 Jonathan Franzen, *Freedom* (New York: Farrar, Strauss and Giroux, 2010), 218.

7 Ibid.

8 Ibid., 346.

9 Gerard Moorey, "Aging, Death, and Revival: Representations of the Music Industry in Two Contemporary Novels," *Popular Music and Society* 37, no. 1 (2014): 74.

10 Franzen, *Freedom*, 533.

11 Ibid., 223.

12 Ibid., 487.

13 Kirschenbaum and Werner, "Digital Scholarship and Digital Studies: The State of the Discipline," 423–425.

14 Jonathan Franzen, "Farther Away," *The New Yorker*, April 18, 2011, http://perma .cc/6M6T-2EE6.

15 Ibid.

16 Ibid.

17 Nicholas Carr, "The Flattening of E-Book Sales," *Rough Type*, August 5, 2013, http://perma.cc/J8RV-P9QK.

18 Ibid.

19 Jessica, Pressman, "The Aesthetic of Bookishness in Twenty-First Century Literature," *Michigan Quarterly Review* 48, no. 4 (Fall 2009): 465.

20 Quoted in Jessica Pressman, "House of Leaves: Reading the Networked Novel," *Studies in American Fiction* 34, no. 1 (Spring 2006): 121.

21 Jonathan Safran Foer, "Author's Afterword: His Book and the Book," in *Tree of Codes* (London: Visual Editions, 2011), 138.

22 N. Katherine Hayles, "Combining Close and Distant Reading: Jonathan Safran Foer's *Tree of Codes* and the Aesthetic of Bookishness," *PMLA* 128, no. 1 (2013): 227.

23 Kirschenbaum and Werner, "Digital Scholarship and Digital Studies: The State of the Discipline," 446.

24 Pressman, "The Aesthetic of Bookishness in Twenty-First Century Literature," 468. Emphasis added.

25 "The 2011 Pulitzer Prize Winners: Fiction," *The Pulitzer Prizes*, 2011, http://perma .cc/K79Y-LVVH.

26 Jennifer Egan, *A Visit from the Goon Squad* (New York: Alfred A. Knopf, 2010), 22.

27 Ibid., 23.

28 Ibid., 336.

29 Ibid., 321.

30 Ibid., 335.

31 Jennie Yabroff, "Jennifer Egan Likes This," *Newsweek*, June 2, 2010, http://perma .cc/SKD6-JMYZ.

32 N. Katherine Hayles, "Translating Media: Why We Should Rethink Textuality," *The Yale Journal of Criticism* 16, no. 2 (2003): 278.

33 Jennifer Egan, "Coming Soon: Jennifer Egan's 'Black Box,'" *The New Yorker Page-Turner Blog*, May 23, 2012, http://perma.cc/TY9Q-TBQX.

34 Kirschenbaum and Werner, "Digital Scholarship and Digital Studies: The State of the Discipline," 448.

35 For more on the tortured translation and reception history of Derrida's "*il n'y a pas de hors-texte*," see Valentine Cunningham, "Sticky Transfers," in *Aesthetics and Contemporary Discourse*, ed. Herbert Grabes, vol. 10, REAL: Yearbook of Research in English and American Literature (Tübingen: Gunter Narr Verlag, 1994), 325–54.

Index